MORE PRAISE FOR
THE VANISHING AMERICAN ADULT

"Ben Sasse is a good senator, a great thinker and an even better writer. His book tells the truth about what truly ails America. It's not partisan politics. It's us—our families, and our loss of confidence in the future. He argues effectively that our national destiny depends less on what happens in Washington and more on what we do at home. But take heart—Sasse offers powerful solutions, both personal and universal, that will restore our faith in the future and our responsibilities to each other as parents, neighbors, and citizens of the greatest country on earth."

—*Dr. Frank Luntz, CBS News & Fox News Analyst*

"Ben Sasse's book is not an angry diatribe against the younger generation. Nor is it a call to return to an idyllic vision of days gone by. Rather, it's a practical, insightful call to all Americans to reject passivity, embrace initiative, and boldly approach the future with purpose and vision."

—*Jim Daly, President, Focus on the Family*

"Ben Sasse is a thoughtful father, historian and senator. And he has written a non-political book about one of the most important policy topics of the day—how to raise self-reliant and adventurous children. Any parent will read this alternating between 'damn right' and guilt pangs. The book is practical, helpful, and conversational. I wish it had been written 20 years ago!"

—*U.S. Senator Tim Kaine*

"Historian, dad, and former college president Ben Sasse has nailed it: we're failing our kids. Each generation must mold the next into solid citizens at home, at work, and in the city square. This book is a well-timed rebuke and a time-tested recipe—just what America needs."

— *U.S. Senator Marco Rubio*

THE VANISHING AMERICAN ADULT. Copyright © 2017 by Ben Sasse. All rights reserved. Printed in the United States of America. For information, address St. Martin's Press, 175 Fifth Avenue, New York, NY 10010.

www.stmartins.com

Cataloging-in-Publication Data is available from the Library of Congress.

ISBN 9781250114402 (hardcover)
ISBN 9781250114419 (e-book)

Our books may be purchased in bulk for promotional, educational, or business use. Please contact your local bookseller or the Macmillan Corporate and Premium Sales Department at 1-800-221-7945, extension 5442, or by e-mail at MacmillanSpecialMarkets@macmillan.com.

10 9 8 7 6 5 4

THE VANISHING
AMERICAN
ADULT

OUR COMING-OF-AGE CRISIS—
and How to
REBUILD A CULTURE
OF SELF-RELIANCE

BEN SASSE

St. Martin's Press
New York

To Melissa McLeod Sasse,
my lifelong partner in the world-changing
work of nurturing little souls.
For there is no higher calling than
two becoming one to create a third.

CONTENTS

Introduction   My Kids "Need" Air Conditioning   1

PART I
OUR PASSIVITY PROBLEM

One   Stranded in Neverland   13

Two   From Little Citizens to Baby Einsteins   31

Three   More School Isn't Enough   57

PART II
AN ACTIVE PROGRAM

Four   Flee Age Segregation   89

Five   Embrace Work Pain   119

Six   Consume Less   151

Seven   Travel to See   177

Eight   Build a Bookshelf   207

Nine   Make America an Idea Again   245

Postscript   Why This Wasn't a Policy Book   259

Afterword   If Teddy Roosevelt Spoke to a High School Graduating Class   265

Acknowledgments   275

Note on Sources and Methods   277

Bibliography   281

Index   297

THE VANISHING
AMERICAN
ADULT

INTRODUCTION

MY KIDS "NEED"
AIR CONDITIONING

WE ALL KNOW THE NOUN "ADULT." BUT I WAS PER-
plexed last year to begin regularly hearing the new verb "to adult." In social media, especially on Twitter and Instagram, it birthed a new hashtag
as well: #adulting. As in: "Doing laundry/dishes/cleaning my bathroom
at midnight #adulting" or "Just paid this month's bills on time #adult-
ing" or "Decided I couldn't watch Netflix for 8 hours straight and went
to the grocery store instead #adulting."

The new word's use spiked so quickly that in 2016 the American
Dialectic Society nominated "adulting" the "most creative" word con-
struction in the entire English language. Alongside slang like "YOLO"
(go for it, since "you only live once") and politically correct neologisms
like "microaggression," the verb-ified version of "adult" is a totally new
addition to our vocabulary.

For those unaccustomed to hearing this term—that is, actual
adults—"adulting" is an ironic way of describing "engagement in adult
behaviors," like paying your taxes or "getting super pumped about home
appliances"—you know, the sort of mundane tasks and tools that responsibility demands. In other words, to a growing number of young
Americans, acting like a grown-up is a kind of role-playing that can be
thought of as a joke.

In a different time, there was decent clarity about what coming
of age into adulthood meant. Leaving childhood and becoming an
adult was conceptually clear. It was a *gift* that older generations gave
to the younger. No longer. Ours is now an odd nation of both delayed

grown-ups and adult-children who create words to mock the idea that we could ever become responsible, civic-minded leaders.

Before going any further, though, I want to puncture in advance a potential misunderstanding about this book. You might think you're about to hear a harrumph against the laziness of the rising generation or about stultifying helicopter parenting. Perhaps you're expecting a fiery harangue about taking away kids' devices, kicking them out of the house, giving parents a spine . . . and all will be well.

Actually, you will hear very little "Get off my lawn!" screaming in these pages. There are few easy answers offered here—and this project isn't primarily about blaming anyone. Nor should you hear in these pages mere nostalgia for some lost golden age, for despite being a historian, I am more interested in the future than the past. Thus, the latter two-thirds of the book offer a gritty but constructive vision, drawn from our nation's traditions, of how parents and grandparents can help build self-reliance into the rising generation going forward.

But first, we need to agree on the problem.

I believe our entire nation is in the midst of a collective coming-of-age crisis without parallel in our history. We are living in an America of perpetual adolescence. Our kids simply don't know what an adult is anymore—or how to become one. Many don't see a reason even to try. Perhaps more problematic, the older generations have forgotten that we need to plan to teach them. It's our fault more than it is theirs.

———

THE IDEA FOR THIS BOOK came when I began serving as president of a liberal arts college in my home state of Nebraska eight years ago. Early in my tenure at Midland University, a group of students in the athletic department was tasked with setting up a twenty-foot Christmas tree in the lobby of our basketball arena. These were hearty and healthy kids, 18- and 19-year-olds. They got the tree up, took out some decorations, dressed the tree, and began to leave, concluding that the job was done. That was when one of the university's vice presidents happened by and noticed something odd. The Christmas tree was decorated only on the bottom seven or eight feet, on the branches the kids could easily reach.

Why, she asked, was the work only half done?

The head of a sorority replied, "We couldn't figure out how to get the ornaments on the top."

"Was there not a ladder in the gym?" the vice president queried. "Was maintenance unwilling to bring one?"

She was met with shrugs. No one had bothered to look or thought to ask.

This day's failure wasn't at all about lacking brains; it was about will. It was about ownership. It was about not having much experience or interest in seeing tasks through to completion.

This startled me. It worried me for the kids. Was this a problem unique to Midland's culture? I turned the scene over in my head, but I couldn't make sense of it. At the risk of sounding melodramatic, I simply couldn't reconcile the decision to leave while the work was still incomplete with how my parents had taught me to think about assignments. I couldn't conceptualize growing up without the *compulsion*—first external compulsion, but over time, the more important internal and self-directed kind of compulsion—to attempt and to finish hard things, even when I didn't want to.

Although I was only 37 at the time, I suddenly felt old—for the very first time—and far more than two decades removed from my own arrival at college. Over my initial handful of months at the helm of Midland, I was noticing that students' limited experience with hard work seemed to make them bizarrely fuzzy-headed when actual, real-world problems needed to be solved. They were regularly and troublingly flat-footed about situations in which smart, lively 18- to 22-year-olds should have had no difficulty leaning in and righting the world. But it turned out that the passivity wasn't at all unique to Midland. As I've become more alert to this problem, I see the story repeated time and again, not only with college-age students but with pre- and post-college-age people as well.

For example, a friend recently shared that he and his wife have become increasingly worried about their kids. They have a 10-year-old boy and a 14-year-old girl who are, by almost any measure, dream kids. They are respectful toward adults, have good friendship networks, work diligently at school, and get top grades. Other parents often comment on how they wish their kids were more like my friend's. But he and his wife are focused on behavior that occurs at home outside the public gaze, namely, their 10-year-old's obsession with YouTube and their 14-year-old's penchant for spending endless hours paging through social media updates and re-watching episodes of *The Office*.

This probably sounds familiar to most parents, but my friend's angst stung more when he explained the primary reason *why* he and his wife have begun to worry. Sure, like all of us they are concerned about screen time being addictive and changing kids' brains. They worry that social media can produce bullying or depression. But their ache is deeper: They are scared of a behavioral change they're observing. They've noticed that all of this screen time seems to imbue their kids with a zombie-like passivity. They detect a decline of agency, of initiative, of liveliness.

Oddly, while the kids know and admit that they are much happier doing other things—playing with friends, throwing a baseball, taking a hike, accomplishing something tangible—they can't find the initiative to get started on these activities on their own. They will do these other things, but only when their parents take the lead in arranging them. In the absence of intervention, the kids remain passive. My friend often arrives home from work (his wife also works but gets home earlier) to find his wife starting on dinner and the kids sprawled out on the floor or couch, their facial expressions blank; attempts to engage them are met with only vague recognition that a conversation is taking place. Even their physical bearing seems to have been altered during these times—normally alert and engaged, they now seem tired, listless, enervated. My friend wasn't complaining; he was actually scared: How will they possibly make it on their own? What magic moment after age 14 will lead them to suddenly switch from passivity to the responsibility-taking of adulthood?

When we hear these stories about other people's children, there's often a "log-in-someone-else's-eye" tendency to quietly assume that a given kid's passivity can be linearly traced to a particular parenting failure in their household. So as an antidote, let me personally own a third and final example that might illustrate that these challenges are not remedied simply by sheer exertion of individual parental will. Because there are forces bigger than any one family at work here: societal affluence that allows us to "entertain ourselves to death," changes in technology, the radical separation of the household and thus kids' upbringing from exposure to meaningful work, and a broader cultural amnesia about child-rearing that makes it harder for individual families to inculcate a sense of self-reliance. How do we awaken an aspiration to self-disciplined independence when the neighbors' kids are almost all suffering from the same affluenza?

One day last summer, my family had returned from a brief trip to Colorado. My daughters and I had taken some eye-opening runs in the Rockies, where it was only forty degrees in the early mornings. When we returned to Nebraska, an air conditioning unit at our house had broken, but fortunately it was cool for August—only high seventies. Nonetheless, our teen and nearly teen daughters arrived in my wife Melissa and my bedroom in the middle of the first night home to announce that they could not possibly sleep in their room, since the A/C was able to cool it down to only seventy-two.

Wait, what?! When I was a kid, we had air conditioning in our house . . . but we never used it. My dad explained that it was a luxury, and it was a nice blessing that the house came with it, but we weren't rich, and so we wouldn't be paying for the extra electricity. Sometimes it would hit one hundred degrees for days on end, and still my siblings and I never really thought to question the judgment that air conditioning costs money—we didn't have much of that, so of course we did not "need" the A/C. By the time I was in high school, my parents decided to begin using the air conditioner for a few weeks most summers—but we still regarded it as a luxury and valued it as such. We would never have been crazy enough, insulated enough, bubble-wrapped enough, to think that it was impossible to sleep without it—especially at seventy-two degrees.

When confronted with our pampered daughters, my wife and I felt a heavy sense of failure. Somehow I had accidentally taught my children, who had grown up with so much, that a functioning household air conditioner is a fundamental staple of life. I had not successfully inculcated that prior moral sense that air conditioning is a "nice-to-have" luxury, not a "need-to-have" requirement.

These seemingly disparate stories about lack of initiative and about the coddling that breeds softness and entitlement, in kids from age ten to twentysomething, are not in any way about politics. And yet the problems identified are problems not merely for these particular kids and parents. This crisis of idleness and passive drift is profound for every citizen of this republic. For this nation is premised on the idea that the government exists not to define and secure the good, the true, and the beautiful, but rather to maintain a framework for ordered liberty—*so that* free people can pursue their happiness in the diverse ways that they see fit.

———

SINCE ARRIVING IN THE SENATE in 2015, my colleagues and I have had discussions on many urgent national problems—from health care to immigration, from cybersecurity to new job creation. All of the proposed solutions to address these problems are meaningless, though, if we lack an educated, resilient citizenry capable of navigating the increasing complexities of daily life. We need our emerging generation to become fully functioning American adults, providing for their families, investing in their communities, showing the ability to raise children who will carry on after them, paying taxes to help government function and fix our broken retirement system. We need curious, critical, engaged young people who can demonstrate initiative and innovation so the United States can compete with a growing list of economic, military, and technological rivals in the twenty-first century.

America wasn't built to enable perpetual adolescence, and America can't long endure this way—even if these were normal times. But let's be clear: these are not normal times. The generation now coming of age is going to need even greater grit and resilience than previous ages. The world of the next few decades is going to be scary for folks as we navigate a truly unprecedented pace of job change for reasons we'll discuss in the coming chapters. And technology, for all its convenience and improvements to our daily lives, has birthed a kind of on-demand consumerism and an ever-growing variety of sources from which we get our news and information. Algorithms in our search engines and social media platforms shape what we receive based on our previous preferences and choice, confirming our natural inclinations to read things that confirm our beliefs rather than challenge them. This is a problem to us as a society—and young people in particular, who will only know this digital world—because of its inherently polarizing effect, its tendency to favor emotion over reason, and because citizen engagement in a republic requires reasoned debate, critical thinking, the thoughtful contesting of ideas, and individuals willing to stand up for what they believe, even when challenged.

Coming of age has always been hard, in every society in every century. But today's challenge is particularly acute, and especially for Americans. America is a creedal nation—that is, it depends on a shared creed or belief set about dignity and freedom. It depends not on the expert rule of a small, faraway elite class, but rather on the virtue and self-reliance of an entire republican (small-r) populace. And in the midst of a radical economic disruption from single lifelong jobs to the demands of lifelong learning for flexible and changing work, solving the riddle of transmitting anew a culture of self-reliance is more urgent than ever before.

We are not ready.

Our kids are not ready for the world they are soon going to inherit. We don't even know how to talk about the daunting tasks of becoming resilient enough to navigate a world with much shorter job durations. This book aims to help frame a national discussion on how to start thinking about these challenges, and some provisional ways to dive in. Everywhere I go across the country, I hear from people who share an ominous sense that something is very wrong with our kids, but they don't always have hooks or labels or a mental framework to discuss it. Some pretend for a moment that the grand fights are political, that what they're really worried about is right versus left, but mostly they know it isn't true. They know that almost all of our kids seem to be distracted and drifting. They yearn for the rising generation of American teens to be grittier, more self-possessed, more self-sufficient, more ready to serve.

They know that we've lost something from our older ways of coming of age, but they're not sure what it is or how it happened. They worry that there are few precise markers of progressively increasing responsibility, expectation, and achievement. They're unpersuaded by fuzzy, directionless claims that more years should be spent in classrooms before ever beginning to work. Yet for most of these worrying parents, there is only a generic sense that we have allowed institutionalized, school-centric childhood to displace the coming-of-age practices, habits, and rituals that defined the American experience in the earlier eras of homesteads, factories, and farms. In short, they certainly believe that there is a "coming-of-age" problem and that adolescence now seems "perpetual." But they usually haven't a clue what to do about it.

I don't have any magic bullets either. And I actually don't believe that there is any one, singular solution. I will unpack some of the methods that my wife and I are using to attempt to address these issues in our home. But please don't misunderstand: I have zero desire to set myself or my kids up as models of execution. We stumble and fall every day. But we have a shared theory of what our family is trying to accomplish: Melissa and I want them to arrive at adulthood as fully formed, vivacious, appealing, resilient, self-reliant, problem-solving souls who see themselves as called to love and serve their neighbors. The thought of them drifting in a state of passive, dependent, perpetual adolescence turns our stomachs. There is much we want to accomplish in life, but failing at this calling would dwarf all other vocations we care about.

Part I of this book is about the problem: How do we know the situation with our kids has really gotten worse; don't all parents always worry about their teens? Why is this coming-of-age crisis especially dangerous for America with our republican (small-r) vision of nationhood? Why can't we simply hope our schools will evolve to fix it?

Part II—the more constructive part—is how we tackle this tangled problem: If we believe that adolescence should be a finite and intentional period for coming of age, what rituals might we recover from the past? What traditions should we reform? And, since technology helped birth many of our newly problematic ways of experiencing adolescence, might there also be solutions these same technologies can bring into being to help parents?

Melissa and I have a working theory of how to raise our own kids—in a way that gives them a fighting chance to become productive adults—and to inculcate the values and beliefs that were at the heart of the American experience since our founding and make life worth living. Generally, our approach to helping them transition from dependence to self-sustaining adulthood—detailed in the latter two-thirds of this book—is organized around the following five broad themes:

Overcome peer culture and wrestle with other life stages, chapter 4. This isn't a virtue so much as prudent advice (which is virtuous). We need to find ways to liberate our kids from the tyranny of the present. One basic way to do that is to know other people, especially older people. Another is to grapple with the reality of our bodies, which are in time—they are born and grow; they suffer and decline. The hypergenerational segregation of our time is bizarre, unhealthy, and historically unprecedented. It takes intentionality and work to overcome it.

Work hard, chapter 5. Almost everyone interesting I've ever met has a substantive and passionate answer to the question: "What was the first really hard work you did as a kid?" Bizarrely, our culture is now trying to *protect* kids from similar hard experiences. We should be running in exactly the opposite direction; we should be figuring out how to help build them a menu of really hard tasks to tackle. They need to know in their hearts and in their bones that suffering is not something to be avoided, but conquered. "As one grows older," Theodore Roosevelt wrote to his oldest son, Ted Jr., "the bitter and the sweet keep coming together. The only thing to do is grin and bear it, to flinch as little as possible under the punishment, and to keep pegging steadily away until the luck turns." Let's go one step further and say that suffering in our work is actually a character-building virtue.

Resist consumption, chapter 6. We already know Americans consume exorbitant amounts of media every day, whether on television, on the internet, on tablets or smartphones. We also just consume too much *stuff.* And yet people remain unhappy and uncertain as to why. Well, we know why. Aristotle knew why. St. Augustine knew why. Rousseau knew why. And we have a raft of contemporary studies from psychologists, neuroscientists, and sociologists that all say more or less the same thing: consumption is not the key to happiness; *production* is. Meaningful work—that actually serves and benefits a neighbor, thereby making a real difference in the world—contributes to long-term happiness and well-being. Consumption just consumes.

Travel to experience the difference between "need" and "want," chapter 7. You can learn a lot about your own culture by experiencing other cultures. Meaningful travel isn't about partying at a dance club in Cancun or walking the tourist-only parts of foreign ports of call on a luxury cruise. It is about engaging people in a culture who have assumptions about life, about economics, about the role of government far different from yours. And it is especially about experiencing premodern economics—that is, subsistence living, connection to food acquisition, nature, and necessity.

Become truly literate, chapter 8. Obviously, you know how to read. But do you know how to read *well*? How to read *critically*—and therefore to think critically? Consider for a moment before you answer. Most of us who read on our phones or tablets do not read deeply or retain as much information as when we read physical books or papers. We skim. We know U.S. students continue to struggle with basic reading comprehension on the National Assessment of Education Progress. We know that literacy has been in absolute decline since the 1960s. But America's Founders understood literacy as a prerequisite for freedom and our form of self-government. Once we know how to read, what we read matters. So let's build some reading lists of books you plan to wrestle with and be shaped by for the rest of your lifetime.

Then, at the end of the book, we'll explore why America, as the world's first modern creedal nation—that is, as a nation built not on shared ethnicity but on a set of shared ideas about freedom, of speech, press, religion, and assembly—is even more dependent on the conscious transmission of precise beliefs about liberty and adult responsibility than other nations. This is chapter 9. Then, in an afterword, we'll resuscitate Teddy Roosevelt—the leading frantic but winsome worrier from the last age of American economic disruption. In a modernized commencement address, the old Rough Rider will humor-scold our children into taking their phones and fashions a little less seriously but their vivacious potential a great deal more so.

The challenges before us are not merely problems for my family or your family to solve—although they are that. The coming-of-age crisis belongs to all of us, even those without children, for the vanishing of a shared sense of adulthood endangers the future of the republic we share.

PART I

OUR PASSIVITY
PROBLEM

ONE

⇒∙◐∙⇐

STRANDED IN
NEVERLAND

*Defining Adolescence * We're All Baby Boomers Now
Their Forgotten Souls * A Broader Character-Building Program*

> WENDY: *You are both ungallant and deficient!*
> PETER: *How am I deficient?*
> WENDY: *You're just a boy.*
>
> —J. M. Barrie, *Peter Pan*

PETER PAN IS A STORY ABOUT A BOY WHO REFUSES TO grow up. We often misremember it as a cheery fairy tale. It isn't. In the end, the Peter of J. M. Barrie's classic is not at all a commendable hero. He's selfish and shortsighted. "I don't want to go to school and learn solemn things," Peter tells us. "I don't want to be a man."

He ultimately cannot remember his past, and thus learns nothing from it. Near the end of the book, Wendy tries to reminisce with Peter:

"Who is Captain Hook?" he asked with interest when she spoke of the arch enemy.

"Don't you remember," she asked, amazed, "how you killed him and saved all our lives?"

"I forget them after I kill them," he replied carelessly.

Though Peter never grows up, each of his Lost Boys does. So does Wendy. She has a daughter, Jane, who visits but eventually flees from Neverland. And Jane has a daughter named Margaret, who similarly refuses to be trapped in Neverland. And on it goes. Everyone moves on. Except for Pan. Peter never changes; he never grows up.

Living only in the present isn't freedom. Living only in the present isn't even human if you think about it. Humans, unlike any other animal on the planet, remember the past. We understand our nature. And we try to build on both of them. We are an aspirational species; we look to the future.

With every crisis comes opportunity, and this time is no different. The challenges before our nation present huge opportunities, not only for fundamentally rethinking how and where we live and work but also how we think about learning, about friendship and social networks, about what it means to be an American. Our goal is for our kids to be *intentional* about everything they do—to reject passivity and mindless consumption and to embrace an ethos of action, of productivity, of meaningful work, of genuinely lifelong learning. In other words, we want them to find the good life.

Now let us begin.

DEFINING ADOLESCENCE

No civilization has ever embraced endless adolescence before. Some spoiled dynastic families have made efforts to cultivate it, but the life of being pampered has rarely ended well for the children of the ultra-rich either. In fact, very few cultures have ever had much adolescence at all, and when they did, they clearly delineated it with communal rituals that forced individuals up and out of adolescence.

Traditionally, the path to adulthood has been clear. There is still an order to growing up, but it must ultimately be an order of events and achievements rather than merely an order of dates. Ancient Roman law explicitly divided the three stages of youth before adulthood into seven-year segments: *infantia* (birth through age 6), *pueritia* (7 to 13), and *pubertas* (14 to 20). This basic framing of these three phases endured until very recently. The first of the three stages was the period when children were most immediately dependent on their parents, and particularly their mothers, for food, care, and safety. Its endpoint was when kids gingerly seized their first taste of temporary independence and began to leave the home for part of the day. When the apron strings were cut, children learned that it was possible to be away from mom for six or eight or ten hours and still survive.

The second stage coincided more or less with the time of apron-strings-cutting until puberty began and bodies signaled the arriving change to physical adulthood. Children exercised more choices in food and fashion and began to demonstrate greater self-control. For children growing up in free countries since the rise of cheap print five hundred years ago, this has been the period when they learned to read, learned to apply logical reasoning, and learned to conceptualize more sophisticated ideas—such as cause and effect, and enduring short-term sacrifices for long-term gain. The maturing children came to consciously believe in things beyond the tangible here and now.

The third stage, adolescence, was the final launching point from childhood into adulthood. The word "adolescence," derived from the Latin verb meaning "to grow up," likely began to be widely used in the fifteenth century, and was meant to suggest the nearing of full maturity—not only biologically, but now also emotionally, financially, and in terms of character. Child psychologist Erik Erikson in the 1950s framed adolescence as a "moratorium on adulthood," a time for individuals to pause in order to experiment and develop their identities, increasingly independent of their parents. Duty could be *understood* as it was embraced; it wasn't merely a burden to bear mindlessly. Adolescence was intended as a greenhouse phase, in which the oldest children could be protected as they worked through the last struggles of maturation. Tolerating or encouraging adolescence reflected the awareness of parents and other community authorities of the importance of a period for children to prepare to leave the nest finally and permanently.

In some cultures, adolescence still involves clear rituals signaling the delineation between child and adult. Their purpose is to vividly impress upon the adolescent the new set of obligations associated with the new phase of life: adult independence rather than childhood dependency. Jews have the bar and bat mitzvah, Hispanics the *quinceañera*. An extreme example comes from ancient Sparta (dramatically portrayed in Zack Snyder's 2006 fantasy-action film *300),* where boys were forced into military academies at the age of 7 and then into the wilderness, armed only with a red cloak, at the age of 12. Spartans expected their budding soldiers to be able to scrounge their own food, which often involved quasi-sanctioned stealing, to demonstrate their survival skills. The Sateré-Mawé, an indigenous tribe in Brazil, celebrates their boys' coming of age at 13 by having them wear gloves containing "bullet ants," which deliver one of the world's most painful stings. They endure the suffering to demonstrate their readiness for adulthood.

Upon turning thirteen, my uncle was allowed to begin camping out at the lakes five miles outside of our town. He and his friends had long been allowed to ride their bikes there in daylight hours, but always with the proviso that they return before the streetlights came on. Now, with that requirement lifted, he came to know the delights of the bright sky, but also the terrors of coyotes howling in the dark in the middle of the night. There were no adults to protect him so far from home—except for, in a way, himself.

A "rite of passage" is a way of marking the transition from one group to another. It is often an occasion for celebration. It entails becoming a full member of a community, whether a tribe, a military unit, a religious group, or a nation. Rites of passage may be sacred or secular, but they serve similar initiation purposes. While they frequently involve hardship, they're not meant to make kids miserable; they're intended to prime them for the inevitable tribulations that come with adulthood and to instill in them the work ethic and perseverance necessary to survive upon leaving home. They reflect—or perhaps, sadly, they once reflected—ordinary parents' extraordinary awareness that children need a realistic sense of what life will be like after leaving the nest before they actually launch. They need an intentional introduction. Today, that sense is dwindling, with potentially grave consequences for society at large.

It's not that Americans don't have coming-of-age rituals, but rather that those rituals have become more automatic, and less purposeful, than achievement-based rituals. Our principle hurdles involve uncomplicated things, like taking pictures before prom or learning to pause the appropriate length of time before walking out to receive a high school diploma—which is granted to virtually everyone who doesn't quit school.

We don't know many folks who have spent a week in the wilderness with a group of elders for an initiation by fire. Some of our communities still push their members toward difficult challenges for a greater purpose: the United States Marine Corps and the Navy SEALs both put young recruits through virtual hell before they become full-fledged members of the service, for example. At the other end of the spectrum, in the Amish tradition of "rumspringa," young people are permitted to leave home and live among outsiders, wear non-Amish clothing, drive cars, even drink and use illicit substances, before being asked to make a conscious choice about whether they want to be baptized back into the community. A membership that began by the accident of birth can now become theirs by deliberate choice—if they opt to become intentionally participating adults.

Of course, external factors can affect the length of adolescence. Children who are born into poverty or experience the premature death of parents often have to step up early, without a supervised transition into adulthood. War-ravaged cultures have neither the time nor the protective space to allow the physically mature to delay full adult responsibilities. If you were a 13-year-old in Bosnia or Rwanda in 1994, it was quite possible that one or both of your parents were killed, and you either became an adult immediately or you perished as well.

Adolescence is different from the earlier two stages of childhood in that its endpoint is more debatable and its length is more uncertain. Adolescence can be nonexistent, or short, or medium-length, or long. Having no adolescence is tragic; a short one can work if it's intentionally focused; a long one is not necessarily a problem if still oriented toward a definable end goal—think a multiyear apprenticeship to master a craft or a series of cross-cultural immersions to become proficient in a language.

Endless adolescence, however, is bizarrely oxymoronic.

Adolescence has always been a means to an end—its point was to aid the transition to adulthood. It was not an end in itself. The Spartans forced their soldiers to go through torturous rituals not because pain was good, but because they wanted to make sure that the adult citizens responsible for defending their society had the knowledge and wherewithal, the toughness and self-awareness, to fulfill their duties and responsibilities. Adolescence was intentional and meant to be finite.

Our situation is different. We no longer have any sophisticated, widely understood purpose for adolescence. We no longer share a definable reason for postponing adult responsibilities beyond biological adulthood. Our kids sense this larger cultural drift and respond with a broad range of time-killers. But if the most precious gift we have is time—earlier generations of Americans after all spoke compulsively about "redeeming the time"—why would we want to kill it?

WE'RE ALL BABY BOOMERS NOW

How did we get to this point—where a large portion of our people in the prime of their lives are stuck in a sad sort of limbo, ordering pizza on cell phones while streaming Netflix from their parents' basements, where they live? There is no simple answer, but we can wrap our minds around the current unraveling of adolescence by briefly considering five big developments in the United States in the first decades after World War II.

First, although the echoes of the 2008 recession remain and longer-term employment instability will likely accelerate, we still have more material surplus than any other people any place in all of history. That's obviously good news—but it also has a large and underdiscussed downside: our jaw-dropping wealth accumulation over the past seventy years has allowed America's youth to indulge in more creature comforts than any generation ever before.

Second, and related to our overconsumption, our kids no longer know how to produce. They don't grow up around work. Today's children are likely to conceive of work as one job, and yet less likely to work the same job as their parents—such as on a family farm or ranch or in the same trade—than ever before. They no longer see up close a broad range of their parents' work struggles, and they do not daily observe their parents' work ethic the way their great-grandparents did. Most kids' hours are spent chiefly in age-segregated environments. This vacuum of adult authority and of the compulsory nature of work has been filled first by the peer culture of the school and more recently by the narcissistic autonomy of the digital world. Ironically, even though many late teens and twentysomethings continue sleeping physically under their parents' roofs for longer than they did in past generations, they have been liberated from the social and moral universes of their elders much earlier.

Third, the warning bells we've been hearing for half a century about the nuclear family being in peril turned out to be right. A stunning portion of our kids now experience the disruption of home life, one that rattles the stable, trusted environment from which they should be finding an orderly launch into independent adulthood. Daniel Patrick Moynihan, the legendary New York Democrat (whose desk I occupy on the U.S. Senate floor), first sounded the alarm about the crisis of black family disintegration. The U.S. Department of Labor published Moynihan's report on why federal officials should panic about household collapse in 1965. At the time, the crisis was an out-of-wedlock birthrate among African Americans rocketing toward one in four, compared with a rate in the low single digits for whites. Five decades later, it's clear that the problem isn't about race—it is nearly universal. The works of Charles Murray, Robert Putnam, and J. D. Vance show that these tragic developments are not unique to any geographic or ethnic community. The share of white births occurring outside marriage is now roughly three in ten, which is higher than the "emergency" black rate in the 1960s. And although the teen pregnancy rate is down, the Urban Institute's "Moynihan Report Revisited" pegs the overall share of black births now occurring outside marriage at more than seven in ten.

Fourth, we have unhelpfully come to so identify our obligations to teenagers with the institution of secondary schooling that we have lost the collective memory of folks who came of age without schooling as the defining formative institution in life. (Note: this was essentially everyone, everywhere, until a century ago.) In most states, year-round secondary schooling went from being voluntary in the 1910s to being a compulsory and near-universal experience by the 1940s. While this obviously brought about much good, an unintended consequence has been that institutionalized schooling displaced work and other multigenerational environments as the context and the culture in which coming of age occurred. Even just after World War II, almost all American families still had many older voices around the dining room table that could—by their own experience—broaden a conversation about growing up to more than just progressing through annual grades in school.

Somewhat paradoxically, even as schooling swallowed most of our mental image of education, it also became shallower in the 1970s and beyond. Some of this evolution toward more secular, bureaucratic schooling followed necessarily from the Supreme Court decisions prohibiting school prayer and religious instruction in the 1960s. Regardless of whether you believe children should have prayer or study religion in school, the removal of those activities had the unintended consequence of removing existential questions about how the individual fits into the bigger, cosmic picture; about our life's purpose.

The moral hollowing of schooling is also attributable to the erosion of secondary education's previously secure place and purpose in preparing kids for steady jobs right after graduation. Education historian Paula Fass traces the drift toward the "warehousing" of our young to schools' loss of their tangible, culminating purpose—to prepare the emerging generation for conclusive entry into adult productivity. Instead, "going to high school became a stop-over during the teen years, with very little to offer beyond academic selection for those who would go on to college . . ." When a diploma was no longer a predictable ticket to a full-time, middle-class job and a set of expectations about adulthood, high schools began to fray. Peer culture metastasized to fill the vacuum of purpose. Instead of learning how to behave from their teachers, who no longer really saw their jobs as moral instruction and instilling wisdom acquired through age and experience, kids were learning how to behave from other kids, with predictable results.

Fifth, the protest era of the 1960s saw an atypical amount of conflict about what America means, about whether our experiment in self-governance was really all that special. Some of the struggles—chiefly civil rights—were essential to America's finally living up to the Declaration of Independence's vision of universal, color-blind human dignity. The nation was centuries overdue in living up to our ideals that all men and women, of all races, are created equal. Other struggles, however—such as debates about the morality of different wars, about the costs of drug use, about the prudence or pointlessness of sexual boundaries—we yelled about for a while, and then we stopped yelling, but not because we came to agreement. Tragically, we quasi-decided instead not to finally decide, not to reconcile. In essence, as the late 1960s eventually became the early 1980s, we navigated some big cultural bumps not by deliberating together and then actually forging a new consensus, but instead by allowing polarization to hollow out much of our discourse. We permitted popular culture and the trivial to substitute as the basis of our shared experience.

To be sure, there remained sparks of renewal in our national consensus: we would eventually resolve to win the Cold War together; our tremendous progress on racial inclusion was overwhelmingly if not unanimously celebrated; the broader inclusion of Catholics and Jews into a previously Protestants-first culture became the norm; and we went to the moon. Nonetheless, national consensus on goals and shared ideals that could unite this diverse nation continued to fray beyond the 1960s. Looking back, the unprecedented consumption, the decreasing presence of work in the lives of young people, and the more frequent broken homes of that turbulent decade mark an epochal divide in the experience of American adolescence. Arguably the most fundamental cleavage in American life is between those who came of age after rather than before the Baby Boom.

THEIR FORGOTTEN SOULS

One final megatrend from a century ago requires special emphasis. Starting around the turn of the twentieth century a battle took place among scholars and practitioners about the ways of educating young Americans. What should they learn? How? Until when? What should be required by law? What should be left to choice and parents in the home?

On one side you had traditionalists, who argued the importance of morality and character-building, that children had souls that needed to be nurtured and habits that needed to be formed in accordance with longstanding ideas about virtue. On the other you had so-called pragmatic school-builders, who believed that these issues were mostly irrelevant distractions—that schools should instead focus simply on churning out workers with a baseline competence that would enable them to live productively in a rapidly industrializing nation. The priority was universal education for everyone, not on the abstraction of what the purpose of that education was. Boatloads of immigrants were arriving, and we needed to get on with the work of building new schools for these millions. The pragmatists won, and their victory would mark a significant change in the way our children came of age.

Ironically, this sidelining of controversial philosophical and theological fights—this alleged cease-fire in ideological warring—was architected by one of the most ideologically aggressive men in U.S. history: John Dewey. To understand coming of age and adolescence as we now practice it, one must first understand Dewey. And to understand Dewey, one must first understand him not as a technical expert, but as a philosopher taking a third position in a grand, age-old debate that had been previously thought to have only two sides.

This book is not about those overarching philosophical questions—yet just behind any analysis of our coming-of-age crisis, and just prior to any suggestions about rebuilding a culture of self-reliance, sit some basic assumptions about what it means to live a good life or to be an honorable person. We are necessarily within arm's length of large questions about whether your kids on their deathbeds will be able to look back on lives oriented toward the good, the true, and the beautiful. This book is not outlining any answers to the grand questions of meaning, but we should acknowledge that adolescents and their parent-guides are inevitably wrestling with the fundamental: What makes a life worth living?

From the moment human beings were able to pause between hunts and harvests to ponder circumstances without fear of imminent death, we have been asking variations of: What is important? What debts do I bear, and to whom? Is there an afterlife? How should I now live? What is the good life? The Apostle Paul added a painfully introspective version to the mix: Why do I not do what I want to do, and why do I do what I do not want to do?

Bearing kids and raising kids and educating kids puts a fine point on many of the existential questions with which some of us regularly struggle, and from which others of us get good at hiding. When your child is stubborn and willful, when she worries about the future, when he regrets the past, when they hurt because of the wrongdoing of another, we are forced to contend with overarching questions about the brokenness of the world and of our souls.

For thousands of years, two broadly competing approaches to the question "*How* is the world broken?" have dominated Western thinking.

To oversimplify, one school of thought says that the corruption origi-
nates inside of us, while the other counters that social structures corrupt
us from the outside. These views need not be completely mutually exclusive, but there is a fundamental fault line at the question of whether human sinfulness—that is, the guilt and corruption that warp all human
beings—is or is not the biggest problem at hand in our own souls and
those of the beautiful babes we're called to nurture. For shorthand, let's
call these millennia-old views of our kids' core natures the *realist* view
and the *romantic* view.

The realist recognizes that much of man's lot in this life is to bear
the burden of suffering and to do his best in the moral quest to turn
away from self-centeredness. He recognizes his inherent weakness and
inclination toward not just vice but full-on narcissism. There is something wrong around here, and it's mostly me. There is only one true
heaven, and it doesn't exist on Earth. Augustine, born in Roman North
Africa in 354 CE, remains perhaps the best exemplar of this view of
the human condition. In his *Confessions,* the troublemaker recounts his
hedonistic youth spent drinking, thieving, and carousing. He famously
prayed, "Grant me chastity and continence, Lord, but not yet." But
Augustine's biggest problem is not his wasted years or that he fathered
a kid out of wedlock; his biggest problem is the egoist desire that predated any action—the yearning he felt to be a law unto himself, to be
autonomous, to be a god. The *Confessions* centers on the story of the
first time he and his friends stole some fruit from a garden. He did not
steal because he was hungry, but rather mainly because the fruit was
forbidden: "It was foul, and I loved it. I loved my own error—not that
for which I erred, but the error itself." Augustine concluded that man is
naturally inclined to sin—to be lustful, greedy, envious, hateful, will-
fully disobedient. Parenting is hard, and it feels like a marathon-long
wrestling match, because all human beings are born with a will that is,
in fact, unruly.

Against this sober worldview stands the romantic view of the world
and of our nature. We could select many archetypes to fill the role of
romantic optimist, starting with Plato. But the French Enlightenment
philosopher Jean-Jacques Rousseau is most instructive in thinking about
where we go wrong with our kids. Rousseau rejected the Augustinian understanding of original sin. He argued instead that the ache or

division in the human soul results not from imperfection inside man, but rather because we have taught the boy-becoming-man to depend on others, to care what they think, to pay attention to social norms. Rousseau's project was to free mankind from this debasement of dependence and from unhelpful introspection. He wanted his boy-becoming-man to be indifferent to convention, to be liberated from status anxiety. His "novel" *Emile* offers a "new system of education," intended to teach us how to bring up the next generation to *be*. With a sweep reminiscent of Plato's grand plan of educating the future ruler in *The Republic*, Rousseau's child-rearing handbook is also a philosophic treatise on human limits and on the aspirations of our mortality-fearing souls.

Emile is one of my favorite books—but not because I like or agree with much of what Rousseau has to say about educating children. Some of it is insightful, but much of it is harmfully encouraging of narcissism, in my view. Other parts of it are downright dangerous. I love *Emile*, though, because it forced me to hone my own thinking about the education Melissa and I were planning for our children—and what we hope for our nephews and nieces, and our neighborhood and nation. Rousseau is someone to argue with. He's someone who helped me make sense of how and why so many other parents' kids flourish in spite of the fact that they (the parents) don't necessarily share my Augustinian perspective on the need for humility. The key Rousseauian principle many seem to understand intuitively is the need to parent and nurture "with the grain"—the need to acknowledge that imposed one-size-fits-all models will simply not work for every child.

"Plants are shaped by cultivation, and men by education," he writes. Human beings aren't commodities; they aren't cogs. Shape a student's environment and he or she can become great—heroic even. Teachers "cultivate" habits of thinking and doing in their students. They don't assemble them; they nurture them. Students are not passive, but active. They are not manufactured; they are molded. This sculpting is what Rousseau attempts to show, in painstaking and clever detail.

The two sides of the parenting coin represented by Augustine and Rousseau—the need to rein in our kids' lesser, self-absorbed impulses while cultivating the grand potential of their self-sufficiency—are at the center of a vital, age-old debate: How can man be so glorious *and* so devilish? So full of beauty and of darkness? Why does the fit between my child and the world not always work? Why does this hurt—why do we often feel hollow inside?

Then in walks Dewey, casually waving everyone off: Never mind all that realism versus romance stuff. Stop debating how many angels can dance on the head of a pin. We've got real work to do!

American philosopher and education reformer John Dewey is a hard thinker-doer to argue with. There are multiple reasons for the challenge: He was stunningly prolific, but difficult to quote because he was rarely succinct. He was legendary in his accomplishments, yet he constantly refused to have a debate about the big steps he was taking—which are themselves premised on a precise vantage point in a debate vanquishing all alternative views.

One way to survey the complexity of the man and his thought is by trying to define his profession and primary work over 93 years of life. Dewey was a philosopher—his *New York Times* obituary in 1952 noted that many regarded him as perhaps "America's foremost philoso-pher"—with interests and expertise in subdisciplines from aesthetics to logic, and epistemology to linguistics. He didn't merely theorize; he built institutions, such as the path-breaking Laboratory Schools at the University of Chicago. He was a sociologist and a union organizer and a recognized theorist on the role of journalism in modern society. He was a cultural ambassador, lecturing hundreds of times on scores of subjects in many countries on multiple continents. An atheist, he nonetheless published on many religious topics. He held distinguished professor-ships at the University of Michigan, the University of Chicago, and Columbia. Eventually, he became the intellectual leader of Columbia's Teachers College, from which his educational philosophy spread like kudzu through teacher training textbooks and programs across the land. A self-described champion of the downtrodden, he was a legal crusader for immigrants, the poor, and women's suffrage. And though he in-vested long hours in the practical tasks of trying to build a new socialist-inclined political party in the United States, he was widely respected in academia as the president of the American Psychological Association.

But more than anything else, John Dewey was, as one obituary put it, "the chief prophet of progressive education." He was passionate about teachers being passionate, an evangelist for the view that educa-tion needed to become a defined, esteemed profession in the way that medicine and law had then become. His overarching motive seems to have been to secure quality, universal schooling for everyone. Laudably, he wanted to ensure that there was no second-tier schooling for some portion of the American public, and he worked to guard against school becoming merely a means to the end of job training, which he worried would cement the socioeconomic status of the poor and the immigrant. He has, in my view, the single best claim to be the father of the modern American public high school. But ultimately, I will argue, even if you share his progressive goals down to the last one, he is responsible for allowing schools to undermine how Americans once turned children into adults.

What's the problem? To the degree that we have forgotten the fact that a school should be a tool—a means to an end, not an end in itself—Dewey is the culprit. For him, the school would become everything—the literal center of the world, he said on occasion. In Dewey's dream, the school ceased to be an instrument supporting parents and became instead a substitute for parents.

A BROADER CHARACTER-BUILDING PROGRAM

Dewey is a tough guy for me to love. He's blunt and honest in certain ways, but he never directly admits to his readers what is obviously one of his ambitions. He's an experimental oncology surgeon masquerading as a smiling school wellness nurse. His goal: He doesn't want the school any longer to be in the handmaiden role, aiding parents in *their* goal of passing literacy and tradition and deferred gratification on to their progeny. As we'll discuss more fully in chapter 3, his schools now have the socially transforming purpose of displacing the parents, with their supposedly petty interests in their children as individuals.

As the son and husband of public school teachers, I hold nearly the opposite view of the place and purpose of schooling in American life. School is obviously an important tool—for intentionally exposing kids to an entire range of content and subjects, for adding structure to days that can become Jell-O, for being the context in which socialization with peers and with authorities beyond your family occurs—but it is still a tool. It is only one of many tools. And it is most fundamentally a tool in the service of parents—and grandparents and neighbors and local communities. For these deeper communities are ultimately responsible for nurturing children toward the kind of living and serving that befits free and independent nearly-adults with big and complicated souls. Great teachers don't try to be the exclusive center of life, but rather instrumental servants of a larger life. Great school administrators know and honor the limits of their institutions; they don't try to displace families and the deeper and wider institutions of life that are based on love.

I have no interest in my children being formed by the *zeitgeist,* by the majoritarian sentiments of any particular moment, by what Dewey celebrated as an abstract "social consciousness of the race." Instead, I want my children to be formed by ideals and principles that are definable and debatable—by me and by them—even if such ideals and principles are not always in vogue. I want my children to be introduced to the enduring debates between Augustine and Rousseau, not to have these debates hidden from them, as Dewey seeks to do.

In full disclosure, one of my children is named Augustine (although we call him "Breck," since Augustine seems a bit theologically heavy for a 6-year-old). I'm a Christian and embrace my religion's traditional view of fallen human nature. I worry deeply about my children's character—I want them to struggle mightily against the self-absorbed, Adamic yearning for forbidden fruit. But I have deep and abiding respect for the optimistic and enlightenment side of the Western tradition as well. For human fallenness is not the whole story. There is also pre-fall and post-redemption, and Rousseau does a splendid job of nudging us to raise our sights to the possible. Hence my fondness for wrestling with him, even though I disagree more often than I agree with him. My wife and I frame many questions in our parenting in terms of our children's souls. How do we help them put aside mindless video games and YouTube fads to devote more time to reading deeply and critically, to struggling with ultimate questions, to persevering in their callings even amid hardship, and to living lives of true meaning and service? Rousseau would differ from many of the tentative conclusions in our household—but he's big, and thus he's worthy of debating. He is not making a total claim of ownership on my kids without any existential acknowledgment that they are *my* kids—which is basically the claim on them that Dewey is making.

The purpose of this book is not to persuade you of any theological points. Every reader will address the larger questions of life on their own timelines. But I do believe that good parenting includes a basic desire for your kids to reach a *satisfying* answer to the bigger questions, as opposed to merely an accidental, impromptu, along-the-way provisional way of living. Thus serious adults have long guided their children to prioritize the weighty over the trivial as they transition to becoming young adults. If one is going to deny the brokenness of human nature that Augustine explained or reject the grander possibilities for true human freedom that Rousseau elevated, those choices should be made explicitly—not because Dewey's schools distracted our offspring from these enduring questions and the self-aware character that exemplifies independent adulthood.

THE FAILURES OF DEWEY'S VISION for our kids weren't as obvious when America's economic upward trajectory was climbing at a historically unprecedented pace. The Industrial Revolution helped birth an anomalous world superpower in the Western hemisphere. And as European powers battled over land on a crowded continent, America created the largest middle class the world had ever known. Jobs were plentiful. The quality of life, compared even to what it had been only a generation earlier, increased dramatically.

No longer. We cannot assume the middle class will easily self-perpetuate in the future. We are living through what is surely the greatest economic disruption since the Industrial Revolution—and what might end up being the largest economic disruption since nomadic hunter-gatherers first settled down to plant crops. We have seen flat median wages and shaky labor demand for nearly three decades—even as folks are being forced to change jobs more frequently than ever before. Economists and sociologists haven't even settled on what to call this era we're living in. It's the Information Age or the Age of Globalization—or the Postindustrial Age, which is really just another way of saying that it comes "after the industrial age," but we don't really know what to call it or how to think about it. No one knows what comes next.

Work instability will become an even more regular feature of future experience. Contrast our present work experiences with those of our grandparents and their ancestors: For most of human history, people did the same work as their parents without choosing it for themselves. Hunter-gathering and then farming were inherited callings. And for millennia, people never even reflected on this reality; it was simply the sea in which they swam. Only after the Civil War—that is, only 150 years ago—did people first broadly develop the concept of picking a job or vocation. But even then it tended to be a one-time decision as a teen that defined one's life until death or retirement. As recently as the Carter administration in the late 1970s, a very large share of the population still worked with their hands, and the average duration at a firm for most primary breadwinners was decades.

That world of once-for-a-lifetime jobs is not coming back. Today, manufacturing represents less than 8 percent of U.S. employment. We live in a time in which the average duration of a job is about four years. In this new world, college graduates will change not only jobs but industries an average of three times *by age 30*. When I was born (in the 1970s), three-quarters of Americans had a high school diploma or less—and the vast majority could find meaningful work and afford a middle-class lifestyle with that level of educational attainment. Mid-career job retraining didn't exist because it wasn't necessary. Today, a combination of market pressures and bureaucratic mandates has spurred a credentialing race that makes even a bachelor's degree insufficient for a large set of jobs. The inflation-adjusted earnings of workers with bachelor's degrees have fallen over the past decade.

We all understand that the evaporation of agricultural and industrial jobs means we will guide more of the young in our care toward "knowledge work." But we are underappreciating that just as technology has steadily eroded the need for human hands on farms and in factory lines, so too is automation already upending the "knowledge economy" as well. A recent study by McKinsey Global Institute looked at seven categories of high-end knowledge workers—doctors, lawyers, engineers, scientists, teachers, etcetera—and found large portions of their roles susceptible to displacement by machines as well. The analysis predicted some truly jaw-dropping advances in communications, manufacturing, and medicine, but one headline from the study will strike mild terror in the hearts of many people already anxious about providing for their families a decade from now: by 2025, "we estimate that knowledge work automation tools and systems could take on tasks that would be equal to the output of 110 million to 140 million full-time" workers. The increasing digitization and automation of our economy will remake work as we know it.

This is truly a critical time in the history of the United States. We are going to need even more nimble and entrepreneurial workers and citizens than we have raised in the past. Yet just as the economy is laying the demand for a society of truly lifelong learners at our collective national feet, we have decided to orphan the rising generation of the American idea of universal dignity and the possibilities of resilience, innovation, and renewal. Tragically, we're in the process of abandoning our children to Neverland, blissfully unaware of their past or their future, living only in a smothering present. It's not fair to them, and it won't work for us. It is nothing short of a national existential crisis.

As a historian, I realize that's a bold statement: everyone typically (and usually wrongly) believes the moment they're living in is the most critical time in human history. Indeed, historians most often have the dreary, balloon-puncturing task of informing people that the great turmoil we are supposedly experiencing has happened many times before. After all, these kinds of challenges—technological change, unequal distribution of wealth, disruptions in the economy—though acute, have afflicted every generation in some form or another.

But this time really is different. This is almost a re-founding moment in American life. Chapter 2 outlines why.

TWO

FROM LITTLE CITIZENS TO BABY EINSTEINS

The Older Idea of Children as Little Workers
*Making Kids Softer * More Medication * More Screen Time*
*More Pornography * More Years under Mom's Roof * Less Marriage*
*Less Religious Participation * Little Citizens No More * More Intellectually Fragile*
*Softer Parenting * Who Birthed Softer Parenting?*
*A Flatter World * What to Call Not-Quite-Yet-Adults?*

What Orwell feared were those who would ban books. What Huxley
feared was that there would be no reason to ban a book, for there
would be no one who wanted to read one. Orwell feared those who
would deprive us of information. Huxley feared those who would give
us so much that we would be reduced to passivity and egoism.

—Neil Postman

TO THE EXTENT AMERICA HAS ANY CLEAR DELINEA-
tion between the final stage of childhood and arrival at adulthood, it is
only that after living 6,574 days on Earth, we become an adult in the
eyes of the state. To be considered mature under the laws of our land,

an individual must have attained the age of 18. Whatever other traits or markers of adulthood you might exemplify or lack, as an 18-year-old American you are, strictly and legally speaking, an American adult, with all the rights and responsibilities attaining thereto—except drinking alcohol or renting a car.

Anyone who has turned 18 knows you don't wake up one morning and suddenly feel like an adult. Nobody shows up to shake your hand and present you with a signed, notarized "adulthood certificate" to hang next to your birth certificate. You're still not fully in control of your destiny. Most Americans will turn 18 during their final year of high school, in the midst of their struggle to figure out what they're going to do once they graduate. An 18-year-old isn't necessarily more responsible than a 17-and-a-half-year-old.

Our laws say otherwise, however. Turning 18 is a concrete *legal* milestone: It confers the right to own property, the right to make contracts (usually including marriage), the right to vote, and, for young men, the obligation to register for the draft. These are all rites of passage—and all important in their own right. But . . .

Something is lost when we allow the automatic and unstoppable turning of the calendar to distract us from the more important matters—the decisions and accomplishments—that ought to be firmly at the front of our minds and our worries as we contemplate development. For adulthood is not an age, and shouldn't be treated as one. It is something to be earned after going through various milestones that mark a mature, autonomous human being.

Sociologists talk about many markers associated with becoming an adult. Consider eight big ones:

- moving from parents' home,
- leaving school for the final time,
- getting a full-time job,
- reaching economic self-sufficiency,
- loss of virginity,
- getting married,
- having children,
- establishing an independent household.

Some of the markers straddle categories but they can be mostly clustered around education, work and money, sex and family, and residence. Think of the teens and twentysomethings you know: How many of these markers have they successfully cleared? Which of them are they intentionally delaying? Which of them have they mindlessly drifted through?

I suspect that most of us stumble through them rather than approach them with any purpose. To be clear, there is not necessarily a right order to the sequencing of the entire progression of these events. There is not a morality about the phasing of when one gets a full-time job and when one firmly establishes a household independent of mom and dad's. Prior to the twentieth century, a young person's first significant work regularly began while still living at home—usually working on a farm, tending to younger siblings, or apprenticing with a skilled tradesman. Similarly, there is not a right or wrong answer to getting married or not before the end of college or graduate school. Conversely, loss of virginity has traditionally been a heavier matter—and its timing for the young was therefore often shaped by older members of the community when they still had substantial control over teens' physical environment. Beth Bailey, in her fascinating *From Front Porch to Back Seat: Courtship in Twentieth-Century America,* has demonstrated that the bigger sexual revolution in modern America was not the 1960s, but rather the arrival of the automobile half a century earlier, which created unsupervised spaces for unmarried people, so that many young adults had the opportunity to have their first sexual experiences well before their wedding nights.

Even though loss of virginity began to happen at an earlier average age over the twentieth century, the series of other typical markers of adulthood remained relatively unchanged: Most Americans finished high school, began full-time work, became economically self-sufficient, got married, moved out of their parents' house, and established their own permanent household, in roughly that order. Having children overwhelmingly occurred after getting married, but they sometimes came before and sometimes after moving out from under mom and dad's roof.

The predictability of these steps provided a structure for finishing adolescence and coming of age. It set expectations and clarified duties. The milestones represented steps toward maturity and independence—an ending and a beginning. Mere conventions were sometimes inappropriately moralized into absolute rights and wrongs, but the reality is that most young people benefited from the structure and predictability of expectations provided by older members of their communities.

THE OLDER IDEA OF CHILDREN
AS LITTLE WORKERS

There is nothing God-ordained about adulthood beginning at the age of 18. We tend to forget that the twentieth-century American convention of having most people arrive at adulthood in their late teens or early twenties has not been a permanent fixture of human experience. Different cultures, in different eras, have helped children transition into the progressively increasing responsibilities of early adulthood at much earlier ages than we do.

The deep imprinting of age 18 on our psyche is the product of two innovations in the first decades of the twentieth century. First, the spread of secondary schooling—and then the passage of compulsory attendance laws—forced firm grade and age divisions onto the experience of "teenagers" (a term that didn't enter Americans' collective vocabulary until just seventy-five years ago). In the late 1890s, less than *10 percent* of 14- to 17-year-olds attended school. Think about that—nine out of ten people between age 14 and 17 were already working. By 1930, more than half of teenagers attended school; and by 1945, three-quarters would be enrolled. Second, the rise of factory work in the late nineteenth century—and then the passage of extensive laws against child labor early in the twentieth century—created new mental markers suggesting precise ages before which (nonfarm) kids should be insulated from work.

This new formula of "much school, little work" until age 18 would have felt strange to Americans in the centuries before the Civil War. Our ancestors didn't talk about age this way, partly because they often didn't know their own ages. The celebration of "birthdays" is a recent, Victorian practice. Many people prior to 1800 simply didn't know precisely when they were born; in some communities, almost no one recorded it. (In a largely agricultural economy, one's age mattered less than one's ability to complete specific tasks. Farming constituted 90 percent of the workforce in 1790, 70 percent in 1840, and less than 40 percent in 1900.

Today it is between 1 and 2 percent.) Few legal categories surrounded age. The questions were whether someone could complete their work; whether he or she was mature enough to marry; whether he or she was perseverant enough to navigate the challenges of adulthood.

Children in colonial times and in the early years of the republic were treated less as "precious" and more as little workers who were just not yet very good at their work. It is a very different way of thinking about childhood as a training ground. Young people were expressly viewed as "little citizens"—not to be coddled, but to be encouraged to contribute more and more to the greater good of their communities. Families were large partly because farms needed more working hands, and sadly many children would die young. Think for a moment how bizarre that sounds to modern ears. Kids—as fun, vivacious, and rewarding as they can be for parents, and no doubt were back then just as they are today—were ultimately necessary for making economic ends meet, and they were treated as such. Their worth was judged partly in terms of their output for their communities. When was the last time "citizenship"—fitting into broader society—was a goal we had for our kids?

As late as the 1870s, when industrialization had already begun squeezing out many apprenticeships and smaller skilled trades, it is estimated that children between the ages of 10 and 19 were still providing at least one-third of family income. The economic contributions of youth would eventually be minimized—by the arrival of the Great Depression, by teenagers' exit from the factory floor, and by the increasing use of technology on American farms—but for most of U.S. history, the basic assumption has been that kids were born to work. Families needed their output, and parents assumed it was good for kids to learn to work. Communities believed that children were naturally self-centered and needed to be shepherded toward the adult end-state of becoming self-disciplined and self-controlled.

European parenting theories diverged widely from the stern American approaches of the late colonial and early national period. According to historian Paula Fass, "European children of the middle classes were being treated as precious objects of solicitude, needing careful protection." American children, by contrast, even those "who later became presidents, doctors, writers, and reformers were exposed to [demanding] adult work and responsibility" as an intentional part of their upbringing. They were in training to become tough. Resilience didn't come naturally; it had to be cultivated. Steven Mintz, in his history of American childhood, notes that unlike "the Romantics, who associated childhood with purity and innocence," the early Americans "adopted a fairly realistic view, emphasizing children's intransigence, willfulness, and obstinacy."

Parents and other cultural leaders worked to minimize those naturally selfish tendencies. When a boy was old enough to work, he participated in a ceremony called "breeching"—after which he no longer wore the gown of an infant, but began to wear pants that would enable work. He would henceforth be outside and under the supervision of his father or another older male. In nonfarming families, children as young as 7 or 8 could be sent away to relatives for more than a year to work as apprentices and to learn a skilled trade. *Johnny Tremain* captures this experience for our children to relive today.

In this frontier nation, literacy was prized, but long schooling was scarce. In the early 1800s, as the new nation sprawled westward and would soon begin the radical transition from an agricultural and artisanal economy to a market-driven factory economy, Americans trusted their early teens to manage significant chores. Parents "at this time assumed that children needed less supervision and direction" than we now assume, Fass notes. "This was true for girls as well as boys." American children would be given meaningful tasks to accomplish and they thus matured early out of necessity, which led Alexis de Tocqueville to claim that Americans appeared not to need an adolescent stage at all.

Such framing helpfully nuances the simple picture we painted earlier: "Adolescence" as a time for rigorous preparation for adulthood doesn't need to come exclusively *after* puberty. In many times and cultures—including pre–Civil War America—what we now mean by adolescence actually straddled puberty. The preparation phase for adulthood could begin much earlier. Thus some historians claim that the modern notion of adolescence as a distinct phase of human development didn't gain currency here until the late nineteenth century, as formalized public education spread and more Americans began to adopt the wealthy European model of protecting children *from* work instead of socializing them *into* work.

We do not need to render a judgment on the stern, realistic, work-centric parenting of early America. We will simply profit by understanding that the child-centered, nurturing approach most of us take for granted today is a choice, and would have been quite foreign to earlier generations. They did not know the separation of children from the adult world that our work environments now presuppose. And they certainly did not presume that the classrooms of secondary education were the sole route to maturation and a middle-class lifestyle.

MAKING KIDS SOFTER

In addition to the ascendancy of schooling, there are now many other indicators of the longer but less rigorous approach to child development. We could detail the explosion in childhood obesity, rocketing 500 percent from less than one in twenty teens in the early 1960s to more than one in five today. We could trace the increased buying power of young adults—which began with Baby Boom consumerism. Toy sales were almost non-existent in the late 1930s but surged to become more than a billion-dollar annual industry by 1960, and have climbed higher ever since.

But let's limit ourselves to brief summaries of nine indicative changes of our less intentional approach to shaping our offspring as they come of age.

More Medication

Before 1980, you rarely heard of kids being diagnosed with behavioral ailments such as ADHD, OCD, depression, and the many other now common mental conditions. We simply didn't think of children's problems in these mental-health terms, except in the most extreme cases.

As diagnoses proliferate, so too do the remedies: Prescription medications from Ritalin to Adderall to Prozac and from Wellbutrin to Xanax, designed to calm anxieties, focus attention, and quiet the mind, are big business. A 2015 report by the market research firm IBISWorld found that sales of ADHD medications alone have grown 8 percent per year since 2010. They topped $12.9 billion in 2015, and are expected to exceed $17.5 billion by 2020.

Is the explosion of pediatric diagnoses based in fact? Or is it a way for Big Pharma to keep selling drugs? It's complicated, and we lack the data to make a fully informed judgment on the level of overdiagnosis. Every kid is different, and as your child's parents, you're the only ones with a well-rounded understanding of their particular needs and personalities. But before putting a kid on these drugs, one should at least have a theory for why the diagnoses and prescriptions are exploding.

There are credible arguments for competing views. The American Psychological Association's 2014 "Stress in America" survey found that 30 percent of teenagers report feeling "sad or depressed," and an even higher share feels "overwhelmed." What's more, teenagers report feeling more stressed across the board than their parents. A 2012 survey by the Association for University and College Counseling Center Directors found that 95 percent of college counselors say the number of students with severe psychological problems on their campus is rising rapidly. Anxiety and depression are now among students' top life concerns. More than 24 percent of students who arrive for counseling are taking some kind of psychotropic drug. They're under pressure to perform and many believe that the price of failure—rejection from their preferred college, falling short of a competitive internship—is too high to contemplate.

They and their parents are turning to drugs to cope—producing the most medicated generation of youth in history. The medications might or might not be an appropriate response to the underlying problems, but even in cases where they are net positive, the side effects—which can include everything from fatigue and lethargy to worsening depression—are spreading across large segments of our young in ways that constitute a public health crisis. It is hard to imagine that a generation with this pervasive medication-induced haze will be fully prepared to navigate the challenges flung at it by an unforgiving world.

More Screen Time

Any parent or grandparent who has witnessed the hostage-taking hold computer and mobile devices have on adolescent attention doesn't need macro data to be persuaded that screens have transformed sensibilities in the last decade. Many children are obsessed to the point of addiction.

One study of more than four hundred eighth- to eleventh-graders found that teen texters exhibit behaviors similar to those of compulsive gamblers, including "losing sleep . . . , problems cutting back on texting, and lying to cover up the amount of time spent texting."

But it obviously isn't just texts. Screen time is consuming more and more of their lives. According to a Common Sense Media 2015 study of 2,600 young people, "American teenagers (13- to 18-year-olds) average about nine hours (8:56) of entertainment media use, excluding time spent at school or for homework. Tweens (8- to 12-year-olds) use an average of about six hours' (5:55) worth of entertainment media daily." Given that most of them sleep slightly less than ten hours per night, this means kids over 13 are spending nearly two-thirds of their waking hours with their eyes tied down and bodies stationary. These obsessive-compulsive digital consumption habits are now rapidly invading young adulthood as well, with Nielsen Research finding that the average adult has "increased his or her time on smartphone applications by 63 percent in just the last two years."

Whether to label all of these behaviors "addiction" is debatable, but social psychologists Philip Zimbardo and Nikita Coulombe estimate that many relatively average young American males have played more than 14,000 hours of video games by the time they turn 21. That's 583 days, or 1.6 years—not an insignificant portion of one's time on earth. Another way of conceiving of this: since they are awake barely 100 hours per week, this translates to half of all waking hours for 280 weeks (more than five years) over the course of their childhoods. Just one month after the release of *Call of Duty: Black Ops* in 2010, the game had been collectively played for *68,000 years*. More and more young American men are opting out of higher education, work, and marriage in favor of electronic amusements. For men with less than a four-year college degree, "leisure time" completely dominates the hours they're not working. And 75 percent of this expanding category of leisure time, according to University of Chicago economist Erik Hurst, falls into one category: video games. A substantial share of low-skilled young men now play video games upward of thirty hours per week. A staggering 5 million Americans—more than the combined populations of Nebraska, South Dakota, North Dakota, Wyoming, and Montana—consume forty-five hours of video games per week.

More Pornography

The relatively recent ubiquity of digital pornography has pernicious effects. A University of Alberta survey of teenagers found that 90 percent of boys and 70 percent of girls report having accessed sexually explicit material. More than one-third of the boys report watching pornographic videos "more times than they could count," as do 8 percent of girls. A Barna survey found that 63 percent of men age 18 to 30 view pornography more than once per week. Half as many women in the same age bracket view pornography regularly (34 percent), but with less frequency—monthly for women versus at least weekly for men.

Consumption of pornography was very different in the pre-digital age when the acquisition of elicit material often required a social interaction that inhibited a large percentage of potential consumers, particularly among the young, who previously could not travel far enough to gain anonymity.

More Years under Mom's Roof

Although there are many strong arguments to be made for intentionally intergenerational households, the increasing trend of the young staying in the parental nest does not seem to be driven by reflective choices about those intergenerational values. Rather, the increasing habit of 18-year-olds to early thirtysomethings to remain dependent or to return home is caused mainly by decreasing initiative, the absence of economic alternatives, and a deficit of the life skills required for self-reliance.

Pew Research data shows that "for the first time in more than 130 years, 18- to 34-year olds in the U.S. were more likely to be living in their parents' home than with a spouse or partner in their own household." Fully one-quarter of Americans between age 25 and 29 now live with a parent—compared to only 18 percent just over a decade ago. And in the next older age bracket, Americans 30 to 34 years old, 13 percent still live at home, compared to 9 percent ten years ago. The last time there was any comparable trend of not leaving home, it was the Great Depression, with its radically limited opportunities for new jobs and thus new household formations. In addition to delaying departure from the parental cocoon, surveys show, millennials are also increasingly likely to "boomerang" back home after failing in school, losing a job, or having a bad breakup.

Less Marriage

Not only are young people waiting longer to set out on their own, they're waiting longer to marry and start families. In 1968, 56 percent of Americans age 18 to 31 were married or heads of households. By 2012, that number was down to 23 percent. More Americans 18 to 34 are living with their parents (over 32 percent) than with a spouse or partner. The *Washington Post* reported in 2016 that the percentage of young men who are unmarried and living at home is now higher than at any point since the 1800s. Take a moment to think about that.

The average age of a newlywed couple in the United States in 2013 had grown to 28, up a full six years since 1950. A Pew Research poll finds that 20 percent of all Americans over 25 have "always been single" (that is, about 42 million people), more than doubling from 9 percent a half century earlier. Among African Americans, the number is even higher: 36 percent say they have never been married, a quadrupling from 9 percent in the 1960s. Social scientists estimate that about a quarter of millennials are unlikely ever to wed. "When today's young adults reach their mid-40s to mid-50s, a record high share is likely to have never been married," Pew analysts Wendy Wang and Kim Parker wrote. Some of these middle-aged unmarried adults will still eventually tie the knot, but Wang and Parker's analysis predicts that the odds of a first marriage after one's early fifties is very unlikely.

Many young people delay or reject marriage because they are themselves the products of broken homes and say they want to be absolutely certain before they make a lifetime commitment. But many others simply privilege their schedules and express disinterest in a "burdensome" partner. Some think the pool of marriageable mates is unattractive. Others worry about their financial well-being, not liking the idea of becoming tethered to someone with tens or even hundreds of thousands of dollars in student-loan debt. Women frequently articulate a desire to marry only a man who is gainfully employed. That is less achievable when more young men are struggling to find employment.

Many younger people are now simply concluding that marriage isn't terribly important, either individually or communally. Various Pew studies ask whether America is just as well off if people have priorities other than marriage and children. About half of all respondents now say yes, with younger Americans far more likely than older Americans to express indifference to the institution of marriage.

Less Religious Participation

Millennials are now identifying as agnostic, atheist, and "spiritual but not religious" at rates far exceeding previous generations. These various ways of rejecting traditional religion further erode young people's participation in what were once common social institutions like the church or synagogue, thereby exacerbating their segregation from older generations and authority figures. (To be clear, I regard theological ideas and belief as significant matters in their own right, but for purposes here, I am discussing merely the *social benefits* of participating in organized religion.)

The generation coming of age identifies less with the faith and organized religion of their parents and grandparents and more with an amorphous spirituality—what NYU sociologist Michael Hunt calls "a 'do-it-yourself' attitude toward religion." Other studies suggest that millennials are now the prime movers behind the growth of "religious nones." In 1965 less than 10 percent of college students said they "never" attend any religious services, compared to nearly 30 percent today. The Pew Research Center's Michael Lipka reported that about 35 percent of adult millennials (born between 1981 and 1996) identify as atheist, agnostic, or "nothing in particular." "Far more Millennials say they have no religious affiliation compared with those who identify as evangelical Protestants (21%), Catholics (16%) or mainline Protestants (11%)."

Many of the young still report a "deep sense" of spirituality (more than 80 percent) and "wonder about the universe"—but they are much less likely to join congregations or participate in religious events with their neighbors. Just 27 percent of millennials say they attend a religious service "weekly or more"—compared with 34 percent of Generation Xers, 38 percent of Baby Boomers, and 51 percent of their grandparents and great-grandparents in the Greatest and the "Silent" Generations.

Religious communities have traditionally drawn firm distinctions between childhood and adulthood, immaturity and maturity, both in Scripture and in practice. St. Paul admonished the Corinthians: "When I was a child, I spoke as a child, I understood as a child, I thought as a child, but when I became a man, I put away childish things." In many churches, the first communion is a major rite of passage; confirmation "seals" a baptized person to the church and the Christian community. The Jewish bar mitzvah and bat mitzvah are quintessential coming-of-age rituals. Under Jewish law, when a boy turns 13, he becomes accountable for his actions. Ages vary slightly for girls, who become subject to the law at age 12 or 13, depending on Orthodox, Conservative, or Reform customs. Traditionally, the child is called up during a Sabbath service to read from part of the Torah. A huge celebration follows, for the service participant is now a full-fledged member of the Jewish community, with the duties and obligations thereof.

Adolescents who are participating less in communal ceremonies tend over time, not surprisingly, to place a lower premium on the value of these communities and their beliefs. Only 40 percent of millennials, in current Pew surveys, say that religion is "very important" in their lives. Christian Smith and a team of Notre Dame sociologists are finding that an individualistic sense of religion and local community tends to bleed over into a highly individualistic understanding of right and wrong. The generation coming of age has an extraordinarily selective understanding of what God might demand of them. "Six out of ten of the emerging adults we interviewed . . . said that morality is a personal choice, entirely a matter of individual decision," Smith writes. "Moral rights and wrongs are essentially matters of individual opinion, in their view."

Little Citizens No More

A hard truth about our public life today is that millennials and the generation coming of age know exceedingly little about the nation they're inheriting. The founding principles and governing institutions of the United States are only vaguely familiar to them. Every four years, the U.S. National Center for Education Statistics administers the National Assessment of Educational Progress in civics, geography, and history to fourth-, eighth-, and twelfth-graders across all fifty states. Known as the

"Nation's Report Card," the NAEP shows where students are proficient and where they fall short. For more than two decades, our students' civic and historical knowledge has been superficial at best. Nationwide, just 18 percent of eighth-graders are graded "proficient" or better in U.S. history, 27 percent score "proficient" or better in geography, and 23 percent score "proficient" or better in civics.

Partly as a result, their love of country is tepid. According to Pew Research, only 49 percent of millennials say that "patriotic" describes them very well. We should be worried about that other 51 percent and the historical and civic ignorance they carry with them into the voting booth. It's no accident that we see a resurgence of interest in socialism. Although only 16 percent of millennials can define what socialism is, nearly half of them (42 percent) conclude that it is preferable to capitalism, according to a 2014 Reason Foundation-Rupe poll. For those with no knowledge of how the two systems have performed historically, this preference seems to be driven merely by an impressionistic sense that socialism sounds gentler. Whatever your views on politics and economics, this skin-deep approach to issues of critical importance should concern us.

As will be explored more fully in later chapters, the American experiment depends on engaged, informed, fully participating citizens—what President Eisenhower called the obligatory "part-time" political calling for all of us in a republic. Yet among our young, nearly half now profess an indifference even to whether they live in a democracy.

More Intellectually Fragile

From college students' demands for "trigger warnings" on potentially offensive literature to "safe spaces" with psychological counselors at the ready in case they should encounter uncomfortable speakers or ideas, our campuses are encouraging an entitled attitude that one is "free from" any duty to hear one's beliefs challenged. Cornell professor Kate Mann made what at face value seemed like a reasonable case for trigger warnings in an op-ed for the *New York Times,* pointing out that they merely give a heads up to students experiencing major post-traumatic stress that could be exacerbated by class discussion—the warning gives them a chance to prepare. But I'd argue in response that the very idea of trigger warnings marginalizes honest discussion of big and hard topics, insulating people not only from exposure to new ideas but also from the intellectual—and character—development that comes from being forced to articulate, defend, and potentially revise one's views and positions. And understandable efforts to protect people who have survived specific traumas—rape and genocide, for example—morph into more general and often parody-able suggestions that we should guard against discussion of war, death, childbirth, or spiders.

The crank in me wants to underscore the obvious truth that the real world isn't going to offer any trigger warnings or safe spaces, so you'd better learn how to deal—and just leave it at that. But more importantly, the lover of knowledge and country in me aches that we are forgetting that a life well lived, that basic participation in the modern knowledge economy, and that the future of our democracy all depend upon an open and unfettered intellectual climate.

Similarly, we've read a lot in recent years about "microaggressions"—small, fairly insignificant actions or word choices that are now seen as akin to assaults or violence. According to the University of California, microaggressions include such supposedly offensive statements as "America is the land of opportunity" and "I believe the most qualified person should get the job." The effort to eradicate "microaggressions" and to police language on campus is more than just a species of political correctness. As Greg Lukianoff and Jonathan Haidt argue (in the second-most-read *Atlantic* story ever), the movement

> is largely about emotional well-being . . . it presumes an extraordinary fragility of the collegiate psyche, and therefore elevates the goal of protecting students from psychological harm. The ultimate aim, it seems, is to turn campuses into "safe spaces" where young adults are shielded from words and ideas that make some uncomfortable . . . [T]his movement seeks to punish anyone who interferes with that aim, even accidentally. You might call this impulse *vindictive protectiveness*.

Ultimately, this movement yields "a culture in which everyone must think twice before speaking up, lest they face charges of insensitivity, aggression, or worse." I realize that many contemporary students find these trends as annoying and even as worrisome as I do, and that not all students should be tarred with this brush. The important point here is that in a culture that demands this level of sensitivity, it becomes increasingly easy to just go along rather than think about the unintended consequences of movements of this kind. I would argue that we've yet to come to terms with the downside of our overarching need to make our lives as protected as possible, and that our campuses merely offer the most appalling evidence.

This grooming not to speak about hard or controversial matters—instead of speaking, and being challenged, and debating, and revising—is almost the exact opposite of what productivity in the coming workplace will demand. As our intellectually insecure students leave the bubble of campus and arrive at full-time work, they are now demanding constant feedback and tender reassurance. They dislike the formality of waiting for the review periods and cycles that might fit the needs of their coworkers and supervisors.

No one enjoys being "bossed" around, but employers report that millennials who have grown up on a steady diet of participation trophies and self-esteem boosting seem uniquely unable to adapt when the feedback and coaching comes in forms they don't like. The generation's shared sense of entitlement in the workplace seems to reflect a reduced sense of toughness, grit, and resilience compared to that of their ancestors.

And on the societal level, we can all agree that polarization is a problem. To put it simply, if every side becomes determined to protect itself from offensive or troubling ideas, we are going to be a country of increasingly walled-off groups. And that never ends well.

Softer Parenting

As explained earlier, this book doesn't lay the blame for our coming-of-age crisis chiefly at the feet of those now moving toward adulthood. Quite to the contrary, these problems are very significantly the result of broader cultural assumptions that made parenting, paradoxically, more time-consuming and ever-present and yet simultaneously less goal-oriented. Although well-meaning, our indulgent practices have tended to encourage complacency among our pampered offspring. Many of us are accidental "helicopter parents," hovering over our children, making sure they're safe and protected, never bored, and on schedule. And it's understandable. If a family has only one or two children growing up in a highly uncertain and competitive world, the parents naturally want to do everything possible to ensure that they succeed, particularly if all of the other parents appear to be doing the same thing.

If our kids are having a hard time in school, we call the teacher to make excuses, or we agitate until they receive special attention. Fortunately, some pockets of the culture at large have begun to wake up to the fact that our intrusions are often accidentally sapping our kids' agency. In our desperate quest to ensure their educational and financial futures, we undermine both. Our actions reduce their initiative to buckle down and work harder at challenging subjects, because they know we're standing beneath them, arms out and ready to catch them if they fall. One of the biggest surprises I had upon becoming president at Midland was finding out that parents call *professors* to complain about grades, and sometimes even contact residence hall directors to negotiate better rooms or intervene in roommate problems. I'm not that old, but the idea that my parents would have even considered doing such a thing is mind-blowing to me.

After spending the better part of two decades micromanaging and choreographing playdates, dance practices, extra tutoring for standardized tests and college entrance exams, music lessons, martial arts, select soccer and travel baseball, track meets, swim meets, art classes, language enrichment, and all the rest, it should come as no surprise that the kids have only the vaguest idea of how to make decisions for themselves. All that many of them have ever had to do by age 18 is be dressed and in the car at the appointed hour. There are shoots of hope—the mother who makes her young kid take the subway alone in New York, the moves for unscheduled play time for kids, the schools like the one in New Jersey, where a friend of mine sends his children, that make a point of telling parents that they are forbidden to intervene on behalf of their kid until the kid has made a reasonable effort to do so him- or herself. But again, it's hard for individual parents to do this in a wholesale way if every other parent seems to be advocating at every turn for their kids.

It is hardly any wonder that publishers are putting out guides for perplexed parents with titles such as *When Will My Grown-Up Kid Grow Up?* and *Parenting Your Emerging Adult: Launching Kids from 18 to 29.* If a generation of Americans has "failed to launch" (there's an entire genre of literature now devoted to this concept), it's due in no small part to parents unintentionally failing to clear the pad for takeoff.

WHO BIRTHED SOFTER PARENTING?

Let's go back to our history for a moment. Over the last century and a half, the gritty parenting of early America has gradually given way to a more nurturing approach. The change began because of a broad set of shared experiences and social evolution: The Civil War produced hundreds of thousands of orphans, and as reformers came to their aid—and to the aid of the children of former slaves—a greater collective awareness emerged about the needs of the poor and neglected; mass urbanization raised questions about the older idea that children were sturdy enough to fend for themselves as they grew, as cities turned out to have more predators and dangers than the countryside; and mass immigration provoked urgent discussions about programs for assimilation and meeting basic needs. In this way, industrialization and the shift from rural to urban work prompted much of the progressive movement, and the exploitation of child laborers focused the collective mind on how substantial the need for nurture was. At the turn of the twentieth century, a surge of institution-building—ranging from the Society for the Prevention of Cruelty to Children to the Women's Christian Temperance Union, from the Rotary Club to the Boy Scouts and the YMCA—nobly helped chart a national agenda of better care for neglected youth.

But none of these societal worries and philanthropic responses fully explain the changed parenting practices *inside* families that were not impoverished. Parents made actual choices that drove the increasingly permissive shepherding of the young. What drove this? In short: Dr. Benjamin Spock and his like-minded peers, who told parents that the emerging peer culture they feared wasn't that fearsome.

The steady rise of mass schooling—less than 2 percent of the population were high school graduates in 1870; well over three-quarters were by 1950—was spawning a new youth culture. The boom in high schools—a new one was built every day in America between 1890 and 1920—served as an incubator for that culture. "Rather than a short transition period of personal uncertainty and discovery," Paula Fass observes in *The End of American Childhood,* adolescence was becoming "a prolonged sojourn of development spent among other youth." School was not only about in-classroom learning; it was also—or even primarily—a social hub. "When a teenage majority spent the better part of their day in high school, they learned to look to one another and not adults for advice, information, and approval," observes cultural historian Grace Palladino. "And when they got a glimpse of the freedom and social life that the high school 'crowd' enjoyed, they revolutionized the very concept of growing up." By the 1950s, adolescence was decreasingly a period of moral development under parental authority, and increasingly a period in which unchaperoned peers shaped the sensibilities of those coming of age.

As will be discussed more in the next chapter, postwar prosperity and generational segregation in the schools allowed this youth culture to flower. Marketers and retailers discovered it before most other observers, as it turned out that teens had lots of their parents' money to spend. Television and rock and roll arrived on the scene. Teenagers began setting trends and changing tastes. Instead of adolescence being conceived of as an apprenticeship stage en route to adult life and responsibilities, increasingly teen culture became *the* model or ideal American life. This was new.

Despite the fact that parents in the 1950s more and more frequently wanted to look and act like teens themselves, they still felt anxious about the radical changes from their own upbringings. Social commentators lamented the disappearance of innocent adolescents and complained about the cool "teenage tyrants." Parents began to worry that they weren't raising their children properly, or at all. Were they just producing spoiled consumers?

Psychologists such as Jean Piaget, Abraham Maslow, and Erik Erikson sought to reassure parents that everything was going to be fine, that they were doing a better job than they understood. They encouraged Americans to spend quality time together, to reassure children of their parents' love for them—in short, to make children the center of adult attention. Erikson urged an understanding of adolescence as an introspective time for individuals to explore and develop their own unique identities. Parents did not need to direct this exploration: assure your offspring of your tenderness, he said, but allow them to wander.

No one was more important to the emergence of the new parenting perspective on nurture than Benjamin Spock (1903–1998), one of the best-selling authors in history. Dr. Spock "wanted to liberate both mothers and their children" from worries about kids' increasing reliance on peers. He advised against "excessive mothering" and suggested that teens would be fine without "excessive expertise" from the authority figures of older hierarchical society. His advice on child-rearing shaped the attitudes of a generation of parents and normalized the emergence of a segregated youth culture increasingly "freed" from older expectations of rigor and economic productivity. As teen culture ascended, American youth began to find a wider popular culture that catered to them as independent consumers rather than as subordinates in their parents' households. Any urgency about learning to produce before one consumed slackened.

A FLATTER WORLD—OF ADULT-CHILDREN AND CHILDISH ADULTS

Neil Postman is arguably the most prescient analyst of the transformation of American childhood, and his *Amusing Ourselves to Death: Public Discourse in the Age of Show Business,* although three decades old, remains a must-read on the trivialization of American culture and the evaporation of shared ideals. In his view, childhood fully flowered in this country beginning in about 1850 but began a rapid decline in 1950. What does he mean?

First, we should acknowledge that he is talking not universally but narrowly about parenting in the majority white culture; in other places, he laments the horrors of slavery that sapped human dignity and undermined the agency of black parents to raise their children according to their visions and dictates of conscience. But Postman's general point in *The Disappearance of Childhood* and other works is that in the mid-nineteenth century, (white) parents began adding a good and needed bit of nurture to the older ideals of objectively toughening up their kids for an adulthood of self-sufficiency. The initial impulse to get children out of factories and into classrooms—and the better intentioned of the attempts to help immigrant children assimilate into American society—must be celebrated.

But by the middle of the twentieth century, two developments had swamped that earlier wedding of warmth to tough love. The nurturing perspective had spun out of control and made cultivating self-esteem paramount, marginalizing competing concerns about cultivating virtue. (Importantly, though "virtue" has come over centuries to mean "moral living," it evolved from an older Latin term meaning "strength." The two are inextricably linked.)

In addition, most of us radically understate the degree to which visual media—first television, now everything—eroded thoughtful childhood. The "disappearance" of childhood is traceable directly, Postman insists, to the rise of electronic media. What separated childhood from adulthood previously was a secret or guarded knowledge about full adult reality that was understandable only by literacy. Adults knew much that children did not—things about sex and money and violence and death. But mainly sex. In a literate culture, secrets are kept in books. If you wanted to know what those hidden secrets were, you had to be able to navigate books. Learning how to read—an act of a budding adult—was a prerequisite to acquiring the new knowledge. Because reading takes work, self-discipline was at the heart of gaining access to complex adult worlds.

Television changed all that, because it is a "total disclosure medium," operating around the clock, demanding and broadcasting a nonstop supply of new and titillating information. Practically nothing is taboo or off limits. Because television doesn't know or care who's watching, the medium effectively "adultifies" children while infantilizing adults; it doesn't judge its viewers, nothing is shameful. Postman argues that childhood's innocence is lost and the idea of shame becomes "diluted and demystified." Deliberate adulthood was turned into an affliction to be avoided, even a joke.

We are thus left with a nation not only of childish adults but also of adult-children. "Without a clear concept of what it means to be an adult," there can then "be no clear concept of what it means to be a child." As so-called adults become ever more childlike, neither child nor adult knows how to transition, not just biologically but socially and morally, from child to adult. Everyone ends up confused and dissatisfied.

Paradoxically, even as America was becoming more child centered, "childhood" itself was beginning to disappear. "Everywhere one looks," Neil Postman wrote, "the behavior, language, attitudes, and desires— even the physical appearance—of adults and children are becoming increasingly indistinguishable." Models of well-lived adult lives are less clear in our shared consciousness. Not surprisingly, adolescents put off adult responsibilities for as long as they can, sometimes by choice but more often as a result of circumstances and trends beyond their comprehension. In the face of unprecedented prosperity and freedom from convention, the generation coming of age is stuck in a hazy, extended adolescence, never allowed simply to be children, and yet also rarely nudged to be fully adult.

WHAT TO CALL
NOT-QUITE-YET-ADULTS?

Psychologist Jeffrey Jenson Arnett has coined the term "emerging adulthood" to describe the space between traditional adolescence and formally definable adulthood. Emerging adulthood is marked by longer "and more widespread education, later entry into marriage and parenthood, and prolonged and erratic transition to stable work." This demographic is "on the way to adulthood but not there yet." According to Arnett, emerging adulthood is not a universal feature of human development, but rather "a life stage that exists under certain conditions that have occurred only quite recently and only in some cultures."

Translation: It's a rich-nation problem. The more affluent the society, the more likely young people will experience an extended drift toward adulthood. Wealthy societies, for reasons largely well-intentioned but now producing unintended consequences, are making it easier for their teens to avoid the rigors and responsibilities of becoming a grown-up. Arnett calls those years the "self-focused age," when there are few real responsibilities, few "daily obligations," limited "commitments to others." In a stage when young people were once supposed to learn to "stand alone as a self-sufficient person," they find themselves increasingly paralyzed by over-choice. There are nearly unlimited personal-social options yet too few concrete work-related accomplishments.

A new subgenre of self-help literature is springing up to assist them in facing their so-called "quarter-life crises." A host of books with titles like *Men to Boys* or *How to Raise an Adult* are trying to help parents and cultural critics get a handle on this new phenomenon, now described as "extended adolescence," "pre-adulthood," "adultescence," and "emerging adulthood." Kathleen Shaputis painfully labels millennials "the Peter

Pan Generation" and "the Boomerang Generation" for their reluctance to become independent and for their tendency to rush back home after trial runs venturing out.

Studies of thousands of emerging adults since the mid-1990s find that the vast majority of 18- to 25-year-olds admit they are anxious when asked if they've reached adulthood. Jeffrey Jensen Arnett finds that the young aren't sure who they are or are supposed to become. Most emerging adults do not see any concrete markers such as marriage or conclusively finishing school as signposting arrival at adulthood.

In full disclosure, Arnett himself is not as convinced as I am that this new stage of "emerging adulthood" is a problem. He instead sees in it a mix of both challenges and opportunities—among them a "sense of boundless potential" that they are free to venture anywhere. Notre Dame sociologist Christian Smith and his team find a similar optimism to what Arnett and his collaborators discovered in their study of emerging adults. Happily, this generation is inheriting a world free of the totalitarian specters that cast long shadows over the twentieth century and free of the racist legal barriers that held back many Americans from exercising full rights as citizens for so much of U.S. history. Add in a more global society and an economy increasingly rewarding innovation and "disruption" and it's not hard to see why some youth look out and see "boundless potential."

The problem, unfortunately, is that Smith's team also found a dark underbelly to this "fun and freedom" of early adulthood. For most young people, this boundlessness is actually experienced as a kind of loneliness. The dominant feelings are not hope but "personal struggle, confusion, anxiety, hurt, frustration, and grief." Many of these young people sense that they are morally adrift, "captive to consumerism," chasing pleasure through binge drinking and casual hookups, and disengaged civically and politically. They do not think they can sufficiently focus either inwardly or outwardly. They are feeling the worry we all feel for them— that they risk leading unproductive, unfulfilling lives.

We've talked about the sometimes useful ways of thinking about one's life in stages. The ancient Athenian statesman Solon divided human life into ten seven-year stages: For the first seven years, a boy is "the man, unripe"; for the second seven, his "signs of approaching manhood show in the bud" as he learns self-control; from age 14 to 21 he completes his physical development; from 21 to 28 he is at the lifetime height of his strength; in his fifth seven years, he is best positioned to marry and reproduce; and so on. Solon had precise views about how long a man should continue to seek workplace guidance from his elders, as well as when he would himself be best suited to run the show (basically in one's late forties and early fifties). After age 63, he should acknowledge his decline—his slower speech and fading wit—and hand over leadership roles.

The real world has always been messier than tidy Greek ideals. But there was something to be said for the way older citizens helped younger and even middle-age folks think in advance about the transitions they would be called to navigate. As our life expectancies grow, and as our duration in jobs and at particular firms inevitably shorten going forward, we need to rethink many of our assumptions about ages and roles. But it remains true that inherited markers of maturation can aid us as we navigate the world, provide for our families, and seek to serve our neighbors.

At a time when these markers are becoming even more important, we are instead now just sloppily muddling all of them together. As Postman observed, the American understanding of life progression has collapsed into just three categories—distinguishable mainly only by one's abilities to manage elementary bodily functions: infancy, adult-childhood, and senility. None of them are defined or crisp enough; there is instead simply drift and stupor. Babies learn to control their bowels and get to become "adult-children"—a category they will inhabit until old age when they can again no longer control their bowels.

This kind of pessimism overstates things a bit, but it is clear that the stretching and distorting of late childhood, the sapping of intentionality from coming of age, and the formlessness of early adulthood yield an experience that generations of Americans from book-centric rather than image-centric ages would have trouble comprehending. Childhood is no longer so much the nurturing, goal-oriented period tapering by the late teens; it is instead an amorphous period between infancy and the age of 25 or 30, interrupted temporarily by the biological awkwardness of puberty (which is confusingly now arriving three to five years earlier for girls than historical norms).

ONCE UPON A TIME, immigrants arriving on these shores were stunned at the independence Americans granted their young children. The migrants, typically from more class-based and hierarchical societies, were accustomed to precise rules for children, whereas Americans tended to focus on the outcome of their growing children's labors. Our national forebears "were more open to endowing their children with greater independence and flexibility in choice because they believed that the future held better possibilities and opportunities for their children," observes historian Paula Fass. The assumption that kids were capable of big things, she writes, "established a baseline" for future generations of American parents to work from, "even as the initial circumstances [of economic compulsion] that created it changed and then finally disappeared."

Tenderly but intentionally introducing our children to the responsibilities of adulthood throughout their adolescence would be the better pathway forward again today. We want them to learn that although being grown-up has its challenges, they have the mettle to meet those challenges. The goal is to build up within them a well of strength from which to draw in times of future crisis as they voyage into the wider world. Most of our millennials have the intelligence to navigate the bumps that are coming, but only if we also instill in them the grit that the new era of uncertainty will demand.

Conversely, denying meaningful rites of passage and obscuring the distinction between childhood and adulthood cheats the generation coming of age of something vital. Lowering expectations, cushioning all blows, and tolerating aimlessness not only hurts them, it also deprives their neighbors, who desperately need their engagement. As we'll see in the next chapter, allowing formal schooling to seep into all of adolescence has created as many new riddles and obstacles as it has solved.

THREE

<hr/>

MORE SCHOOL ISN'T ENOUGH

*Schooling and Education Aren't the Same Thing * Are We Spending Enough?*
*Time Is the Most Important Limited Resource * Dewey, Again * But Is It Working?*
*"If Mediocre Education Were Imposed on Us" * The Digital Revolution and Hybrid Learning*
*Against Grade 13 * Learning How to Learn * Training Wheels Are Made to Come Off*

<hr/>

I have never let school interfere with my education.
—Mark Twain

MELISSA CRIED HERSELF TO SLEEP EVERY SINGLE night for nearly three weeks when she started the new job. Some mornings she'd cry before work too. It was 1998, and my wife and I had just moved to New Haven, Connecticut, where she had become a teacher and administrator at a brand new public high school, and where I began graduate studies and teaching undergraduate history. She had felt a calling to schools in troubled neighborhoods for much of her life and had been a teacher and/or school administrator for three years by this point, but what she found at this school was soul crushing.

There was the full-time "security guard" who collected a check but had almost no actual responsibilities at the school—except to drop off food in the principal's office. His real job was night-shift manager at a neighboring fast-food restaurant, and he would bring an ample supply of free food by the front office each morning before heading home to sleep. There was what became known as the "ghost-town math" classroom where the teacher quit the third day and was not replaced for an entire semester—with the affected students receiving an extra study hall in place of the class. There was the student who, upon asking why there were no challenging classes he could take, was told to stop complaining and be grateful that his senior year could be mostly free time. There was the union representative who spent the majority of each workday going classroom to classroom raising funds from teachers for local politicians. There were the assemblies that would start hours late, with student fights breaking out during the unscheduled, mostly unsupervised waiting periods.

Melissa could tell a dozen more stories of this kind, but one experience angered her above the others: When the school had moved from an old building to a gorgeous new facility a mile away that summer, all of the academic records for six hundred of the high schoolers had been lost. School officials not only had no papers to show who was signed up for which classes, but they also didn't have documentation confirming what grade each student was in. Enterprising underclassmen declared themselves to be seniors, with only a semester or two of credits left to earn before graduation. When senior administrators learned this was not a small but a systemic problem, no one built any method—parent interviews, birth certificates, testing, cross-referencing any records at the system central office—to tackle the chaos. The attempt to skip two or three years of school was treated as a harmless prank, even as actual grade levels and credit totals remained unknown. More tragically, most students had almost no classes for the six weeks until the scheduling files were finally found. Their time was simply wasted.

A friend had told us similar vignettes from the Baltimore schools the year before, but it hadn't seemed real. We hadn't known the faces of the kids being robbed or of the many heroic teachers being forced to work against rather than with the system. My crusading wife quietly approached a reporter at a city newspaper but was informed that fraud and waste in the local schools had ceased to be news decades ago. Melissa, long a self-styled "bleeding heart conservative," first thought of writing a book, but then dejectedly concluded that the reporter might well be right. Though scandalous, what if this wasn't news? What if we have already just given up?

Depending on where you stand, you may be nodding your head knowingly with this story, or wondering where I'm going with it, so let me be clear what I'm *not* saying. Of course all public schools are not like this, and my goal is obviously not to question the necessity of public funding for universal education. I'm the product of public schools, and I know there are many great teachers and administrators in virtually every school—Melissa wasn't the only teacher upset at what was happening and determined to turn it around. I'm certainly not suggesting that this school is representative of the thousands of healthy ones across the nation. But I do believe the existence of such a school must be placed at least partially at the feet of a system that hasn't mustered the courage to admit that all motion is not progress, that hasn't been willing to acknowledge that lots of what we're doing isn't working. Who is ever held accountable for glaring failures? Why does this school drift "forward" on autopilot year after year when any institution failing this spectacularly in other professions—from grocers and cabdrivers to dry cleaners and driving school operators—would obviously face real consequences?

SCHOOLING AND EDUCATION AREN'T THE SAME THING

Before we rush to our partisan corners, let's agree that countless folks across the ideological spectrum genuinely care about America's kids and sincerely worry we are failing too many of them. As we drill deeper on the particular factors underlying educational failure, we'll surely get to meaty disagreements—but let's agree first that our schools are not performing as we all wish they could and would. Acknowledging the problem need not immediately prompt partisan fissure.

Because of Melissa's painful experience teaching in New Haven, I began reading about America's educational history. As a product of Fremont High School (go Tigers!) and the son of a lifelong teacher and coach in Nebraska's public schools, I've always had a deeply protective impulse toward the selfless teachers who filled my house after games on Friday and Saturday nights in my youth. I've seen heroic teachers turn kids' lives around, at times even becoming their surrogate parents. I'm a conservative, but not because I care much about the marginal tax rates of the richest Americans; rather, I'm a market-oriented localist because I believe in cultural pluralism and the First Amendment, in voluntarism over compulsion whenever possible, and in as much decentralized decision-making as conceivably feasible. One of my unexpected discoveries reading educational history was learning that many of the first skeptics of the effectiveness of homogenized, one-size-fits-all high schooling were genuine leftists.

Paul Goodman, an intellectual godfather of the New Left, spoke for a movement of doubters fifty years ago when he began describing the homogenizing effects of America's public school system as "compulsory mis-education." Known for his wildly popular 1960 book *Growing Up Absurd,* Goodman looked at what he called the "Organized System," by which he meant the application of the centralizing techniques of large corporate and governmental bureaucracies to the structuring of little kids' daily routines. He countered: Couldn't we possibly "have more meaning and honor in work? To put wealth to some real use? To have a high standard of living of whose quality we are not ashamed?" He wanted a free society to be raising kids who would love poetry and beauty and neighborliness, not just bigger stores and deeper walk-in closets.

He blasted the stifling uniformity that had overtaken schooling. One can almost hear the nasally teacher droning on with "Bueller? Bueller?" in *Ferris Bueller's Day Off* as you read Goodman. "We have been swept and are being swept on a flood-tide of public policy and popular sentiment into an expansion of schooling" that is not thought out. What was happening, Goodman warned, was "an aggrandizement of school-people that is grossly wasteful of wealth and effort and does positive damage to the young." Goodman recognized that the bells ring at exactly the same times every day, like a train schedule, but that a love for poetry is probably not discovered on the same timetable. He feared that we were merely crafting the next generation of "organization men" and sheep-like consumers. Why can't we use our wealth to ask big questions about "social justice for those who have been shamefully left out?" Why can't we raise our kids to find "a use of leisure that is not a dismaying waste of a hundred million adults?"

Why was the postwar homogenization of life and schooling accelerating? At some point in the life of our nation, Goodman argued, we ceded too much authority on the critically important subject of what and how our kids need to learn to "professional educators." He makes a crucial distinction between schooling and education—the former being a large-scale institutional tool, the latter the goals and dreams we have for our kids. The trouble is that those who earn their living in the schools are probably the least likely to honestly acknowledge this difference, because we're all unlikely to call attention to things that might raise hard questions about the sources of our funding. Goodman wrote: "When, at a meeting, I offer that perhaps we already have too much *formal* schooling and that, under present conditions, the more we get the less education we will get, the others look at me oddly." Discussion ignores the purposes for which schools might or might not be effective and proceeds immediately to questions of "how to get more money for schools" and "how to upgrade the schools." And the superstition persists that more money correlates to better outcomes despite overwhelming evidence to the contrary, he lamented.

Goodman envisioned alternate programs by which adolescents could be educated more diversely in fields and in cities than in homogenized buildings filled with homogenized classrooms. But before unpacking his ideas further (and before my father reads that I became intrigued by the hippies' "un-schooling" movement), we should first pause to consider his then-contrarian declaration that insufficient funding isn't the core problem in our educational underperformance.

ARE WE SPENDING ENOUGH?

As Melissa and I were aching over the New Haven schools, many national observers were simultaneously reading about those in Kansas City, where a twelve-year test case of the theory that more funding equals improved outcomes was playing out. In 1985 a federal judge in Missouri took control of the Kansas City school district as part of the settlement of a desegregation case. Noting the divergence in educational results between black and white students, the judge ordered taxpayers to spend an unprecedented $2 billion over the next twelve years to build fifteen new schools and renovate fifty-four others. Included was not only more instruction but also the construction of nearly sixty new schools, which would feature such amenities as an Olympic-sized swimming pool; a robotics lab; recording, television, and animation studios; a planetarium; an arboretum; a zoo; and even a twenty-five-acre wildlife sanctuary. Upward of $11,700 on average was devoted to each pupil, the highest spending level of any school district in the nation at the time.

What was the result? "When the judge, in March 1997, finally agreed to let the state stop making desegregation payments to the district," journalist Paul Ciotti reported to the nation, "there was little to show for all the money spent." Black "students' achievement hadn't improved at all, and the black-white achievement gap was unchanged."

Broader studies suggest that the Kansas City experience isn't an outlier. Contrary to popular assumption, per capita spending by school districts is not correlated to student outcomes nationally. Nor does increased spending over time lead to better outcomes. In 2013 the United States spent over $620 billion on public and secondary schools, or $12,300 per pupil in inflation-adjusted dollars. Although the federal government contributes only 12 percent of direct expenditures, the federal role in education policy continues to expand—again with no discernible improvement in outcomes. Congress appropriated, in inflation-adjusted dollars, $67 billion to the U.S. Department of Education in fiscal year 2014, up from $56 billion in 2004, $25 billion in 1994, and $14 billion in 1984 (again, all inflation adjusted). And yet there was no substantive improvement in the reading or math scores of eighth- through twelfth-grade students on the National Assessment of Educational Progress over the period. To reiterate: nearly a quintupling of federal spending over thirty years produced nothing quantifiably better.

Angst about whether we get sufficient value for our educational investments is a century-long national worry. With little to show for it, inflation-adjusted spending per pupil increased from $440 at the end of the First World War to more than $8,000 at the end of the twentieth century, an increase of over 1,700 percent, or an average yearly growth rate of nearly 6 percent. Albert L. Bell, a Pennsylvania educator and self-appointed ombudsman on national educational quality in the 1930s and 1940s, documented that per-pupil expenditures in the United States grew 600 percent from 1890 to 1930. "Are we accomplishing six times as much?" Bell worried. "Are the present graduates six times better able to think and act for themselves than the graduates of 1890?"

In 1958 the successes of the Soviets in the space race prompted another round of soul-searching—as did the late 1970s debate surrounding President Carter's push to create the U.S. Department of Education. (Carter believed the critical importance of education demanded federal coordination, while skeptics worried that the federal government had no constitutional mandate over K-12 education and, more fundamentally, that the federal tendency to crowd out other levels of government would ultimately harm rather than help local education.) Move forward a couple of decades and you find President Clinton joining forces with conservatives worried about the "social promotion" by which middle schools send unprepared students on to high school, a concern that now extends to colleges. Four-year universities, despite having lowered standards for freshmen-year performance, now place one-third of their incoming students in remedial reading and mathematics courses. About half the students entering two-year colleges require some degree of remediation. Family expenditures on remediation during just the first year of college now exceed $1.5 billion annually, according to a 2016 study by Education Reform Now.

The unsatisfactory payout from these investments is widely understood. Our international performance consistently ranks near the bottom among industrialized nations. Among members of the Organization for Economic Cooperation and Development, the United States ranks twentieth in science and twenty-seventh in math (2012), after France and the United Kingdom and well behind China, Singapore, Japan, South Korea, and Vietnam. Even in other metrics ranging from "cognitive skills and educational attainment" to general literacy, the United States never cracks the top ten. Our long-running aspiration for "world-class" public education has never come to fruition. We're not close.

Readers might not agree with the view that funding isn't the fundamental problem in the underperformance of American schooling. Some will persuasively argue that if teachers were among the highest-paid professionals in American life, the prestige and performance of our schools might skyrocket. If there were compelling evidence that the overriding issue affecting American education was underinvestment—if increased spending could be shown to drive better results—I would be enthusiastically for increased spending, toward the ends of greater international economic competitiveness, enhanced national security, and more vivacious and ambitious youths.

Still, what we experienced in New Haven—and what we have seen up close in many other systems—did not seem to be about money at all. In fact, Connecticut generally and New Haven particularly at that time had among the best-funded schools anywhere in the nation, public or private. This crisis was about something else. It was about mission. It was about hollowing out. It was about sclerosis and lethargy, apathy and atrophy.

TIME IS THE MOST IMPORTANT
LIMITED RESOURCE

Melissa cares about taxpayer dollars, but that was not why she wept. She cried because she was seeing kids' lives—their hours and their days and their wills—leaking away at that New Haven school. There is nothing more frustrating to an educator than to see lives wasted simply because the system is messed up.

Paradoxically, the expansion of American high schools centered largely on a different worry about teenage time—how to occupy it. Mass secondary education in the United States spread chiefly in response to two profound disruptions in the seventy-five years after the Civil War. As discussed earlier, between 1870 and 1940 the United States transitioned from a predominantly farm-living nation to a largely city-dwelling one. The American population was 85 percent rural on the eve of the Civil War, but only 40 percent rural by the end of the Second World War. The "big tool" industrial economy displaced the older farming and workshop economy that had driven the nation's growth over the previous century.

Just as profoundly, from 1880 until 1924, the nation experienced the so-called "great wave" of immigration. More than 25 million Europeans—Italians, Greeks, Poles, Hungarians, Germans, Irish, and Jews—arrived in America, disproportionately city-bound. As context, our entire population had been less than 25 million people in 1850. Americans had very mixed feelings about outsiders coming in such large numbers. In cities especially, alcohol abuse, prostitution, and crime surged.

The Progressive movement emerged in response. Although high schools had served a very small portion of the teen population prior to 1870—as noted earlier, less than 2 percent were graduates, and almost all citizens were engaged full time in what would be their life's work by age 15 or 16—social reformers seized on mass schooling as a solution to many riddles. Some motives were altruistic, others leaned more toward social control. But all reformers and school-builders agreed that we needed a massive program to help the tens of millions of immigrants learn English and assimilate into American culture. Moreover, there was widespread understanding that there were no longer enough jobs for the young males already crowding our cities, let alone for the waves of new ones arriving from Southern and Eastern Europe. Mass schooling was explicitly conceived of as a safe and meaningful place to go in the absence of a job. Immigrants needed to have their time accounted for; idle hands needed to be occupied.

Classroom hours were boosted, school years extended, and attendance increasingly made mandatory. The school-building boom was visible in almost every town. Stunningly, total public high school enrollment doubled every decade from 1890 until the 1930s. Urban schools began to look like the institutions we know today, with students separated into grades by age. Curricula evolved toward the practical. Administrators curtailed Latin and chemistry to make room for the teaching of supposedly practical subjects, like general science, home economics, bookkeeping, and typewriting. These vocational and commercial classes became more common during the economic worries of the New Deal.

Massachusetts before the Civil War, led by its ambitious education commissioner Horace Mann, had sought to establish a national model by mandating that every town construct schools and announcing that parents could be fined—and potentially even have their parental rights terminated—for refusing to send their kids. Most states didn't seriously debate compulsory schooling until the 1890s and early 1900s, but all eventually followed suit, with Mississippi in 1918 becoming the last state to pass a compulsory attendance law. The Great Depression marked the final triumph of the high school, as the youngest workers were typically the first to be laid off. In the cities, school thus became every teen's shared alternative to the factory.

DEWEY, AGAIN

We met John Dewey in the first chapter. His overriding goal was universal public education for a growing nation, but in pursuing it, he turned the school into the literal center of the world for children, crowding out roles and responsibilities traditionally carried out in families and communities. The school was no longer there to support parents, but to replace them. School took on the grand cause of "nurture." The community's "paramount moral duty" is to the education of the young, Dewey wrote—but what he really meant was not that education, generally, but "the school," particularly, must become the new "center" of the "social life of the child." The intrusive reach of this kind of schooling would be deep, because when "others are not doing what we would like them to or are threatening disobedience, we are most conscious of the need of controlling them and of the influences by which they are controlled."

Dewey's worry list is not what one would expect from a champion of teaching. He worried aloud about content and academic "subjects," because they can seem to be handed down from on high rather than discovered by students. He was a skeptic of the obsessive need to teach children reading, calling it a "perversion." Schools should "not any longer bear the peculiar relation to books and book knowledge which they once did." Ultimately, "it is desirable to postpone the child's introduction to printed speech until he is capable of appreciating and dealing with its general meaning."

Many readers of this book might be laboring—and worrying and struggling—to get their kids to set aside sparkling images and to take words more seriously, but Dewey didn't share this anxiety. He wrote, "I believe that the image is the great instrument of instruction," by which he meant to raise doubts about the alleged priority of the literary over "the hands-on." Similarly, he doubted the usefulness of inherited debates from civilizations past, because he doesn't think the purpose of education should be "to transmit and conserve the whole of its existing achievements." In other words, he wanted to ensure that endless theoretical debates did not distract from the practical skills to be honed. In fact, even having Johnny do his memory work can be, Dewey decreed, a selfish act: "The mere absorption of facts and truths is so exclusively an individual affair that it tends very naturally to pass into selfishness. There is no obvious social motive" for the individual to learn more about where he or she came from. Dewey wanted everything in the school focused on how it can be instrumentally put to the cause of evolving Hegelian "social progress."

If Dewey's agenda is starting to sound almost like a theology, that's because it is: "I believe [that] . . . the teacher always is the prophet of the true God and the usherer in of the true kingdom of God." (Reminder: he's an atheist.) Although his style was usually dense, his totalizing goals can be seen in *Democracy and Education,* in "Self-Realization as the Moral Ideal," in "The Primary Education Fetich [*sic*]," and in *The School and Society.* But the most revealing thing he wrote—the most subversive thing—was "My Pedagogic Creed" in the middle of his career (1897). Constructed around five sections, of seven to eighteen declarative "I believe" paragraphs per section, this 4,000-word essay lays out his *theology of the school.* Although he claims to know nothing conclusively—only a "process" for kids to explore—all of life, from sewing and cooking to philosophical and ethical reasoning, is nurtured in and only in the school. There are no other institutions in his "Pedagogic Creed." Everything about the child's life centers on the modern school. The teacher exists not "to impose certain ideas" but to "select the influences which shall affect the child and to assist him in properly responding to these influences." As Dewey explained in *Democracy and Education,* society will eventually realize that "the school is its chief agency."

Dewey's student ultimately has no soul. The only thing that matters, in the end, is man's relation to his society. The societal here and now is the all in all. The goal is expressly *not* the full flowering of the individual, but rather "all education proceeds by the participation of the individual in the social consciousness of the race." Or, as Dewey and his colleagues put it in *The Humanist Manifesto,* "There is no God and there is no soul. Hence, there is no need for the props of traditional religion. With dogma . . . [now] excluded, then immutable truth is dead and buried. There is no room for fixed and natural law or permanent moral absolutes." (Wow.)

Although most parents today are unaware of the overarching, family-skeptical ambitions of that seminal generation of progressive educators, this is the ethos that Dewey and his colleagues aimed at and succeeded at instilling in America's education system in the early twentieth century. Their work produced some concrete benefits—namely, millions of students who otherwise wouldn't receive a formal education now could—but it also, we should now admit, had some seriously undesirable consequences as well.

BUT IS IT WORKING?

Just as secondary education was finishing its ascent to universal experience in the 1930s, observers had the first pangs of doubt as to whether their grand experiment was actually producing—either in terms of cost or quality. Many parents—to the consternation of progressive theorists—were expressing their disappointment that the large school-as-factory didn't resemble the localized, intimate education they remembered from the elementary schoolhouses across the countryside in the nineteenth century.

Many education experts agreed that the outcomes were inadequate, but for precisely the opposite reason: George Counts, a progressive champion who led the American Historical Association, complained that public schools continued to reflect the values of their local communities, which he found to be too complacent about social progress, too interested simply in their own kids. Education, in his view, was not primarily about helping individuals, but rather about molding the collective. The schools, he protested, were not nearly uniform or centralized enough to advance social transformation.

Even Columbia University's Teachers College, the cockpit of John Dewey's thought and long the Mecca of secondary schooling theory in the United States, worried that civics and math outcomes were inadequate. In 1930 the university's esteemed professor Thomas H. Briggs delivered a scathing assessment of the nation's great investment to date in high schools: "There has been no respectable achievement, even in the subjects offered in the secondary school curricula." He then rattled off an indictment of high schools' defects that sounds depressingly familiar. No competence in science. Schools were failing to produce any "permanent taste" for literature, and student writing was abysmal. He identified performance "of the sort which, applied in business, would lead to bankruptcy" or perhaps "the penitentiary."

Education reformers went through a regular cycle for decades: utopian optimism, failed new programs, a return to theorizing, and then renewed optimism. Diane Ravitch, one of the most exhaustive chroniclers of failed American reform efforts, concedes that some progressives began to have doubts, worrying that their grand designs "might be useful for teaching animals and very young children . . . but would ultimately prove wholly inadequate for the education of a strong and vigorous people." In spite of their decidedly mixed record, the champions of factory-era mass schooling have managed to maintain fairly uniform control over almost all teacher training institutions up to the present day. Thus, despite widespread public worry over the quality of secondary education, no alternative model has ever gotten substantial investment or even crystallized attention.

Our education debates have tended to conflate support for government-funded schooling on the one hand with a commoditized approach to the school day, year, building, and curriculum on the other. This is an unfortunate muddying of an important distinction between funding and form. (By analogy, we don't decide that since we fund food stamp programs, we will allow only olives and peppers, but never fruits or grains.) Because state schooling has played an outsized role in most of our lives and careers—91 percent of U.S. school-aged children will enroll in a taxpayer-funded elementary or secondary school this year—Americans have zealously affirmed public investment in schooling for eighty years. But along the way, needed debate about whether more homogenized schooling is what our kids really need to thrive has unfortunately been driven away from the contexts where public money is allocated. Parents across the country worry about whether the hours and years their kids spend in school are being sufficiently well spent, but there are few clear alternatives about other ways to be investing this time.

Arthur Bestor, one of the satisfied prophets of the triumphant model of secondary schooling, summed up the new consensus: "Universal, free, public education is part of the democratic creed," and it is now not easy to question. Universal, free, public . . . at face value, all of these things seem downright American. "Universal" suggests that everyone gets access to the same quality of education. "Free" suggests not, of course, that it's actually free, but that access should be equal no matter how rich your parents are. And "public" suggests the opposite of private or exclusive.

The problem with all of this is that it again assumes without questioning that education can be reduced to schooling—that they are synonyms. It presumes a particular tool is the answer to how most of our teenagers should spend the vast majority of their time—even before the students who will need to seize that tool have even agreed what problem *they* are seeking to solve. Again, Dewey has answered with a specific institutional form before we have even agreed what the question is.

"IF MEDIOCRE EDUCATION WERE IMPOSED ON US FROM ABROAD . . ."

In the previous chapter we talked about the role our schools play in removing students from the guiding influence of the multigenerational families of previous eras. Today our students spend more annual hours in the classroom over longer and longer academic years than at any previous point—yet they leave high school for college or the workforce less prepared and less able to cope with the next stage of their lives. This isn't working.

Paul Goodman, in *Growing Up Absurd,* predicted the dire consequences of ceding too much authority to the schools fifty years ago. Most of us won't agree with all of Goodman's prescriptions—he advocated, for instance, repealing all compulsory attendance laws and was a fierce critic of professionalized teacher licensing. But his calls for rethinking our passive expansion of homogenized schooling demand our consideration.

The "model of Athenian education" assumed a great deal of real-world interaction, he explained while touting his field-trip-heavy idealized educational program. Get out of the building and use "the druggist, the storekeeper, the mechanic" to introduce your children to multiple sectors and to a broader "grown-up world." Find the kind of enthusiastic teachers who know how to "use the city itself as the school—its streets, cafeterias, stores, movies, museums, parks, and factories." Again, many of his ideas would frighten cautious parents—for instance, he proposed restructuring school funding formulas to enable city children to be sent to "farms for a couple of months of the year." But he helpfully challenged us to reconsider how much of the comprehensive education we desire for our offspring is really reachable inside whole-day, one-size-fits-all schools.

Goodman, an intellectual on the left, found an unexpected compatriot on the right in John Taylor Gatto, who taught for thirty years in the public junior high schools of Manhattan's Upper West Side. Named New York City's teacher of the year in 1990 and then New York State's teacher of the year in 1991, Gatto showed courageous inventiveness in launching what he called the "guerrilla school program." He required apprenticeships and independent study, and expected his students to perform 320 hours of community service each year. He remains a passionate advocate of education, but he has evolved over time into an implacable skeptic of *schooling*.

Everyone should annually ask again, "Do we really need school?" he urged. The answer is probably yes, but if so, we should be able to explain why and what for. He wasn't questioning the necessity of educating the young, he clarified—"just forced schooling for six classes a day, five days a week, nine months a year, for twelve years. Is this deadly routine really necessary? And if so, for what?" School can't possibly solve every societal problem, so we need to know precisely what we're expecting from our schools. Too often, for too many kids, he worried, school accidentally becomes "a twelve-year jail sentence where bad habits are the only curriculum truly learned."

Soon after winning his awards, Gatto concluded that he wasn't making enough of a difference in heavily bureaucratized schooling. So he quit. In *Dumbing Us Down*, a volume of speeches published after he left the New York City public schools, he confessed that even though he was certified as a teacher of "English literature," he mostly just taught "school." What does he mean? "Teaching means different things in different places," he said, "but seven lessons are universally taught from Harlem to Hollywood" in our cookie-cutter schools. The main consequences for students are: emotional confusion, social class disparity, indifference, passivity, intellectual dependency on experts, conditional self-esteem, and surveillance by those in charge. This is the very opposite of what we should expect from public education, and it is actually antithetical to American democracy. Dejectedly, Gatto shouted that school has become the "prime training for permanent underclasses, people deprived forever of finding the center of their own special genius."

If we're inculcating passivity like this, it "should be little wonder we have a real national crisis," Gatto wrote, referring to the 1983 report by a national blue-ribbon commission that had been tasked with surveying the quarter century since the panic over Sputnik led the nation to declare poor educational quality our preeminent national security vulnerability. *A Nation at Risk* famously warned that "a rising tide of mediocrity . . . threatens our very future as a Nation and a people." The authors cried out: "If an unfriendly foreign power had attempted to impose on America the mediocre educational performance that exists today, we might well have viewed it as an act of war." A decade before No Child Left Behind and two decades before Common Core, Gatto sounded the alarm: Our "young people are indifferent to the adult world and to the future, indifferent to almost everything except the diversion of toys and violence. Rich or poor, school children who face the twenty-first century cannot concentrate on anything for very long; they have a poor sense of time past and time to come."

Expecting that his readers who heard "commitment to public education" and "commitment to the schools we have today" as synonymous would view his questioning of our current model as somehow indifferent to the poor and underprivileged, Gatto clarified that his goal is "radical" only in the original sense of the term—that is, returning to the root, or the fundamental nature of education. He called on Americans to do just that: Ask what the purpose of education is. And what portion of that purpose can reasonably be accomplished by formalized schooling? And what kind of schools? He understood that not everyone would agree on the answers to these questions. But, he argued, competing ideas, and competing models, will be not detrimental but rather constructive to more effectively tailoring our offerings to more of our kids.

He called therefore for more diversity of institutional form. What does that mean? We need more choices: "family schools and small entrepreneurial schools and religious schools and crafts schools and farm schools [should all] exist in profusion to compete" with the standardized large public high school. "I'm trying to describe a free market in schooling exactly like the one the country had until the Civil War, *one in which students volunteer for the kind of education that suits them,* even if that means self-education" (emphasis in original).

Polling shows that tens of millions of American parents consistently worry that we are churning out indifferent, distracted, passive, dependent young adults. They don't usually articulate their reform hopes as systematically as Gatto did, but the level of dissatisfaction with the current model of schooling our adolescents is stunning. Gallup annually asks how pleased we are with the overall quality of education that students receive in kindergarten through twelfth grade. Only once in the past two decades has a solid half of the public expressed satisfaction with what our schooling now delivers (53 percent were satisfied in 2004).

Homeschooling is now the fastest-growing segment of American education, having evolved from a fringe movement of hippies and "unschoolers" in the 1960s and 1970s to a diverse movement of nearly 2 million students from all walks of life today. With a population that has more than doubled in the past fourteen years, homeschooling is now nearly as common as Catholic schooling, and there are almost 40 percent as many homeschooled kids as there are kids in private and religious schools in America.

(Full disclosure: As will be touched on in part II, Melissa and I now homeschool two of our three children. We do so partly because our lives are geographically complicated, as we split time between Nebraska and Washington, DC. But we also do it because we are able to get our older two a broader array of educational experiences at 13 and 15—time working on cattle ranches, intergenerational travel experiences, a mix of in-person and online curriculum, language saturation, a wide range of athletic and musical experiences, and so on.)

THE DIGITAL REVOLUTION AND THE HYBRID LEARNING TO COME

The combination of the public's lack of confidence in the quality of our schooling and the unpredictable ways the tech industry is upending economic and social life will likely drive a profound reshaping of American education. The digital revolution's disruption of other businesses—from stock brokerages and travel agencies to journalism and music publishing—will also fundamentally transform schooling.

As a sneak peek into what hybridized learning will probably come to look like, consider the story of Salman Khan and the Khan Academy, which he built almost by accident. As a 27-year-old working at a hedge fund, Khan began tutoring his niece from afar in algebra on the internet, recording short video lessons in math and then science for her to consult. His videos were compelling, and soon many other folks, both known and unknown to him, began accessing them online.

Once his tutorials had been viewed a few hundred million times (!), Khan decided to quit the hedge fund and build his global academy full time. With funding from the Gates Foundation, Google, and a few quiet philanthropists, Khan has now produced nearly 7,000 videos on a range of subjects. They are all free, making him a familiar tutor to kids around the world—and an invaluable source for homeschooling parents, free-range parents, and school-supplementing parents everywhere. *Forbes* and *Time* have repeatedly labeled Khan one of the most influential people on earth. His YouTube channel now has 3 million regular subscribers and his video view count will soon top 1 billion. Although just turning 40, he is almost surely already the most important math "teacher" (not to say researcher) in human history.

While Khan's videos are not without their critics—some have criticized him for focusing too much on procedure and not enough on theory—it's inarguable that he has created an important new educational resource for contemporary students. And he is but one of hundreds of similar new content providers.

So, in the face of this crowd-sourced revolution in remediation and tutoring in America, what is the education establishment talking about? Where are the incumbent power brokers in American education—and especially at the university education schools—trying to take our national conversation about reform?

AGAINST GRADE 13

The "P-16" framework, launched in many states in the late 1990s and now picking up adherents all across the country, is the newest fad among self-styled education reformers and school administrators. In the place of old K-12 state bureaucracies that focused on kindergarten through the senior year in high school, P-16 proposes an expansion of the current model on both ends—"P" is for preschool while "16" is for the fourth and final year of college. This logic demands a reworking of the college freshman year into something conceived of as a new "grade 13," which would focus on needed remedial work and more counseling to help students better transition into college.

P-16 proponents rightly note that many students arrive at college unprepared. The grand irony, of course, is that this intended remedial instruction would use almost exactly the same model of student passivity that failed the students in high school in the first place. What assurance do students have that grade 13 will be more productive and better taught than grade 11 or grade 9? What guarantee, in other words, do we have that this deferral of responsibility-taking for our own learning won't turn into a grade 14, or grade 17, or grade 23? And if we do fail again, and thus kick the can farther down the road—that is, if we defer adolescence longer yet again—who will be held accountable next time? Who? Because we aren't holding anyone accountable for current or previous failures. Put another way, shouldn't the obvious question before us be: How can we address the existing and underlying issues of education without adding more broken education on top? Shouldn't we be asking why grade 12 isn't working rather than making its failures the model for "grade 13"?

More than forty states have now adopted some sort of a P-16 framework—and the folks pushing these initiatives mean well, without question—but this is not going to work. The trouble with P-16—but especially with grade 13—is this: Instead of admitting that our one-size-fits-all model is extending the period of adolescence rather than producing active learners, we are lazily deciding to invest even more power and authority in the same one-size-fits-all model. Unfortunately, centralized education bureaucrats tend to see every failure as a product of *still not enough* centralized bureaucracy. Most of these experts are blind to the possibility that perhaps we are still trying to spoon-feed young adults who we should instead nudge to travel and to read, to work and to become the kind of students who ask questions before being handed a three-point formulaic answer. The argument of P-16 advocates is that students have had a tremendous amount of guidance and support from preschool through high school, but then they fall through the cracks when they receive less hand-holding during the transition from grade 12 to "grade 13." Their answer then is that we should extend the training-wheels period. The (again, well-intentioned) argument is that the students can't simply be cut loose to tackle college or the job market on their own: "Young adults cannot be expected to know or understand the full ramifications of their roles in the economy without close guidance, particularly in the early years of their careers," wrote Matthew Lynch, a Virginia education expert.

I disagree. I think the problem is that we already overmanage the lives of young adults rather than that we are not offering them enough bubble wrap. I take issue with the notion that young adults are incapable of making choices or acting independently. It is clearly true that they aren't very good at it, but that is because we failed to help them learn how to seize the reins and do it themselves much earlier—in primary and middle school—and doesn't mean that we should still be choosing and acting for them after high school. We're already shifting people from high school graduation into college without requiring them to make thoughtful choices about work or career training or how they'll learn. It's a new kind of mindlessly passive "social promotion." Right now, about one-third of fall freshmen do not return as fall sophomores. What happens next?

The experience in my home state of Nebraska is illustrative of the bumpy transitions for 18-year-olds: We've seen the percentage of graduating seniors that go to college increase by roughly 25 percent over the past fifteen years. At first glance, this is a tremendously encouraging sign. But how many more people have actually graduated from college in Nebraska during that period? Until recently, *none*—most simply drift into college unintentionally and then drop out in their freshman or early sophomore year rather than having first made an intentional choice whether or not to try college at the end of high school.

Proponents of grade 13 have a noble desire to help smooth these bumpy transitions, but they fail to admit and learn from the obvious imperfections in our system. They fail to acknowledge the Socratic insight that at a certain age, learning cannot be force-fed; it needs to come in response to genuinely asked questions by genuinely curious people. Experts can't educate your kids until the kids have the desire to be educated.

Are we satisfied that we've gotten secondary education right, and if not, why would we make it the model for further expansion? Yet, the P-16ers' answer is more schooling, more standardization, more time in the classroom. They seem to think a homogenized institutional form is right for every 19-year-old in America. But it feels like they don't know many 19-year-olds. They want to standardize college the way we standardized K-12, creating mass tertiary schooling the way we homogenized mass secondary schooling. But the mass secondary schooling we have right now doesn't work very well for most 16-year-olds; why would we think it's the right model for most 19-year-olds?

I'm suggesting that we should be having a completely different conversation. Instead of spending our energy building hermetically sealed bubbles in which to protect our adolescents, we should be building in advance the kinds of experiential tools that we hope to persuade them to ask for—without them even realizing that we were orchestrating affairs to get them to discover their need. In the former vision, they're passive; in the latter, they're progressively more empowered—and we're helping them lay a foundation on which they themselves will further build.

I believe that the increasing institutionalization of the teenage years has made many young Americans less like citizens and more like cogs in a machine. It isn't surprising that so many are floundering in such stultifying environs. More time in a bureaucratic setting means less family life, less time in the community, and less effort invested in thinking about what coming-of-age work experiences could and should look like. Grade 13 becomes a substitute for the plural institutions in which young people can be challenged and can find special strengths and gifts. Past a point, more years spent in school does not reap better outcomes. Too much formalized schooling inevitably crowds out communities of the heart and soul, voluntarism, flexibility and choice, cross-cultural experience, exertion, success and failure, and time—essentially everything for becoming a fully formed adult, an empathetic citizen, and a worker-learner flexible enough to navigate the accelerated pace of job expiration and change in the new economy.

LEARNING HOW TO LEARN

Since I'm suggesting removing part of a diseased organ, it's on me to suggest how to replace it. What's needed is, first, more awareness that adolescence is neither fully childhood nor fully adult; and, second, a clear sense of what we want our kids to accomplish and internalize during this tweener stage. At the risk of oversimplification, I think we are largely hoping to help them learn how to learn—so that *they* can go out into life as autodidacts now able to tackle a whole new set of challenges that will be thrown at them. We need to affirm and refine their agency. We need to help them develop their self-confidence, not as an emotional abstraction but as a realistic assessment of their newfound abilities to ably navigate a world where nimbleness, inventiveness, perseverance, and grit will be demanded.

In arguably the most important essay on education written in the last century, English author Dorothy Sayers railed against the power of educational "specialists" who act like the rest of us couldn't or shouldn't fully own our own process of learning. Education, she argued in 1948 in "The Lost Tools of Learning," is inherently about the goals of lives well lived; it is about the good, the true, and the beautiful. It is not the private domain of the experts. It belongs to all of humanity.

In education, "too much specialization is not a good thing," she insisted. Lamenting the "artificial prolongation of intellectual childhood and adolescence into the years of physical maturity," the novelist and playwright presciently argued that a societal decision to "postpone the acceptance of responsibility to a late date brings with it a number of psychological complications."

Education that focuses on tools and techniques at the exclusion of the student's role in directing his or her own learning is destined to fail. As Socrates taught, it is almost impossible to educate someone with an answer until he or she is invested in asking a question. Similarly, it is difficult to put the tool that is school to the proper use until we agree what the problem is that requires a tool to begin with. As the momentum behind P-16 builds, we would be well served to pause and question, Sayers' work teaches us, to identify our goals and the specific problem we're tackling. How can juvenile people be expected to self-govern or to navigate an advertising-saturated market economy full of propaganda and untruths? How can they determine fact from opinion or what's been proven from what might be possible?

While Dorothy Sayers was writing in 1948, her commentary feels as if it could have been written yesterday. She worried that the education system sanitized learning by taking it away from the real world, allowing students to artificially and unhelpfully silo various subjects "by watertight bulkheads from all other 'subjects'" in their minds. She feared that modern schooling was substituting frenzy for achievement, encouraging kids to check a great many subject boxes—piling "task on task and prolong[ing] the days of labor"—but without the students ever coming to learn anything about how they themselves actually learn so that they might eventually do it on their own without the training wheels of the classroom. She acknowledged that students needed to master the core subjects but believed it was more important for them to first "learn how to learn."

Sayers lamented the loss of the historic "trivium," a model of learning that recognized very different strengths and inclinations at different stages of childhood. The trivium consists "of three parts: Grammar, Dialectic, and Rhetoric, in that order." "Grammar" means not just the grammar of language, as we think of it, but basic facts, such as the alphabet, or the forty-five presidents, or multiplication tables through 12 times 12 equals 144, or the two hundred countries on a map. "Dialectic" is another way of saying "logic," the interplay of facts. "Rhetoric" means learning how to present a logically accurate case persuasively. In learning a foreign language, for instance, it is silly to learn "just how to order a meal." Rather, first you need to learn some words, as well as the structure that underlies how to conjugate a verb. Second, you take that grammar and begin to assemble some initial sentences. And only third do you string sentences together into an effective argument. But once you've learned to do this in an initial language, and once you understand how the parts of a language interact, then it becomes markedly easier in each subsequent language. The same progression of grammar, then logic or dialectic, then rhetoric applies to virtually every subject. A student needs to become conscious of learning how he or she learns.

By contrast, modern schooling typically defines clearly the roles of teacher and student, the one active—"to teach"—and the other passive—"to be taught." There is almost something perverse about wanting to teach everyone to read but not to teach them to think clearly—leaving "them at the mercy of the printed word." We were, she feared, creating young people without the mature tools of logical discernment about good versus weak arguments.

Harkening back to an educational psychology or an anthropology that predated Dewey and mass factory-model schooling, she argued for a distinction among "three states of development" for 5- to 15-year-olds:

"the Poll-Parrot, the Pert, and the Poetic." She was not waging any political or policy battle, but rather urging us to ask, first and foremost, about the basic nature of children and young adults. About how much sitting still aids their development? What is the role of physical self-restraint for a 6-year-old? For an 8-year-old? For a 10-year-old? It is obvious that there are prime periods in childhood development for the memorization of facts, especially set to jingles. In Melissa's and my experience, allowing kids to march and stomp around while they memorize is far more effective than trying to get them to sit still.

Sayers's first stage, the babbler or the

> Poll-Parrot stage is the one in which learning by heart is easy and, on the whole, pleasurable; whereas reasoning is difficult and, on the whole, little relished. At this age, one readily memorizes the shapes and appearances of things; one likes to recite the number-plates of cars; one rejoices in the chanting of rhymes and the rumble and thunder of unintelligible polysyllables; one enjoys the mere accumulation of things.

Her dialectic-centric "Pert age" comes second, and "is characterized by contradicting, answering back, liking to 'catch people out' (especially one's elders); and by the propounding of conundrums. Its nuisance-value is extremely high."

Third and finally, and most significantly for the purposes of this book, comes the Poetic or the "difficult age." Budding teens are self-absorbed, increasingly independent of their nuclear families and yearning to express themselves. This age "specializes in being misunderstood; it is restless and tries to achieve independence; and, with good luck and good guidance, it should show the beginnings of creativeness; a reaching out towards a synthesis of what it already knows, and a deliberate eagerness to know and do some one thing in preference to all others." If we are going to parent with the grain during this adolescent-poetic stage, we had better first grasp that there is indeed a budding romantic in there trying to define his or her own identity.

This third stage is directionally oriented, aiming to leave the child behind and find a self-possessed young man or woman at its end. As that earliest edge of adulthood arrives, there is a new—partial but real—humility, as "the pupils will probably be beginning to discover for themselves that their knowledge and experience are insufficient." They will begin to realize not just what they know but also—marvelously and in a humility-inducing way—all that they do not know. They realize "that their trained intelligences need a great deal more material to chew upon." The late rhetorical or Poetic stage is the time to throw open the "doors of the storehouse of Knowledge," as subjects "once learned by rote will be seen in new contexts; the things once coldly analyzed can now be brought together to form a new synthesis; here and there a sudden insight will bring about that most exciting of all discoveries: the realization that truism is true."

If there is a patron saint of the educational philosophy underpinning this book, it is Sayers. She yearned for a great education for all, but she knew that such a dream could be realized only once children were individually and personally engaged. If this book ever sounds critical of schoolteachers, then I'm probably not arguing very effectively—because the intended argument is *against the mindless assumption made by too many of the rest of us* that schools and their teachers can awaken all of our kids alone inside just one institutional form. Rather, all of us need to be more engaged at helping spark these awakenings. Sayers knew that teens themselves must come to realize that both cultures and vibrant individuals "cannot live on capital forever." If a free people is going to be reproduced, it will require watering and revivifying and owning anew older traditions, and awakening the curiosity in the soul of each citizen.

National greatness will not be recovered via a mindless expansion of bureaucratized schooling. "We dole out lip-service to the importance of education," Sayers grieved seventy years ago. Sure, we demand another "grant of money; we postpone the school-leaving age, and plan to build bigger and better schools"; we demand that teachers "slave conscientiously in and out of school hours"—but to what end? "I believe," she lamented, "all this devoted effort is largely frustrated," because we have *no definable goal* for each child to become an adult. We "have lost the tools of learning," sacrificing them to the "piecemeal" subject-matter approach of bureaucratized schooling that finally compromises to produce passive rather than active emerging adults.

Our kids are not commodities; they are plants—they require a protected environment, and care and feeding, but most basically an internal yearning to grow toward the sunlight. What we need is the reequipping of each child with those "lost tools"—the "axe and the wedge, the hammer and the saw, the chisel and the plane"—to construct a logical argument and to present coherent positions passionately. "For the sole true end of education is simply this: to teach men how to learn for themselves; and whatever instruction fails to do this is effort spent in vain."

TRAINING WHEELS ARE
MADE TO COME OFF

People who have taught kids to ride a bike can debate the merits and demerits of using training wheels in the process. I've taught multiple children, and I'm now a decidedly "no-training-wheels" guy. This has been my method for all three of my own kids: Dressing them in *Ghostbusters*-level coats and ski pants, I then run behind them, straddling the back wheel of each little bike. I knock them side to side in the shoulders as we shoot down a slightly declining street until suddenly they find their balance, mostly by accident. And then they can ride! It's a beautiful moment—notwithstanding the great damage the straddle-running inflicts on dad's aging lower back.

This technique probably yields a few more bloody knees and chins (for all of us) at the beginning than the training-wheels technique, but my way is both efficient and effective. The kids all learned fast. But even if you are strongly in the pro–training wheels camp, we would surely agree that training wheels are a tool—an interim state—rather than an end or goal. Training wheels are made to be shed as quickly as possible. The final definition of success is the first time you see your kid coming back around the block alone in one piece, training wheels–free, beaming from ear to ear.

So it is with launching an adolescent into adulthood. Nobody wants eternal training wheels. Yet allowing our culture to devolve from one that encourages self-sufficiency into one that indulges permanent dependency is to tolerate a disengagement of the soul akin to permanent training wheels. Letting the next generation believe someone else will solve their problems imperils not only them but our whole society. What we want is to see them soar, training wheels–free, beaming from ear to ear, ready to ride next to us as independent adults, able to provide for themselves and to benefit their neighbors and nation.

PART II

<del>——⟫◆⟪——</del>

AN ACTIVE
PROGRAM

WE HAVE DAUNTING CHALLENGES BEFORE US—AND
it would be useful to embrace a notion of adolescence as a series of
training-wheel-removal exercises. What tasks are we parents and guides
doing for our kids now that we want to help them learn to do well,
but without our hand-holding? We have a bottleneck of young people
to help transform from children into productive, responsible men and
women. Our problem today is not just that we are failing to foster good
character but also that we are failing even to imagine together what success would look like.

We seem collectively blind to the irony that the generation coming of age has begun life with far *too few* problems. No one should regard the eradication of polio as anything but a glorious blessing, but we
should also be able to recall that many older folks we know grew their
character by fighting through their polio—and many of their generation who didn't contract the paralyzing infection learned to count their
blessings because of what they didn't have to fight through. Similarly,
there are many household chores that we no longer need to complete
today—such as feeding and watering and warming the horses who
would pull our carriages. And while the absence of particular tasks is
individually a happy development, the overall absence of meaningful,
character-building, household-centered tasks is not.

What alternate necessities are we helping our kids see, tackle, and
conquer? We're not shepherding very well on this score, and thus our
offspring know neither the experience of work nor even their ignorance

of the hidden work that keeps their grocery aisles overflowing and geo-political tormentors at bay. There is simultaneously a great blessing and a real curse in living in an exceptionally prosperous nation.

The riddle before us is how to construct alternative ways of build-ing long-term character in an era when the daily pursuit of food and shelter no longer compels it. While some schools are trying to emphasize character development, and are to be applauded for doing so, genuine character-building can't be taught—certainly not in two class periods per week for forty-two minutes each. It has to be lived and breathed and struggled with—modeled and mentored.

MARRIAGE—AND TEACHING A LION TO HUNT

Marriage offers a useful analogy. Learning to be married—I mean here something beyond the passionate, infatuation stage of the first couple of years and learning to actually share an entire life of thick and thin times, successes and failures, even boredoms—is a lot like coming of age. And though the decision to get married for those of us who do feels like a natural step in our adult lives, this doesn't mean that we instinctively know *how* to be married. It turns out that substantial instruction, and practice, is required.

People who choose to get married rely on a range of social constructs, laws, and customs, beginning with courtship, to show them how to act. They seek help and advice from older married couples, religious leaders, friends, and family members. Candid talk about the likely challenges ahead is a healthy way to prepare for life together. I remember, before I got married, having an older couple laughingly tell me that what I *meant* to be communicating and what my future wife might be hearing could be quite different things. After two decades of marriage, awareness of this gap now seems second nature, but back then I don't think I'd ever heard the distinction before. Intentionally seeking advice from those older and wiser is both artificial and yet not at all contrary to the natural work of two learning to become one—the hard but satisfying work of unity.

Somewhat surprisingly, nature works in a similar way. Wild animals don't reason as humans do, but they don't act purely on instinct either. Mothers teach their offspring how to survive on their own. Mama birds instruct their babies how to fly. Some birds teach their chicks how to associate specific sounds with calls for food versus other warning pitches against impending danger.

What's true for marriage or for animal flight training is truer still for coming of age. Teenagers need help. Growing up is actual, hard work. I would venture to guess that most of our teens don't need more therapy or more antidepressants. They need direction about how to acquire the habits essential for navigating adulthood, and experiences that introduce and instill those habits.

FIVE CHARACTER-BUILDING HABITS

We can conjure dozens of ways to help teens learn to be tougher and grittier adults, to develop into more thoughtful and empathetic neighbors. Humans have done it for millennia. Almost every culture in history has adopted rituals and customs to mark the transition out of childhood: Go to war. Learn the value of hard work. Go on the big hunt. Take on a bully. Leave home. Prepare to give birth. Experience subsistence. Comfort someone struggling at the door of death. Build something large.

Shaping the budding adult's character has always and everywhere been a matter of great gravity. In a rich and accidentally spoiled society like ours, though, it is even more momentous, because it doesn't happen by inertia of motion; it requires forethought. And at exactly the moment when we need it most, we've begun to neglect both any definition of what adulthood means and any shared tending to the markers of transition to it.

Though we rarely admit it in polite company, I suspect most thoughtful parents know that we've placed excessive faith in schools' ability to remake our kids for us and to solve almost every serious social problem. A misplaced hope about what schools can and cannot accomplish has led to recurring cycles of disappointment, disagreement, and public disengagement. The schools are less to blame than we are, for we are the ones who have asked them to deliver more than any mass institution is competent to produce.

For the remainder of this book, I will focus on five uses of a teen's time—five habits to cultivate—to transition from childhood to adulthood. There are dozens of other experiences and habits we could unpack here, but let's focus on these five because each of them is at least as important as schooling. These five habits demand an active posture—all require discipline—but every American can develop them.

All five require building scar tissue on purpose. Call them body-building for the mind and soul.

First, discover the body—its potential and its frailty, and the many diverse stages of life that lie ahead—by breaking free of the tyranny of one generation. Teens need to appreciate the joys of birth and growth and the tragedy of pain and decline. The most natural and obvious way we're limited is by our own mortality. Death is the hardest reality all of us must confront—the "last calling," writers used to label it. It's typical of young people to think of themselves as indestructible. That's always been true. The difference today is that our emerging adults are cut off from older generations and the reality of human frailty. They're immersed in a culture created by their peers. If your experience is limited to spending time only with people roughly your own age, then your understanding of life and joy and pain and suffering—and death—will be severely attenuated.

Second, develop a work ethic. Hard work, manual labor, working outdoors—on a farm, say, or a ranch—is an education in itself. The goal is to learn the habits that lead to the discovery of meaning in work. Your aim is to become *free to* work with delight rather than seeking to be *free from* work.

Third, embrace limited consumption. "Luxury is the bane of republics." At some point we forgot the difference between *needs* and *wants* and decided that acquiring things could bring us happiness. It's not true. Gluttony is a danger we've forgotten to guard against. But even more basically, consumption alone cannot make us happy; meaningful production can. Knowing how our species overcame subsistence and necessity, and why the United States developed from a small agrarian republic into a commercial powerhouse, is an asset in recovering an older understanding of how to limit your desires and how to find satisfaction and gratitude in the meeting of a limited set of true needs.

Fourth, learn how to travel and to travel light. To understand the difference between *need* and *want,* you need to know what it's like to subsist. To understand your own culture better, it's essential to experience other cultures so that you can look back at yours. Literature is a key way to gain that perspective, but the best way to shock open young eyes is to travel. Pick up a backpack, take only the eighteen pounds that are needed, and go. The traveler finds the larger world, but also his or her own.

Fifth, learn how to read and decide what to read. Just as you learn to appreciate necessity and your own culture better by experiencing the cultures of other places, books offer a kind of literary travel. You can visit ancient Athens and Jerusalem in books. But there is a difference between learning how to read and how to read well. Your kids need to become obsessed with the habit of reading; they need an appetite. And then they need a list of great literature and great nonfiction. The best way to develop that appetite is for them to start playing an active role in building and explaining and defending their menu—so they can then fall in love with and return again to some of their entrees. Let's wrestle over what your list should include.

Bodybuilding for the mind and soul—the scar tissue of character—happily awaits.

FOUR

FLEE AGE SEGREGATION

*Lonely with Our Peers * "I Can't Not Be There for That"*
*Death as a Central Fact of Life * The Gut Punch of Beating Dad*
*Preparing to Die Well * The Three Purposes of Sex*
*Experience a Birth * How Adults Escape*

It's not by strength or speed or swiftness of body that great deeds are done, but by wisdom, character, and sober judgment. These qualities . . . grow richer as time passes.

—Marcus Tullius Cicero

IF SEVENTEENTH-CENTURY SETTLERS FROM PURITAN Massachusetts or Anglican Virginia were transported to the present day, much would obviously confuse them—the lights, the sounds, and the technology. Our vast market system, which overtook the subsistence agricultural economy of their time, would baffle and impress them. They would probably not believe their eyes upon seeing the endless supply of food in our supermarkets and the infinite product list on Amazon.

But once our time travelers got past the shock of material plenty, I suspect they'd be even more disoriented and distressed by two changes in how we organize our social lives: the way we separate work from home and then, consequently, the ways we segregate the young from older people in our communities.

First, work has become tremendously specialized and thus increasingly centered—at least prior to the new revolution in mobile digital devices—in factories, offices, and other specialized workplaces. Think about this: Three hundred years ago, nobody commuted to work. People worked where they lived—downstairs, upstairs, or just outside the house or tent. Everybody in the family was engaged in activities for the betterment of the family and possibly the village—hunting, farming, fetching water, gathering firewood, barrel-making, butter-churning, etcetera. Separating work from the home—taking the artisan out of his shop and putting him in a steel mill, for example—was a stark shift in not just economic but also social and family life. Children who had grown up around their parents' world of work were now divorced from it. In the process of the economy shifting from farms to factories, and Americans moving from the countryside to cities, habits changed, and the family culture was altered. Dad—and then increasingly mom—headed off to "work," by which they meant the production line or office. Children didn't see adults' gainful employment up close anymore. Apprenticeships waned.

We tend to focus on our children's lack of motivation to work, but at least as large a hurdle to developing a work ethic is their simple lack of exposure to different kinds of work. We have, undeniably, prospered materially because of specialization. But an underappreciated unintended consequence has been a sharp reduction in opportunities for kids to work and, in turn, to reap work's diverse benefits. The next chapter will tackle that loss, and propose some better ways forward.

But this chapter will focus on the second cultural practice that would shock our seventeenth-century visitors: As work left the home, it became more sterile and our ever-wealthier households much less intergenerational—and our children's entire lives drifted into age-segregated ghettos. As young and old became separated from work, young and old became separated from workers and from each other. Young people now spend the majority of their waking hours in and around schools and, thus, mainly with people their own age. We first separated youth from the broader population by putting them into schools as the primary consumer of their time, and then we began further separating students within schools by age as well. It's only within the past century that schools started grouping children by age as opposed to learning ability or the specific skill they were trying to acquire—and yet kids have been given the false impression that this is how life has always been.

LONELY WITH OUR PEERS

Today, young people's lives are driven by one predominant fact: birth year. Instead of helping with the family business or apprenticing, teenagers are now hanging out, in person or online, with friends, most of whom are their same age and year in school. Correspondingly, senior citizens live out their years in nursing homes where they also interact mainly with their age peers. Retirees buy condominiums in age-segregated communities like Sun City, California, and Kings Point, Florida, where people under 55 are prohibited unless accompanied by an older adult.

Over the last thirty years, Americans' "discussion networks"—a fancy term for the people in whom we actually confide—have declined substantially. A study in the *American Sociological Review* essentially asked, Do you bare your soul to anyone? Do you have friends? Painfully, the authors found that fewer and fewer of us do. The number of people who report that they have no confidants at all has nearly tripled, to fully a quarter of all Americans in recent years. Even among those of us who do have genuine friends, the average person now claims only two confidants—versus an average of three just two decades ago. According to another study of Americans 60 and older, only a quarter of them had discussed anything "important" with anyone under 36 in the previous six months. And when the question excludes relatives, the percentage drops to a jarring 6 percent.

This hollowing out of friendship is genuinely tragic.

Other cultures, even highly hierarchical ones, have not segregated young and old this rigidly—and our marketers and advertisers now aim to increase that segregation. As will be explored in chapter 6, consumption categories—both the "what to consume" and the "who consumes like I do"—profoundly shape the lenses through which we see the world. I recently heard a teenage girl announce "I like Jessica but we cannot be friends because Jessica is 22." Could we perhaps define "friend" first, before rejecting a meaningful relationship with someone who doesn't happen to be in the same grade or shop at the same retailers?

Generational segregation now touches upon all facets of life, from the ways we socialize and work to the ways we worship. Fifty years ago it was the norm for multiple generations of a family to worship together. But that began to change in the 1980s and 1990s. The rise of mega-churches illustrates the ways retail categories have remade our conceptions of community. Just as "mom-and-pop stores" and neighborhood supermarkets evolved into "big-box" anchor stores with demographically targeted specialty shops arrayed around them, mall-like churches now offer services and programming tailored to the market segments inside their congregations: high schoolers, college kids, GenXers, Baby Boomers, and even holdover "liturgical traditionalists." (Perhaps only chains like Starbucks transcend intergenerational divides, anchoring the corner curb of the strip mall and the lobby of the megachurch.) Worship services are differentiated primarily by musical style and volume—the younger the crowd, the louder the amplifiers.

But the costs go beyond possible hearing loss, as studies show that generational segregation weakens faith commitments. According to the Fuller Youth Institute, "involvement in all-church [intergenerational] worship during high school is more consistently linked with mature faith in both high school and college than any other form of church participation." Fewer and fewer of our young people have intergenerational experiences in the pews, with both theological and sociological consequences. As community density weakens, contexts for sharing wisdom also sadly evaporate.

At a dinner party discussion a few years ago, when I was agonizing about the extended adolescence of some of our students at Midland, I asked a long table of opinionated friends how they determine whether a teenager is "mature." The conversation quickly evolved to gender, and one woman announced, "Well, it's easy to know if a 13-year-old *boy* is or isn't mature: if I would trust him to watch my baby for 90 minutes— that is, long enough that there might be a diaper change on his watch." It wasn't a variable I'd considered, but almost every woman at the table immediately agreed. Another mother added, "Yep. Basically all 13-year-old girls can. But if a boy can, he's mature. If not, he's still a child." This sorting criteria ended up having broad utility, as it quickly became apparent many of these mothers regarded lots of 25-year-old "men" as boys too. (One childless thirtysomething began to shift awkwardly in his chair.) They were really asking if these young men have the vision and awareness to see and feel beyond their immediate needs and beyond the social world of an often narcissistic peer set.

Social science confirms that adolescents *acquire* vital social skills by interacting with people outside their peer bubble. University of Arizona anthropologist Alice Schlegel has studied 186 preindustrial cultures and found that age segregation is closely correlated to "antisocial behavior and to socialization for competitiveness and aggressiveness." Conversely, older kids who spend time with younger kids learn to be nurturing, while younger kids learn concrete lessons about the coming stages of intellectual development and economic productivity, as well as how to navigate communities larger than themselves.

"I CAN'T NOT BE THERE . . . FOR THAT"

When my wife was 8 years old, she struck up a relationship with the Killians, an elderly couple next door to her childhood home in Birmingham, Alabama. Mr. Killian, a gardener, taught her to prune branches, trim leaves, and till soil. But they also talked and laughed and, over a few years, developed a friendship. When Melissa was 12, Mrs. Killian developed Alzheimer's disease, and her husband became her primary caretaker. Melissa continued regularly visiting and helping out around the house until she left for college. She had long, meaningful conversations with Mr. Killian as his wife's memories gradually disappeared.

Alzheimer's is brutal not only for the person afflicted, but also for their loved ones. One day, upon observing Mr. Killian's exhaustion, Melissa mustered the courage to speak frankly to the old man: "She doesn't know you anymore. She has *no idea* who you are. You're not in the best of health. You're frail. The burden of caring for her is too much. You're exhausted. Why not put her in a home and get some rest? You can't keep doing this."

Mr. Killian took a deep breath. "You're right—sort of," Melissa recalls him saying. "Most of the time, it's very hard. But, I'll tell you, she often wakes up in the middle of the night and asks me for water or she'll need help to the bathroom. And for ten minutes, perhaps two or three times a month, she'll know who I am again. I could never miss those moments. I can't not be there for her, for that."

That conversation profoundly impacted my wife. Looking back, she can't imagine not having had that "aha" moment, ugly though the context was.

When Melissa and I started dating in 1992, she was living in an apartment in Boston across the street from a nursing home. Many afternoons, she visited the residents. I occasionally went with her. Some were blind, so she read to them. She was well aware that mortality was real, that these people were lonely, and that *our* attempt to pretend that decline isn't real is actually much stranger than the fact of their decline. We have a duty to care for our elders. They shouldn't simply be warehoused and forgotten.

Melissa has kept up the habit of visiting the elderly and the sick. She also visits prisons and helps chaplains organize services. The first time I brought her back to my hometown in Nebraska in 1993, she insisted that I take her to the local rest home and introduce her to some of the elderly people I'd known growing up. My grandparents had long taken communion Sunday afternoons to folks too weak or infirm to attend church services—so I had learned the hallways of Merrick Annex and Arbor Manor well back in elementary school.

I'll never forget the evening over Christmas week in 1993 when my childhood piano teacher, Clara Druhe, came ambling down the nursing home hallway. Upon seeing me, Mrs. Druhe, age (and probably weight) 83, slapped herself so hard in the forehead I sincerely wondered if she might crack one of her frail vertebrae. She couldn't believe that this individual from her past—this "young" person, full of vitality—had come to see her. I was delighted—and I was ashamed. Why had I not done this before?

Some religious communities across America have taken pains to ensure that their elders are respected and not forgotten. A number of Lutheran churches throughout the Midwest utilize retirees at schools to help with the drop-off line of cars in the mornings and pick-up line in the afternoons. A Dutch community in San Diego County purposely built an elder-care facility on the same site as an elementary school. The idea is straightforward: Let the elderly who are able help in the classroom. Let them do the vital work of reading—and listening—to children as they stumble through the trial and error of sounding out words, of becoming literate and articulate.

It's true that most older people cannot do everything that came easily in their youth. But the great Roman orator Marcus Tullius Cicero observed more than 2,000 years ago that "surely there are activities suitable for older minds even when the body is weakened." Education is one of the most suitable. "People who say there are no useful activities for old age don't know what they're talking about," Cicero argued in his dialogue *On Old Age*. "They are like those who say a pilot does nothing useful for sailing a ship because others climb the masts, run along the gangways, and work the pumps while he sits quietly in the stern holding the rudder."

Cicero's wisdom comes with no expiration date. It takes work, of course, to build—and rebuild—relationships with the elderly. Yet once you've done it, you won't regret the effort. We work at it in our own family, and it pays real dividends—for all parties. Time provides perspective. The pain of a peer-cultural slight, for instance, is diminished when articulated to someone who's been there, felt that, and healed from it. "Let's bake some cookies with Mrs. Peters—or for the Dillons," is a suggestion that almost instantly snaps our kids back from a navel-gazing obsession with some peer trivia that will quickly fade. Those shared cookies, and shared minutes and words, end up being therapeutic and wisdom-imparting for all involved.

DEATH AS A CENTRAL FACT OF LIFE

Thomas Hine, author of *The Rise and Fall of the American Teenager*, believes that American adult anxiety about growing older leads us to undermine our own kids' growing up. We have very shallow "coming-of-age ceremonies" partly because we the adults are unsure how we would "enact what it means to be an adult" in this culture ourselves. Folklorist Ruth Benedict believes our anxiety about aging, compounded by the desperate need of thirty- and fortysomething parents to "see themselves as still young," makes us "particularly reluctant to acknowledge the maturity of our children." In our flatter culture, the broader authority of parents is called into question, and many opt for peer relationships with their own children, well before the child has demonstrated sufficient adult maturity and capacity for peer-like status with an adult. Channeling Bob Dylan's 1970s soul-searching, we ignore the hard questions and just prefer to think of ourselves—to delude ourselves—as "Forever Young."

Death is the hardest question, and in an age that gives short shrift to the transmission of wisdom from old to young, it is not surprising that death is the single most obvious fact of life from which we constantly insulate our kids. We have, to our detriment, created a cult of denial about our own mortality. Life needs to be lived and prioritized with the understanding that it is limited. An awareness of one's mortality makes life richer because the important can be emphasized and the trivial marginalized.

What is a child's typical first experience of death today, excluding TV or movies? Maybe the loss of a pet or a much older relative. For a young child, the death of a frail great-grandparent hardly seems real. They are just so different, which makes relating to them difficult. They're abstractions, not flesh-and-blood creatures who really left a mark on the world. The loss lacks immediacy.

Often a child's first shocking exposure to death comes in the accidental passing of a relative or friend. When I was eleven, my cousin Jana died from a head injury in a motorcycle accident. Jana was as full of life as anyone I have ever known. She and I loved to water-ski together. Ten days before she died, we had literally run our dads' boat out of gas twice as we attempted to set an all-time record on the lake for total miles skied. And then she, of flying-tackle-hug fame, was gone. It wasn't natural; it wasn't right. Her tragedy was the first time I had known anyone who had died who wasn't already feeble. Jana's abrupt death forced me to reflect on my own mortality and that of other family members. I still remember going for a walk under the stars with my dad the night we got the call and how he reflected on mortality in ways I had never heard him speak before.

Historically, for most Americans, a young person's first real exposure to death was through hunting. A young hunter's first kill is one of the few identifiable rites of passage we have left. After that first kill, some deer hunters have the blood of their casualty dabbed on their foreheads and cheeks in a ritual called "blooding." While that may sound morbid, hunters tend not to be wanton killers. They respect both their game and the environment in which they hunt. Farmers know this respect for death and cycles as well. They live off the land. For the farmer, killing isn't an arbitrary choice; it's a necessity. Crops need to be protected from insects and wild animals. The beef, chicken, turkey, and pork on your plate came from somewhere; it didn't slaughter itself.

When we stop and reflect, we're surrounded by life and death: the nightly news reports on casualties from conflicts overseas and radio updates about fatal traffic accidents. But unfortunately these are treated as just passing pieces of information, forgotten as quickly as they're heard. Death at "too early an age" was prevalent prior to the twentieth century in America. Fatal food poisoning and infections were commonplace. Many of our grandparents are old enough to remember neighbors living under quarantine with scarlet fever, measles, or whooping cough—ailments that today, if they occur at all, can be easily treated with antibiotics. For the generation coming of age, the wonder of vaccinations has all but eradicated the terrifying threat of smallpox, diphtheria, and polio. Happily, infant mortality in America is a fraction of what it was in the past. The rate is so low, in fact, that we measure it in terms of deaths per 1,000 live births, which in Boston, for example, is now 5 of 1,000. In seventeenth-century Boston, the metric was more like 300 per 1,000.

We forget that when death was routine, Americans dealt with it—though still fearfully—regularly and forthrightly. If twenty-first-century Americans are blithely "spiritual but not religious," the early colonists agonized over the possibility that death was their doorway to eternal damnation. Children were constantly reminded—as if their lived experience wasn't harsh enough—that time was not on their side. Puritan minister Cotton Mather was severely blunt: "Go into Burying-Place, CHILDREN; you will there see Graves as short as your selves. Yea, you may be at Play one Hour; Dead, Dead the next." In the seventeenth century, a schoolbook maxim reminded students, as if previewing a Monty Python sketch, "Tis not likely that you will all live to grow up." Alphabet books taught the letter "T" as: "T—Time cuts down all / Both great and small." Of the 102 pilgrims who landed at Plymouth Rock in 1620, half of them were dead before the first winter ended. Conditions improved in the coming years, but a twenty-first-century time traveler would still find the outlook bleak.

Given death's ubiquity, people were more matter-of-fact about it. One Puritan custom was to display the body of a deceased individual in a kitchen for a week as family and neighbors gathered to pay their respects. Another was to give pairs of gloves as invitations to funerals. Ministers would receive these gloves as well, and Andrew Eliot of the famous North Church in Boston kept track of the gloves he received. In his thirty-two years as minister, he collected nearly 3,000 pairs—that's just shy of two pairs per week over his career.

People not only commemorated death, but created "other reminders of the frailty of life" too. Funeral guests sometimes received rings for their attendance. These weren't cheap party favors; they were typically made of gold and inlaid with designs of skulls, coffins, and skeletons. Death masks—wax, plaster, or metal casts made from a dead person's face—were popular *memori morti* in America until about 170 years ago. After the emergence of photography, families often had portraits taken with deceased loved ones, especially the babies. Postmortem photography seems odd to us now, but it nonetheless highlights how far removed death is in our current culture relative to its depiction in other times and places. Happily, vaccines, food safety, workplace safety, automobile enhancements, decreased public violence, advanced medical procedures, and better technologies across the board have all added up to longer and healthier lives for more and more Americans—but death is not going away. The Grim Reaper is merely being asked to wait, and our downplaying of death to the point of its disappearance from consciousness is not a healthy development.

In our age-segregated era, we spend enormous energy, time, and money letting the young and middle-aged pretend eternal youth is attainable, rather than actually grappling with the inevitable, and rather than comforting those actually declining. The century-old critique of fashion photography still hits the mark: It creates impossible expectations. Consider the silliness of "age-defying" makeup. The American Society of Plastic Surgeons reports that Americans spent a record $13.5 billion on cosmetic procedures in 2015. Women account for 90 percent of the total, with breast augmentations, liposuctions, rhinoplasties (nose jobs), blepharoplasties (eye lifts), and tummy tucks making up the lion's share of the surgeries and the spending. And the frequency of these procedures is growing three times faster than inflation.

Every generation of adolescents has likely toyed with their invincibility—early libido is a powerful drug—but what's different today is that almost all of us, of every generation, entertain these fantasies. We latch onto evidence hinting that aging can be put off, perhaps indefinitely. It's no surprise then that our young today inherit a fear of growing up and growing old, and a near allergy to confronting honestly the only certainty in life besides taxes.

THE GUT PUNCH OF BEATING DAD

I spent thousands of hours from elementary school through sophomore year of college wrestling, and I had hundreds of matches with my peers, dozens of them still easy for me to recall. My toughest matches, though, were not in any gym or practice room, but rather in my family living room. At least three or four times a week, my wrestling coach dad and I would clear the room, pushing furniture to the walls, and grapple on the floor. (We had alternate rules for wrestling in the lake, with variations for ankle-deep versus waist-deep water.) Week after week, month after month, year after year, dad defeated me. Just when I thought I had him in position for me to win, he would find a way to get sufficient leverage on my shoulder or neck to triumph. He was bigger, faster, and had years of experience. He had coached multiple state champions and one state championship team. How could I compete? He was definitely not the type to let someone win to boost self-esteem.

Little by little I improved—eventually going a year in competitive matches without anyone ever riding me for an entire period—and the matches at home got closer too. I was obviously also getting bigger, stronger, and quicker. Dad shared some important techniques, and I was sent away to some elite camps, despite our tight family budget.

It became increasingly apparent that my growing strength could enable me to pound his neck with an aggressive front half nelson. I refined the move, and finally, one Saturday morning when I was 16, I added my left hand to my right wrist for additional leverage on the back of his head, pushed him face downward, and beat him. What a rush! The student bested the master. It was in no small way a turning point in my life, a true rite of passage.

But almost as quickly, a feeling of dread rushed over me: This is *horrible*. It meant my dad—my provider, my protector—was starting to decline. I hadn't won just because I was 16 instead of 12, but because he was 41 instead of 37.

The benefits of better nutrition, medicine, and exercise notwithstanding, our parents won't always be there for us, serving as a safety net and security blanket when things go wrong. I have been blessed, both to have great parents always there for me when I've been in need, and also to have had that painful experience of my father's diminished strength, a discovery in my teens that crystallized my understanding of his mortality, and all of ours.

I worry that most adult-children and many childish adults haven't figured this out yet because none of us really want to know it, and our communities are becoming too thin to lovingly nudge each other toward seriousness. At some point, it is harmful rather than helpful to keep shielding people, to keep tolerating their attempts to distract themselves from the examined life.

PREPARING TO DIE WELL

What might rouse younger Americans from their slumber? Teddy Roosevelt was a charismatic figure who believed passionately in determining the most important things and then tackling them head-on. Unsurprisingly, he never blinked in the face of death. He led men charging into battle in the Spanish-American War. Less well known, when running for president for a third term in 1912, he was shot at point-blank range in the chest by a disgruntled Milwaukee saloon owner. The bullet was slowed but not stopped by the fifty-page speech folded up in his front pocket. "It takes more than that to kill a bull moose," Roosevelt told the crowd that witnessed the shooting. He was determined to finish his speech, and only after speaking for ninety minutes did he finally allow himself to be taken to a hospital.

Roosevelt in his *Autobiography* tells of the first time he hunted dangerous game. He doesn't recommend it for amateurs. He conceded that he was only a mediocre marksman because of poor eyesight and had several near misses with wild animals, including one charging elephant. The risk, he says, is the nerves of an inexperienced hunter when game first comes into view. "Any beginner is apt to have *buck fever,* and therefore no beginner should go at dangerous game," Roosevelt writes. "Buck fever" is a state of intense nervous excitement "which may be entirely divorced from timidity." Imagine the thrill and anxiety of doing anything for the first time: your first trip to the zoo, first visit to the dentist, first time behind the wheel, your first kiss. Roosevelt mentions the first time speaking in front of a large audience and the first time in battle. That's "buck fever," and there is really only one cure, Roosevelt explains: "habit." "What such a man needs is not courage but nerve control, cool-headedness. This he can get only by actual practice. He must, by custom and repeated exercise of self-mastery, get his nerves thoroughly under control."

For one of my kids, it was helping kill a large, jaggle-toothed possum in the garage. Ordinarily, we'd try to scare and shoo the creature outside and away from the house. But this particular possum was a nuisance, attacking our pets, consistently eating their food, nesting where it wasn't wanted, befouling the air and floor. It had to go. One night I heard our daughter Alex yelling from our garage, where she had been refilling her cats' food and water bowls. There was the possum, in the corner, hissing and screeching. What happened next involved a shovel and a lot of jumping around. In the end, the rodent was dispatched and my kids learned something about the necessity of pest control. It wasn't pretty, but it had to be done. (And then the corner wall of the garage had to be repainted.)

Killing an animal is one thing—but, of course, killing another human is a different matter altogether. Everyone who joins the armed forces will have different reasons for doing so. For decades, the U.S. military emphasized the scholarship opportunities that came with four years of enlistment. Join the army, go to college. It was and remains a good deal. After 9/11, joining the military meant a much higher likelihood of deploying to a combat zone overseas. Whether in peacetime or wartime, every enlisted man and woman learns quickly that the purpose of a soldier, sailor, airman, coast guardsman, or marine is to fight, kill, and quite possibly die in the service of the nation. Death may not be always at the forefront of a service member's mind, but it's always there, lurking. Even a supply clerk or cook must pick up a rifle and fight if need demands.

Proximity to death compels one to ask foxhole questions that demand honest answers about life, meaning, relationships, insecurities, priorities real and neglected. Our kids shouldn't wait until their own existential panic to wrestle with such questions; they should be gaining perspective on life as they age by sharing in the stories of those who've already had such experiences. Meaningful questioning forces us to come to grips with the knowledge that we are not the person we wish we were. At the very least, we're apt to repeat the enduring phrase: "There but for the grace of God go I." This observation is intended as an expression of humility and reliance on God's compassion. Contemplating the end brings into focus the chasm between the righteousness of the eternal law and our own unrighteousness and inadequacy. Some part of us fears what comes after life. The prospect of the infinite and the unknown is daunting. Confronting it doesn't require courage so much as humility.

Powerlessness to forestall death has a cousin in admitting our weakness before worldly powers. Even a modest understanding of tyranny puts our petty worries in perspective and engenders gratitude. My wife and I work to inculcate in our children thankfulness for our many freedoms in America. After Melissa read them *Escape from Camp Fourteen*, a biography about the only person born in the Kaechon internment facility (that is, concentration camp) in North Korea to ever get out, they began to read a great deal more about the present evils of Kim Jong-un's regime. Contemplating the evils of totalitarianism necessarily reorients you. Jay Nordlinger's *Children of Dictators* painted a picture for them about how horrifically some of the world's inhabitants have suffered under despots like Stalin, Hitler, Pol Pot, Mao Zedong, Saddam Hussein, and Bashar al-Assad over the last century. Melissa also has our children regularly praying for victims of religious persecution across the globe. As aids to this end, we subscribe to and keep around the house periodicals like the *Voice of the Martyrs* and publications from organizations such as the International Justice Mission, which advocates for and seeks to rescue trafficked persons.

If we recognize that we're going to die someday, the least we can do is prepare to die *well*. "Why is it that the wisest among us die most calmly," Cicero asks, "while the foolish die in the most distress? Isn't it that the soul of the wise man, with a keener and clearer view, sees that it is setting out for a better world, whereas the foolish soul with its duller vision cannot see where it is going?"

Aeschylus has his chorus in *Agamemnon* announce to us that "he who learns must suffer," and that "against our will, comes wisdom through the awful grace" of enduring pain. Melissa and I have tried to teach our kids that suffering can be virtuous, that nothing worth doing well can be done without a bit of strife. What's true of life is also true of death. The psalmist tells us, "the days of our years are threescore years and ten; and if by reason of strength they be fourscore years, yet their pride is *labour and vanity;* for it is soon cut off, and we fly away" (Psalm 90; emphasis added). In other words, there is no trite happy ending—and thus sucking the marrow out of life requires brutal honesty about the brokenness in which we find ourselves. "Dying isn't dead; it's a stage of living," observes medical ethicist Wesley Smith. "Difficult yes, but so are other times of our lives."

The goal is to develop character that's resilient in the face of adversity yet humble, cool-headed, and tempered by self-control. In 1832, a cholera epidemic broke out across the world. Between June and November, 3,000 Americans would succumb to the disease. The nation's swampy capital was probably harder hit than any city. Nearing the end of his first term as president, Andrew Jackson—65 years old and not in the best of health—was urged by his family to leave Washington and return to the Hermitage, his home just outside Nashville. He finally agreed to leave his work and the city, but only a month after the epidemic had pounded DC. "Knowing that we have to die," he wrote to his family ahead of his journey, "we ought to live to be prepared to die well, and then, let death come when it may, we will meet it without alarm, and be ready to say, 'The Lord's will be done.'" Jackson was not an especially pious man, but here nonetheless expressed a realistic Christian stoicism that we now rarely wrestle through in public.

Why embrace suffering when we have drugs and other means at our disposal to eliminate it? Because suffering will never truly be avoided. If approached the right way, suffering not only can be endured; it can also ennoble. Rod Dreher, a journalist whose career took him to several coastal cities before he and his wife decided to return to their home in small-town Louisiana, wrote movingly about his sister Ruthie's untimely death at the age of 40 from cancer. When she received her terminal diagnosis, Ruthie instructed her three daughters not to be angry with God, but rather to see her affliction as an occasion for grace. Her suffering and death inspired others to acts of charity and compassion—especially Dreher himself.

He began the long process of reconciling with his father, who would end up dying a few years after Ruthie. "Neither one of them were complainers, but in fact both were Stoics," he wrote. His father's decline and eventual death in 2015 led Dreher to meditate on what he called "the mysterious gift of suffering." "For my dad, every day he could not go outside and *do something* was a humiliation," Dreher wrote. "About two weeks before he died, I heard him telling some visitors that he hoped to build his strength back up so he could get out of the house and onto his Mule, a small farm truck, and ride to his back acreage to check on his pine trees." As the father was dying, he told his son "from his hospital bed, that he needed to exercise his arms so he could regain strength in them. I thought: *Are you kidding?* He wasn't."

"He was eighty," Dreher continued, "and indeed the final decade of his life was toil and travail. Yet he endured, as a good Stoic would. What he could not see—maybe because Southern culture is traditionally more Stoic than Christian—is that he was not useless to the rest of us. His utility was in giving us a chance to serve him." This is a profound insight, that the sufferer is serving the servant in the humbling of being served.

Helping our kids flee their generational ghettos is an important part of helping them wrestle with the great teacher that is mortality. Suffering offers us a wake-up call. It imparts patience and humility and puts us in our proper place as servants and stewards of something greater than ourselves.

THE THREE PURPOSES OF SEX

I decided at the outset of writing this book to skip the topic of sex. It wasn't out of reticence about addressing its theory or practice, but I didn't include the subject because it invariably leads to the battlefields of the culture war. We have such a big problem with coming of age.

If we don't first foster a different mentality about what it means to be an adult—if we don't begin talking deliberately about what our teens actually need—we will fail to rebuild our morally shrunken coming-of-age experiences. As such, I have regarded it as imprudent and therefore unhelpful to risk the needed first steps in this conversation by diving straight into any topic that could be considered controversial. I eventually concluded, however, that it is impossible to think deeply about nature, life, and coming of age without at least tipping the hat to the considerable fires and influence of sexuality.

"I think the world would be better off," wrote H. L. Mencken, "if novels and other books could describe the precise process of reproduction, beginning with the hand-shake and ending with lactation, and so show the young what a bore it is." He was being sardonic, but the point is well taken. Our kids are generally not provided with any understanding that sex has *purposes*. To begin a conversation with your children, you should be able to itemize some of those purposes. Melissa and I have tried to teach our kids that, in our scanning across the Western tradition, sex has had three major purposes. They aren't particularly controversial. But it's worth declaring up front that there are three—not two, not eight, not an insane number limited only by our imaginations.

First, from an anthropological or Judeo-Christian standpoint, sex has always been seen as a covenant initiation and a covenant renewal ceremony. Fundamentally, the act of the flesh of two different people becoming one has been to say, in effect, that they are engaged in a unique relationship, one that is different from all others. They are now intimates. They possess knowledge of each other that is different from the knowledge they possess of even other friends, let alone strangers. That's what the loss of virginity on the wedding night traditionally means, and it's also the way sex is used as a way of renewing relationships. The term "make-up sex" is often referenced as a movie joke, but it's actually a critically important kind of reconciliation—a step well beyond smoking a peace pipe together. It bridges the chasm of discord both physically and relationally.

Sex's second purpose is procreation, and its third is pleasure.

Almost everything about sex fits into one of these three categories. Yet in our sex-saturated society, young people don't really think about sex in a purposeful way, in a *meaningful* way. At the risk of gross understatement, sex is a very big deal. We shouldn't pretend to be prudes when we talk with our kids but we should also make sure they know that the idea that sex is only about pleasure is silly, to say nothing of dangerous. Anyone who is the least bit thoughtful and reflective about their sexual history knows that intercourse isn't merely about pleasure. Yet we often callously allow teens to conceive of sex almost exclusively in terms of pleasure, indulged or forbidden, with only some brief pre-flight instructions about the perils of sexually transmitted diseases. It's a terrible disservice we're doing. Studies indicate that those who seek only short-term pleasure through sex tend, over time, to find the most pain. (It probably works in the opposite direction as well, that those in pain might look to sex to fill an impossible void, thus exacerbating disappointment.) Conversely—and contrary to attitudes perpetuated by pop culture—people who take sex's first two purposes seriously also tend to be the people who enjoy the most pleasure in sex.

There is a correlation between sexual monogamy and personal happiness, yes. Causation is impossible to prove—how would you control for adultery? Would you force promiscuous people into monogamous relationships or vice versa? But plenty of studies find a correlation between the security and safety afforded in a monogamous relationship and happiness. Also, we're talking about a particular form of happiness. We reject "follow-your-bliss" hedonism. Mark Regnerus and Jeremy Uecker in *Premarital Sex in America* looked at sexual behavior among young adults and found a significant correlation between monogamy and happiness in general and between promiscuity and depression in particular. (This correlation is much stronger for women than for men.)

These kinds of fruitful insights and debates are unlikely to develop between a 17-year-old and other 17-year-olds. Instead, they need to be confiding in, and questioning, and listening to some folks with much more of life in their rearview mirrors.

EXPERIENCE A BIRTH

Giving birth and navigating death should not be the province of adolescents, the not-yet-adults. And yet preparing to do both well should definitely be on the agenda of adolescents, those who are in the process of becoming adults. To do this planning and preparation well, teens will need wisdom, they will need advisors, they will need deep relationships with people wrestling through older life stages. Birth and death are overwhelming. They overwhelm us with joy and grief. They involve us in something greater than ourselves, greater than we can fully comprehend. For giving life and seeing it extinguished enliven our highest hopes and reveal our deepest fears. Almost incomprehensibly, we get to participate in creating life. But its pace and length still remain entirely beyond our control.

Birth is not a mystery, but it's still surreal. In 1726 an Englishwoman named Mary Toft caused a sensation in her town of Godalming when she convinced local doctors that she had given birth to various animal parts during a miscarriage. A local midwife confirmed Toft's story. A surgeon from a nearby town was skeptical at first but he eventually backed Toft's claims of a *second* miscarriage. He testified that he personally delivered "three legs of a cat of a tabby color . . . one leg of a rabbet [*sic*]: the guts were as a cat's and in them were three pieces of the back-bone of an eel." The surgeon, a fellow by the name of John Howard, spread the news of his discovery far and wide. Before long, word reached the court of King George himself. So the king sent his personal physician, Nathanael St. Andre, and Samuel Molyneux, secretary to the Prince of Wales, to investigate further. Toft explained that she had an intense craving for rabbit, but was unable to catch any. One night, though, she somehow envisioned a rabbit in her lap, and the next day she was giving birth to dead rabbits. Stunningly, in a display fit for reality television, to prove her claims, she gave birth to more rabbit parts with the royal officials present. They couldn't doubt any longer what they had seen with their own eyes.

Toft was brought to London, where she became an instant celebrity. Almost always under supervision now, she suddenly stopped giving birth to rabbits. People became suspicious. Other doctors began to doubt her story and one threatened a thorough examination of her uterus. Toft couldn't keep up the ruse and finally confessed to having surreptitiously inserted rabbit parts in her womb when no one was looking. She simply wanted a bit of fame and maybe a nice pension from the king. She spent a short time in prison for her fraud but was never formally charged with a crime. There was nothing precisely on the books for whatever unspeakable thing she had done while unsupervised. John Howard and Nathanael St. Andre never practiced medicine again.

My daughter Corrie first told me Toft's true story, which she had come across in one of Madeleine L'Engle's fantasy books. Why was my 15-year-old fascinated—almost entranced for a week at one point— by this story? Obviously, partly because it is so odd and hilarious. But also because she had just helped birth a bunch of baby calves (more on that in the next chapter). She was perplexed by why certain parts of sex and conception, gestation and procreation, are discussed clinically while other parts remain shrouded in mystery. Why are some parts of reproduction acknowledged and others not to be admitted in polite company? And why is it different in discussions of humans versus animals? How and why has this varied over time? For us now, birth has been thoroughly demystified. But the L'Engle recounting of the Toft tale shows that things have not always been so.

I'll admit it that early in marriage I was very anxious—embarrassingly so—at the thought of the day when my kids would be delivered. Naturally, Melissa and I talked a lot about having children—and how our definitions of "a full house" might differ. Yet thinking about the joys and blessings of bringing children into the world was offset by the fear of passing out in the delivery room. I got claustrophobic just thinking about getting claustrophobic.

One day, as Melissa was both mocking and threatening me—"Don't you dare pass out when I'm giving birth!"—I asked her, "Wouldn't it be nice if there were a risk-free situation where if I felt queasy, I could just leave at any time? I wish there was some way I could either conquer my fear or just hit the reset button."

We had some graduate school friends, Tom and Teri. They were a few years older than us, pregnant with their second child at a time when Melissa and I were starting to think about getting pregnant. One night with them over pizza, Melissa mentioned that I needed to witness a birth as a trial run so that I didn't pass out at ours. The conversation was mostly in jest at first—but both of them knew my jump-in-with-both-feet persona, and somehow before the pizza was even finished,

Teri—always gregarious—shrieked with delight: "Here's a great idea: You'll come to our next birth! Absolutely! This is a great idea. Birth is a beautiful thing!" She was six months pregnant at the time.

What? "Wow, uh, that would be easy," I thought to myself. And weird. I looked toward my wife. If we were at their blessed event, it would be the risk-free trial we had discussed—and I could just leave if I was getting light-headed. I mean, it wasn't the birth of *my* baby. But . . . were we seriously considering this?

Tom's jaw was on the table. Melissa was laughing hysterically—actually everyone was. Tom's wife had just invited two friends to witness the birth of their next child, and they hadn't had a moment's worth of private deliberation. Later, I took Tom aside and told him if he had any reservations at all, of course we would withdraw. "I know it's weird. I mean, I'm slightly freaked out about it," Tom said. "But I think we're going to think it is okay after some time to consider."

Three months later, the obstetrics nurses were—to put it mildly—surprised to see the four of us arrive in the delivery room arm in arm. But once they got over the awkward giggling, the six of us (the doc was almost never around) had a great evening. It was an amazing experience—and after a couple dozen deep knee bends, I got my sea legs. *I've got this,* I thought. Happily, I did not pass out—either there or at the births of any of our kids. And it's an event we talk about with all of our overlapping friends to this day. (We've never told the boy being delivered, who's now 17.)

I'm not necessarily recommending that you or your kids follow our lead here—although for heaven's sake, if the opportunity presents itself, do go see a birth. Think of it this way: Labor and delivery used to be a communal event, at least among women. It's no accident that a small but growing slice of moms have returned to using traditional midwives to help deliver their babies, either in a clinic or at home. Even though we know seemingly everything there is to know about obstetrics and pediatrics, some doctors treat pregnancy with such intrusive monitoring that it seems they think it's practically a disease. It isn't.

Of course, things can go wrong. It's perfectly understandable that most of us want to deliver our children in a sterile place with trained professionals standing by with life-saving medicine and technology. But complications are statistically rare, and the ability to play defense in case something goes wrong is different from actively treating pregnancy from the outset as a problem to be solved.

Isolating birth from everyday life is neither natural nor healthy. Birth, like death, speaks to our whole person. The encounter with such visceral, bodily functions reveals something undeniable about reality as it is, beyond artifice and contrivance. Birth, like death, forces us to face fundamental human questions. It's a humbling reminder that life is larger than you. As King Solomon counsels in Ecclesiastes, we're all participants in a majestic odyssey of infinite length. "One generation passeth away, and another generation cometh: but the earth abideth forever" (Ecclesiastes 1:4).

Whether or not you know them, there were men and women who made you possible. You stand in a line. You yourself might make possible the lives of countless men and women—and most of these descendants of yours will probably never know your name. But in witnessing birth, you have the honor of being able, if only for a fleeting moment, to touch history and the future.

HOW ADULTS ESCAPE

We were not created for a state of perpetual adolescence—or "arrested development," to borrow the title of a popular sitcom about a perpetually dysfunctional family. We are designed to make sense of the world around us. We are fashioned to redeem our time on earth. As such, we need to make our days matter, make them meaningful. Adults need to pause to reflect. We need to "escape" the tyranny of the urgent and the loud. Thus, soon-to-be-adults need to learn how to manage their use of these escape tools—and they need advisors outside their peer group to help them learn how.

Our brains when most alert are constant prediction machines; they are trying to solve puzzles and to make sense of things. And almost all of the work your brain does is either analysis or synthesis. You are always either cutting something into smaller chunks to understand it (analysis) or putting things together to make sense of how each part fits with the whole (synthesis). By and large, the specialization of our modern work and the plural plenty of our rich material lives drive us to frenzied distraction with seemingly infinite events and ever-accelerating speed. Our whole lives sometimes seem to be either analysis or distraction—but no synthesis. No pause, no peace, no wholeness.

Escapes give us a chance to pause, to reflect.

Consider music. You can listen to music in different ways. Many listen passively, preferring it as background noise, as distraction. Others—professional musicians most obviously—listen actively, as technical specialists.

But the glory of music—the freedom in music—is when it comes together as a whole, as a unity. (That is not to deny the special delights of the trained listener, who can take a piece apart. For music, like reading and writing—or anything else worth doing in life, really—surely rewards close attention. But the purpose of analyzing music is ultimately to synthesize it again, now more meaningfully.) Composer Elliott Schwartz in *Music: Ways of Listening* laments that our listening skills have been "dulled by our built-in twentieth century habit of tuning out"—that is, distracting ourselves rather than focusing ourselves. Schwartz suggests developing a musical "memory" by paying attention to patterns in time. Composers, he explains, provide "musical landmarks" so we can quickly determine the part of a song even if our attention wanders. Ideally, he writes, "it would be fascinating to hear a new piece of music with fresh expectations and truly innocent ears, as though we were Martians. But such objectivity doesn't exist. All listeners approach a new piece with ears that have been 'trained' by prejudices, personal experiences and memories." In other words, we constantly *synthesize* our knowledge, experience, and memories—and incorporate what we hear into the greater tapestry.

Unless you are dead or in the process of withering away in front of your screen the way so many millions of us do, there's an imperative in your soul to unpack life and its endless mysteries. This is an active, not a passive, pursuit. For people who are alive, really alive, their brains are in motion. On the wall in the primary schooling area in our home hangs this apt observation by Ellen Parr: "The cure for boredom is curiosity. There is no cure for curiosity." That's just homeschooling 101. If you're doing it right, you're awakening your kids, and they are alive. Curiosity is the mental mortar for building strength and resilience.

If you're alive, then boredom is impossible. It's practically a sin. Melissa and I do not allow our children to be bored. The phrase "I'm bored" is forbidden from passing through their lips. I personally can't conceive of being bored. Sure, I might experience temporary claustrophobia when I'm captive in an unproductive meeting, but then I remember visiting Robben Island. Robben Island is the South African prison just off Cape Town where Nelson Mandela was held in solitary confinement for eighteen years. Mandela kept his sanity by relying on his memory of William Ernest Henley's famous 1875 poem "Invictus":

> Out of the night that covers me,
> Black as the Pit from pole to pole,
> I thank whatever gods may be
> For my unconquerable soul.
> In the fell clutch of circumstance
> I have not winced nor cried aloud.
> Under the bludgeonings of chance
> My head is bloody, but unbowed.
> Beyond this place of wrath and tears
> Looms but the Horror of the shade,
> And yet the menace of the years
> Finds, and shall find, me unafraid.
> It matters not how strait the gate,
> How charged with punishments the scroll.
> I am the master of my fate:
> I am the captain of my soul.

Contrary to bad movies about classical education, parents who demand memorization are giving their kids a gift that lasts a lifetime.

In dull moments, I also often recall stories my Senate colleague John McCain has told me about his five years as a prisoner of war—tortured and left to languish in the Hanoi Hilton. What's an hour in a windowless conference room compared with day after day, week after week, month after month in solitary confinement? McCain and prisoners in neighboring cells created their own language of tapping, not unlike Morse code, which they perfected over time. They used their new language to tell each other stories and poems and songs from their youth.

("Who cares? What the hell else were we going to do?" the irascible McCain grunted when I asked how long it took to devise their system. "We had infinite time.") Eventually, they managed to secretly dig holes through the walls so they could talk instead of tap. "I'll never forget the tapping to each other, and the leadership and inspiration that I got from those people who were far better and stronger men than I am," McCain said. "We sustained each other."

We all have escapes. Some are healthier than others. Competition is a raw need many of us feel. I find playing sports therapeutic. When I have a bad day, I work out—I even play some of the bad basketball that a washed-up wrestler musters—to gain a different perspective on problems. A new start usually seems possible after the game.

Alcohol is another tool of escape, as is smoking. Many escapes can enslave if they cease to be tools in service of deliberation and reflection, conversation and bonding—and instead become compulsions. Eating well—feasting, rather than merely refueling—is an escape, too.

Sleep is a great escape. Some of the most productive people in history were prodigious nappers. Winston Churchill is legendary for his tireless work ethic. He kept long hours well into the night his whole life, but especially during the Second World War. He drew much of his energy from regular naps. The great statesman once chided an American for his rigid habit of arriving at his desk precisely at eight o'clock every morning and leaving in the evening with only a short break in between. Churchill said it sounded like "the most perfect prescription for a short life he had ever heard." He proselytized for his own habits. "You must sleep some time between lunch and dinner, and no halfway measures. Take off your clothes and *get into bed.* That's what I always do." The idea sounds strange to anyone obsessed with clock-punching productivity, but Churchill wasn't the nine-to-five sort. He was involved in intellectual work that had his mind always churning. "Don't think you will be doing less work because you sleep during the day," he chided. "That's a foolish notion held by people who have no imagination. You will be able to accomplish more" if you nap and then return to working.

The *tyranny of now* steals from us the deeper need we have to take in history and future as well. We need escapes to pause, to reflect, and to synthesize.

Sex is an escape.
Worship is an escape.
Poetry and music are escapes.

———◆———

STORYTELLING IS ONE of the most elemental reflection and synthesizing escapes of all. Why is it fun to repeat old stories? Why is it pleasant to live vicariously or, as Aristotle explains it, to get emotional catharsis at the theater through the shared experience of grief or revenge? Why are people nostalgic? Some storytelling appears hardwired into our brain chemistry. But some of it is habit; some of it is learned behavior to transcend the moment we're in—behavior learned over time, through history.

Jean-Jacques Rousseau unpacks an analogy about a dog lying on a porch in the sun. The dog doesn't have the human capacity for memory and anticipation. This puts him in both a better and a worse position than we are in. For when he is in a good moment—feeling the warmth of the sun shining on him—the present is there and wonderful, without the bad and the disappointing crowding in from the past and the future. The dog feels the sun, and he is satisfied then and there on that porch, with nothing stealing the joy of the moment. Conversely, when he is in present pain, he cannot escape that moment either. He is where he is.

Humans are different. We live not only in the present but also in memory of the past and in anticipation of our future. When the sun is shining on us, the moment is rarely as pleasant and unadulterated a good for us as it is for the dog. For unlike him, the simple is not sufficient for us. Even when the warmth is nice, we still have nagging regrets; we feel loss and remorse; we have memory of many of the bad things past. More urgently, we worry and are uncertain about all the bad that might yet come. And through it all we hear the tick of time, for we know we are mortal. If you have a pessimistic worldview, the costs of the canine's limited historical awareness are less than the benefits: it would be better for you to be the dog. Sure, you wouldn't get to remember all the good things past or anticipate all the possible positives yet to befall you in the future—but your pessimistic view is that there is more bad than good yet to come anyhow.

But regardless of whether you prefer it or not, regardless of whether you are that pessimist, there is something profound for all of us in understanding that we humans have power that dogs do not. Whether we choose it or not, we have historical awareness. And thus we can emotionally flee the bad moments by hope, or by conjuring a happy memory. Our spirit is resilient, and we can overcome great hardship—as Mandela and McCain modeled.

This expansive sense of consciousness, this awareness of time, this remembrance of good and bad from our history, and this anticipation of the pain and pleasure of the future—it isn't automatic. It is also a habit. And one of the markers of a disciplined and an adult life is the learned skill to live in the moment when things are good and to turn to hope or pleasant nostalgia when the present is bumpy.

No adolescent knows how to do this. No young adult is well versed in this habit. And thus no adolescent can learn it from a peer. It requires the transmission of wisdom, which in turn requires knowing and being known by some who are wise and who have experienced more.

STEPPING STONES TO TAKING OFF
THE TRAINING WHEELS

Nudge Their Affections beyond the Moment

When Melissa was pregnant with our first child, we became aggressive students of parenting—observing and questioning everyone we could and reading constantly. We sought expertise on sleep patterns, eating metrics, developmental stages, actual risks, phony risks, how to stimulate the brain, and the probability of raising a college quarterback.

But then three years ago, as our oldest became a teenager, we noticed we both lacked the same intense obsession with learning how to parent through this last still-at-home phase. And this was true of our friends as well: most seem to be winging it with their teen parenting.

So we started compiling a list of principles related specifically to guiding older kids. To our surprise, a hefty portion of our emerging list was comprised of almost exactly the same stuff we tried to get good at with our infants and toddlers.

Here are a few of our rules for nudging teens' affections toward the lasting and the durable:

- Find them going good. It is so much easier (and more effective) to praise good behavior than to correct bad behavior.
- Make them earn the marginal rewards. If you are feeding your baby broccoli and apple sauce, sequence the sweets as a reward for the vegetables. The same principle applies a hundred ways with our teens.
- Learn to talk future-tense about *who they are going to become.* Don't dwell on what's wrong about what they just did. Instead tell and show them what their future right actions and words are going to look like. Tell them that they will succeed—not at being first at everything, but at developing character, because they will in fact succeed if indeed they *will* it and work at it.
- Invite them to ask hard questions of house guests and dinner companions. Although they need to know that there are boundaries between adults and kids, we should also give them authorized windows to ask the hard and messy questions (obviously having pre-cleared this with your guests).
- Sing together.
- Rethink training wheels and life jackets. Instead of always wrapping them in floatation devices, get in the water with them. Let go and re-grab them, let go longer and re-grab them, go again—and then celebrate their survival. They'll be successfully treading water in no time. We've taught lots of kids to drive on ranch roads with the same principles.
- Help them see the value of authority figures beside parents.
- Less helicopter parenting; more stealth-drone parenting. I'm not here to say spy on your kids (but definitely do—with them knowing that you have a right to do so for their good, and that you plan to often). Don't hang over them waiting to solve every problem, but do organize a world where you are likely to have insight into what problems are occurring.
- Memorize poetry together.
- Eat family dinner together as much as possible.
- Envision and talk through alternate futures. Whether they are 3 or 13, observe someone two or five years older with complicated options or problems before them, and role-play it out. Don't tell them the answer; urge them to play forward many steps of a scenario.
- Have digital detox "fasts" as a family (and yes, that means you too—no Netflix after the kids have gone to bed). The absence of easy entertainment leads directly to families that sit and talk and eat and grow together.

- Give them choices. Even if they think they don't like vegetables, giving them a menu of green beans-versus-spinach choices still treats them with dignity and actually helps create more affinity for the vegetable that they—now with acknowledged agency—just chose.
- Mix storytelling with your walking. Whether going around the block with a 4-year-old or climbing a mountain with a 14-year-old, carry a book to read aloud or an audiobook to play on a portable speaker. Shared stories create lasting bonds.
- Model gratitude. Thank people for their work all the time. Go out of your way to do it—go back to stores where you got great service just to say thanks again. They'll absorb and begin to emulate your mature kindness.
- Focus not on one-off mistakes. Focus on habits.

FIVE

EMBRACE
WORK PAIN

A Work Ethic Isn't Inevitable * *"Lots of Hours, Lots of Stress, Bad Citrus"*
The Rise and Fall of Ben Franklin's Nation
"Recreation" Is a More Helpful Word Than "Leisure"
The Detasseling Alarm Hurts at 4:30 a.m.
Lessons from the Ranch * *Make Great Shoes at a Fair Price*

Let us then be up and doing,
With a heart for any fate;
Still achieving, still pursuing,
Learn to labor and to wait.
—Henry Wadsworth Longfellow

MY GRANDMOTHER ELDA KREBS SASSE WAS A GIANT, though she stood barely four feet, eleven inches and probably never tipped the scales at a full 100 pounds. She never raised her voice— except to break into what her six sisters called her infectious "cackle-laughing"—yet her personality always found a way to dominate the room. As a little kid, whenever the many generations of our family assembled on some farm, I remember always wondering how this tiny lady managed to wield such emotional power so effortlessly. Lots of people were feisty, so what made her unique?

Then I began to hear some of the stories of her steely character from her early adulthood—and it became clear why everyone regarded her as unflappable. One of nine kids born to a second-generation immigrant family in windy, rural Diller, Nebraska (population 327), Grandma grew up poor, working the family farm during the Great Depression. But that just made her experience identical to every other family's in Diller. It was at home—and thus work—that she met my grandfather, who was hired as a farm boy by her dad in the 1930s. They were married in May 1941, him at age 22 and her 21. (Incidentally, for those looking for reasons to mock Midwesterners for lacking creativity, it's worth noting that my grandfather was named Elmer; one of Elda's two brothers was Elmer; one of her sisters also married an Elmer; and a third sister married a Delmer. Family reunion pick-up sports were often the three big Elmers and a Delmer versus everyone else.)

Their first leased home had no indoor plumbing or running water. Their plot of land was north of town on Commercial Road, where they planned to start their own corn and bean farm. Just as they were settling down, World War II started up, and Grandpa was on his way to Europe. He would serve for over three years, with stops in Germany and England, as a wartime "mayor" of a regional factory town in the latter. Grandma had just given birth to their first baby, my uncle Roger.

Here's the first thing you need to know about Elda: with Elmer in Europe, she had no choice but to run the farm they had just leased but that she didn't yet know much about. Though she'd grown up on a farm, she'd never driven a tractor. Fall was coming, and no one else was coming to do the work. So she jerry-rigged a way to attach the baby's bassinet to the side of the lumbering old John Deere as she taught herself to harvest.

Here's the second thing you need to know about Elda: She regarded the bassinet-on-the-tractor—this story of a tiny 22-year-old first-time mother learning to harvest that fall and then plant the next spring while simultaneously breastfeeding and relaying war news from her husband's letters to the local community—as 100 percent uninteresting. "It was simply what needed to be done." I know this story not because she ever thought to offer it but because I was always interrogating my grandparents for war stories as a child. I used to ride in the back of their old Chevy Impala on road trips to sporting events, and it became a conquest game to get these pleasant but stoic Germans to tell me tales of their hard-fought youth in the Depression and then the war: tell me about the tornado that destroyed the barns; about having two grandparents, two parents, nine siblings, and sometimes a spouse and someone's new baby in that three-bedroom farm house; about Grandpa's duties during the war; about the men he met on the boat across the Atlantic; about the guy from New Jersey who got shot at the checkpoint; about the time my dad fell out of the car on Highway 15 when he was 8; and so on. Along the way, I learned about Grandma's trial-and-error farming—and about her makeshift bassinet sidecar for the tractor.

Stunning though this ingenuity and seeming danger were, what made an even deeper impression on me as a 10- or 12-year-old in the early 1980s was the fact that the two of them were always genuinely perplexed that I thought their problem-solving perseverance was extraordinary. They did not regard it as extraordinary. Why did I want to hear the story again and again? To them, it was no big deal; there was work that needed to be done, nobody else was going to do it, and that was that. It was just who they were. The "aw-shucks" demeanor echoes the resolve of the "I will work harder" pledges of Boxer in Orwell's *Animal Farm*. There was a matter-of-factness about them that, in fact, wasn't extraordinary for much of their generation. This nose-to-the-grindstone, get-it-done attitude can still be heard today in conversations about work and callings with many aging members of the Greatest Generation I encounter.

A WORK ETHIC ISN'T INEVITABLE

When I was little, mom would leave detailed lists of chores on the kitchen counter each summer morning for my siblings and me to complete before we could play baseball, ride bikes, or go swimming. And when I arrived at college, basically everyone with whom I became friends, a group from a wide range of socioeconomic backgrounds, had also done real work growing up. Not everyone had worked in the field like I had—most had spent summers in retail or taking orders at a fast-food place or sorting the mail or doing some other kind of grunt work at a local office—but it was at least a job with certain expectations and set hours. Because these new friends were from all regions of the country and because they confirmed my own childhood experiences of regular toil, I arrived at young adulthood in the early 1990s assuming that work was a near-universal component of American upbringing and maturation. I didn't presume everyone was as gritty as Elda Sasse, but I knew that my siblings and I hoped we would one day prove as perseverant as she was—and I honestly believed that this was a universal aspiration. Without deliberate reflection, I assumed that basically all young people everywhere had similar placeholder role models in their minds, and thus that the transmission of a work ethic to each next generation was more or less inevitable.

This chapter is about how painfully wrong I was in that assumption. It's also about why failing to transmit an ethic that productivity is essential to human flourishing will leave us at odds with how America and Americans came to be. Finally, this chapter aims to persuade you that there is almost nothing more important we can do for our young than convince them that production is more satisfying than consumption. Indeed, a hallmark of virtuous adulthood is learning to find *freedom in* your work, rather than *freedom from* your work, even when work hurts.

My passive assumption that all kids have some meaningful work experiences as teens was shattered in late 2009 when I arrived as president of Midland University. The university's board of directors had hired me, as a 37-year-old, not because I had any special insight into shaping 18- to 22-year-olds, but because I was a "turnaround" guy who specialized in helping troubled companies become solvent. This liberal arts institution was in big trouble, in terms of both finances and enrollment, the latter at its lowest point in a century. My job was to tackle the college's unsustainable deficits, skyrocketing debt, enrollment shortfalls, and flagging morale among faculty and staff.

None of my initial charter had anything to do with current students and their emotional health. Immediately upon arrival, however, it became apparent that in addition to dealing with other so-called "big picture" concerns of a university in crisis, I would also have to reshape the student affairs leadership and structure. It's an odd experience arriving at a college as president in your thirties. In the first year I was regularly mistaken for a student, and not just by other students. Two visiting professors once asked me if I thought I had made the right choice—to enroll at Midland as a current undergraduate, they thought they were asking me. For many reasons, I didn't have a conception of myself as an old guy, but I soon discovered that my experiences matriculating into college half a life ago, at age 18, were vastly different from those of our students.

When my team and I arrived at Midland, the school had been on the verge of missing payroll four months in a row, which would mean that families would miss mortgage payments. That's a pretty urgent crisis. Yet finances might not have been the biggest problem at the school. More stunning to me was that it was an atypical experience for an incoming freshman to have done really hard work, not even the sorts of elementary farm tasks common to Nebraska kids from the homesteaders of the 1860s until just a few years ago. Teenage life, I soon learned, had been stunningly remade in the two decades since I'd gone off to college. Elda's and Elmer's childhoods were far removed from these kids' experiences and understanding.

Let's be clear that there were many wonderful human beings and delightful students at Midland, but many of the teens I met upon arriving on campus also had an outsized sense of entitlement without any corresponding notion of accountability. For example, a student staged a sit-in in my office one day, announcing that he would not leave until I resolved a scheduling problem for him. He was upset that the registrar wouldn't be offering a particular course he needed the following semester. Obviously, college presidents don't usually solve the Rubik's cube of course scheduling. The student was emphatic that he wasn't leaving, and while I was clear that the course registrar had a job to do and that she did it well, I realized it might be a teachable moment, a chance for the student and me to have a conversation. At one point he proclaimed, "You need to figure this out. I pay tuition to go to this school, which means I pay your salary. So you work for me."

Well, ummm . . . no. That isn't how it works at all. My job did include serving him, but in a defined way. It was not my job, for instance, to wash his car or fetch him pizza on Friday night. I patiently explained that Midland exists for many people and many purposes; the board of directors hired me; and I serve at their pleasure—but that my leadership of the institution as a whole relies on my empowering *a team of people to fulfill their specialized vocations*. (Parenthetically, the registrar was right and the student wrong—the course in question was to be scheduled only every other year.) I then gently pointed out to the student that he was attending the university on scholarship. In truth then, he worked for—or had a debt to—the generous donors who made his scholarship possible. But even if he'd been paying for his education himself, the college is a living institution of partners, with thought-out, intentional divisions of labor. He was approaching the situation and this whole living-learning-working community only as a consumer. He was not thinking or talking or acting like a maturing young man aware of the dignity of the work of the many other people in the equation.

During the five years I was president, we conducted surveys annually about the highs and lows of students' university experience. The survey takeaway that repeatedly woke me in the middle of the night was the aching sense not just that the students lacked a work ethic, but more fundamentally that they lacked an experiential understanding of the difference between production and consumption. Dispiritingly, students overwhelmingly highlighted their desire for *freedom from* responsibilities. The activities they most enjoyed, they reported, were sleeping in, skipping class, and partying. A few mentioned canceled classes as the best part of their four years. I too love a good Midwestern blizzard, but I loved them in college *so that* we could explore the beauty, or ski, or snowmobile—rather than merely be free from class. Almost nowhere did the student surveys reveal that they had the eyes to see *freedom to* categories—to read, to learn, to be coached, to be mentored in an internship.

If you have done any real work, you begin to see a broad range of work differently. And if you've been reflective about your and other people's work, you start to ask questions about where goods and services come from. Who did the work that got these non-Nebraska items to this store in this Nebraska small town? As hard work is baked into your bones, you begin to feel great gratitude for the other workers who built the stuff and plotted the distribution system that got these toasters and sneakers and books to this place. On the other hand, if you've never worked, you are more likely blind to the fundamental distinction between production and consumption. And these students, I learned from interviewing many of them, had mostly not done any hard work prior to arriving in college.

Although it is not universally fair, millennials have acquired a collective reputation as needy, undisciplined, coddled, presumptuous, and lacking much of a filter between their public personas and their inner lives. As one *New York Times* story about millennials in the workplace put it, managers struggle with their young employees' "sense of entitlement, a tendency to overshare on social media, and frankness verging on insubordination."

"Well, what's the alternative? Are you asking us to be fake?" one young woman asked me after a speech in which I'd made a passing comment about the virtues of "deferred gratification." No, of course not. Of course we all struggle with selfishness, and of course there are times to simply have fun, avoid responsibility, and seek escape—or perhaps, as noted in the last chapter, to pause the daily churn to reflect. But growing up involves coming to recognize the distinction between who we still are today and who we seek to become. Our hope is that our young people will begin to own the Augustinian awareness described in chapter 1— that not everything we long or lust for is something we should really want. Healthy people can admit that there are unhealthy yearnings. It is not "fake" to aim to mature. And it is not fake to begin modeling the desired behavior even before it is a full and fair representation of who you are in the moment. I remain selfish and impatient today, but it is surely not fake or wrong to seek to sublimate these traits. I want to grow beyond who I am today, and I aim to begin better modeling that idealized future right now.

"LOTS OF HOURS, LOTS OF STRESS, BAD CITRUS . . . AND I JUMPED AT THE CHANCE"

Our students' coming-of-age crisis is not limited to lacking self-restraint, but more broadly reflects that they do not understand what self-restraint is, why it's necessary for them individually, and why they should be frightened at our lack of it collectively. They don't know and we aren't telling them that working on it—today, tomorrow, and until death—is just part of being a thoughtful, moral adult.

At Midland, we once hired a talented young woman for a critically important position that involved interacting with the public. She had precisely the kind of poise, intelligence, and charisma to represent to donors and incoming students what the college was up to and why they should invest resources in joining our cause. Unfortunately, her obvious talents were undermined by the fact that she frequently left work hours earlier than everyone else with little effort to communicate to her coworkers and superiors when and why, and apparently no concern for or understanding of how her actions affected their work. It eventually resulted in so many missed opportunities and caused such internal dissension that we had to intervene. Her supervisor and I sat her down in my office, reiterated our positive judgments about her potential, but gave her the bad news that we would have to let her go because she was unreliable. She began to cry and pleaded for her job. She said she recognized her failings and promised that if we kept her on, she would improve. Perhaps against my better judgment, we decided to reconsider, concluding that the tough-love truth-telling had gotten through.

Less than a week later, her supervisor watched in amazement as she began to pack up to leave around 2:30 in the afternoon. So she called her out: Didn't we just have a conversation about this? "Well, sure," she replied. "But this is different. My favorite Pilates teacher has her class at 3:00 instead of 6:00 today."

"What?" the boss replied. "I'm confused. How does that sentence align with your pledge last week to work harder and longer, and to communicate better?"

"Well, sure. But no one ever said anything about missing Pilates!"

I recognize that this story seems unbelievable; our jaws dropped too. We were sad to let her go, but our bigger emotion was confusion. How could she possibly think this was tolerable? We knew she had friends—what did they think of such bizarre irresponsibility?

Sometimes stories like these capture the public attention and go viral. In 2016 Talia Jane, a 25-year-old customer-service representative at Yelp's Eat24 delivery service, caused a sensation when she wrote a long letter of complaint to her boss's boss's boss, CEO Jeremy Stoppelman. Ordinarily a complaint from an entry-level employee doesn't reach the chief executive's desk in a large organization, let alone make national news. But Jane posted her letter on Medium (a social media platform), where it quickly attracted tens of thousands of readers. Jane explained that living in San Francisco, where Yelp is headquartered, is difficult on her salary:

> I haven't bought groceries since I started this job. Not because I'm lazy, but because I got this ten-pound bag of rice before I moved here and my meals at home (including the one I'm having as I write this) consist, by and large, of that. Because I can't afford to buy groceries. Bread is a luxury to me, even though you've got a whole fridge full of it on the 8th floor. But we're not allowed to take any of that home because it's for at-work eating. Of which I do a lot.

She claimed that 80 percent of her income went to rent. "Isn't that ironic? Your employee for your food delivery app that you spent $300 million to buy can't afford to buy food. That's gotta be a little ironic, right?"

Stefanie Williams, a 29-year-old screenwriter in Los Angeles, was incensed at Jane's attitude and quickly dismantled her complaints, which Williams attributed mostly to poor decision-making. "She openly accepted the salary promised, chose to live alone in the Bay Area without a roommate, and the hyperbole of her 'poverty' is easily debunked by a quick glance through her Instagram account," Williams explained. Some initial scanning of her sites revealed her showing off a bottle of bourbon, baking cupcakes, and preparing some pretty nice meals. (Rice was nowhere to be seen.) "The great deal of distress she faced was brought on entirely by her own misplanning" and her exaggerated sense of what she deserves, Williams coached. "Try being 35 with a family and getting fired in a recession. That's distress."

Williams contrasted Jane's tale of woe with her own efforts to get ahead in life. Although she dreamt of becoming a writer for television, she recognized that no one was going to pay someone so inexperienced for such a coveted job. So she started work as a waitress. It wasn't her dream, but it was an important means to an end. She didn't think she deserved either pity or charity.

> Long hours, lots of stress, I smelled like bad citrus and stale beer most of the time, I had to miss Christmas Eve, Christmas Day and New Year's Eve with my family and friends, but I jumped at the opportunity. And all

of a sudden, after about a year, I was making enough money to live. And after several years, I was making enough money to live well.

All of this was afforded to me not in the first month I was working at a restaurant, but after I put in the hours, made the sacrifices and sucked up my pride in order to make ends meet and figure out what I wanted to do and how to do it. I was gracious and thankful and worked as hard as I could even if it was a job that sometimes made me question my worth. And I was successful because of that.

Reading Stefanie Williams's words, you hear in your head parents across the nation breathing a sigh of relief and whispering: "Praise her parents. We need more of that." (Some parents may also nod their heads in hearing that Talia Jane was quickly fired from her job.)

THE RISE AND FALL OF BEN FRANKLIN'S NATION

Our Founders would recognize Ms. Williams, and they would panic about the survivability of a nation if we have too many Ms. Janes. Americans long regarded work differently than the rest of the world, but that difference is slipping away. Our national forebears had an almost compulsive preference for productivity over passivity.

"There is probably no people on earth with whom business constitutes pleasure, and industry amusement, in an equal degree with the inhabitants of the United States of America," observed the Englishman Francis Grund in the mid-1830s. "Active occupation is not only the principal source of their happiness, and the foundation of their national greatness, but they are absolutely wretched without it." Historically, Americans have *needed* to be working, to be producing. We need to recover lots of that if we are going to navigate the bumpy—interesting but highly disruptive—economic times that are coming next.

Benjamin Franklin was the most vociferous American booster of hard work and industry. *Poor Richard's Almanac,* the book that made Franklin rich and famous, is a compendium of sound advice and moral suasion. Its aphorisms can feel obvious, and yet most of our generation coming of age have not turned them over and over in their heads or in conversation with adults helping guide them: "Industry need not wish," Poor Richard says, and "he that lives upon hope will die fasting." Elsewhere, "he that hath a trade hath an estate," and "he that hath a calling hath an office of profit and honor."

Franklin's "Poor Richard" represents a secular form of the old Puritan work ethic, which might be summarized with the adage "Idle hands are the Devil's workshop." At the heart of the Puritan attitude toward work was the Apostle Paul's warning against wasting time; we should be "redeeming the time" instead. Puritanism was an *active* and *intentional* faith, one that emphasized guilt, grace, and gratitude. Guilt is the reality that all people have broken God's perfect moral law; grace is the Christian view that Jesus does the saving. But the Puritans were unique in putting intentional rigor into thinking about the gratitude. They were emphatic that human works do not save us, but rather that our works come in response to the grace already shown to us. To them, "redeeming the time" meant ordering your daily life according to godly principles—not to earn salvation, but with the compulsion of gratitude for having already been saved.

We were created to be worshipping and working. Puritans held, in the words of the Reverend Thomas Manton, that "every creature is God's servant, and hath his work to do wherein to glorify God; some in one calling, some in another." "Christianity is not a sedentary profession or employment, nor doth it consist in mere negatives," wrote the Puritan minister Richard Baxter. "Not doing good is not the least evil," he warned—explaining that "sitting still" while there was work that should be done was as risky for the soul as directly running away from your duties.

The Puritan work ethic—and its cousins "Yankee ingenuity" and later "rugged individualism"—helped form a shared identity for the Americans from the late seventeenth to the late nineteenth century as we evolved from thirteen distinct colonies into one common nation that was traversing the continent and finally transcending our slave-holding past. Hard work became a shared experience. It was an almost liturgical touchstone that all Americans, across geography, race, gender, and denomination, came to esteem together. What Wheaton English professor Leland Ryken explicated as "the Puritan doctrine [that] vocation sanctifies common work" became a common creed. *Americans believe in work.* There is not dignified versus undignified work, nor important versus unimportant work; there is only useful versus useless work. And if your work benefits a neighbor, it is useful and therefore dignified, and it can be used as an occasion to glorify. Or, as Baxter preached it to his congregants in one of his famous sermons, "God looketh not . . . principally at the external part of the work, but much more to the heart of him that doth it." The heart of the grateful adult yearns to be productive, to be useful to his or her neighbor.

Benjamin Franklin secularized the Puritan work ethic but kept the obsession with investing all time well. He retained the hardheaded practicality about doing useful tasks, from early until late, that benefit actual neighbors rather than worrying about the opinions or fashions of European elites, but he dispensed with the Puritans' rigorous focus on remembering God while you work. Instead, Franklin was the world's first financial self-help guru, sharing advice and tips on how to pursue and build wealth. He saw great opportunity in marrying worldly, profit-seeking ambition with the Puritans' practical focus on persevering and problem-solving. "Remember, that *time is money,*" Franklin wrote in 1748. "He that can earn ten shillings a day by his labor, and goes abroad, or sits idle, one half of that day, though he spends but sixpence during his diversion or idleness, ought not to reckon *that* the only expense; he has really spent, or rather thrown away, five shillings besides." Max Weber, the German sociologist best known for his *Protestant Work Ethic and the Spirit of Capitalism,* described Franklin's counsel as a "philosophy of avarice," founded upon "a duty of the individual toward the increase of his capital, which is assumed as an end in itself." "Truly," Weber wrote, "what is here preached is not simply a means of making one's way in the world, but a peculiar ethic." The American obsession with efficiency and effectiveness, Weber observed, binds this whole nation together in a desire to be productive, regardless of whether one is ultimately motivated by the secular desire to store up profit, or by a sacred duty to live all of life as a thank offering to God.

Both religious and secular early Americans united around a suspicion of leisure. The Puritans and Franklin agreed with the popular Richard Baxter when he sermonized that "idleness is robbing God" and idleness is robbing ourselves. American children learned the proverb that if you "see a man diligent in his business, [know that] he shall stand before kings" (Proverbs 22:29).

Our ancestors' suspicion of leisure endured until the dawn of the twentieth century, when the Industrial Revolution delivered vast wealth and efficiencies along with a growing middle class that didn't need to work as hard to subsist. But even then, as leisure became more socially acceptable, most Americans seemed to be born with a compulsion in their chests to invest their hours in productive activities. David Riesman explains why he thinks America retained an older work ethic even when surviving no longer required it: In Europe, and in England particularly, there was a large wedge between the gentry class and workers, where the rich were pushing the poor and middle classes to work harder, but the poor and middle classes often simply ignored the pushing. In the United States, by contrast, a large portion of the population felt an inner, religious compulsion to work; they regarded their work as virtuous, rather than merely a means to an end; and they thought of themselves as independent and middle class—not as poor folk looking for direction from elite gentry. The important American cultural cleavage was thus not rich versus poor, but rather dignified working poor versus supposedly lazy, undeserving poor. Americans continued to think of themselves as ambitious for the future, and responsible for the republic, rather than mere cogs in someone else's national experiment. Still, the machines and the wealth of industrialization accidentally posed a large problem—the threat that "the leisure which was once a fringe benefit now threatens to push work itself closer to the fringes of consciousness and significance." There was, many writers feared, a coming "anti-Puritan revolution." These early– and mid–twentieth century worriers were essentially predicting the aftermath of the 1960s.

The change wasn't just that material surplus can breed materialism and sloth—although it can and does (as will be considered in the next chapter). It is also that material abundance and economies of scale, despite all their benefits, also often make our work less meaningful and more disconnected and robotic. Industrial life is fundamentally different from the neighborly work of the village. While Karl Marx misunderstood how destructive government economists could become in trying to engineer happy lives for people, he was surely right to worry about the "alienation of labor"—the idea that people lose out on something vital when they are producing not cherished handcrafts for their neighbors but mere commodities for distant, anonymous consumers. It is possible that our postindustrial "knowledge economy" will restore more thinking and satisfaction to many jobs, but this is not yet a widespread experience for people whose work lives became more cog-like after the rise of factory jobs, and after industrialization forced the greater specialization of tasks—and the increasing separation of *thinking* and *doing*.

Matthew Crawford wrote movingly about this in his tremendous 2009 book *Shop Class as Soulcraft*, arguing that a cultural shift away from teaching "the trades"—the sort of skilled labor people go to vocational school or community college to learn—has made people more passive and dependent, less aware of the satisfaction of completing any manual task well. "What ordinary people once made, they now buy; and what they once fixed for themselves, they replace entirely or hire an expert to repair, whose expert fix often involves replacing an entire system because some minute component has failed." Our global systems of production have radically reduced the prices of almost everything, but they have also come at the cost of promoting a new mentality that everything is disposable.

"RECREATION" IS A MORE HELPFUL WORD THAN "LEISURE"

As people sense that the products of their work and the process of working are being devalued, they often understandably drift toward a sensibility of merely "working for the weekend." While this angst and these escape-seeking feelings are somewhat understandable, it is something altogether different to resign oneself to no longer trying to fix the situation. It is altogether different to conclude that you will never find meaning in work again. It is dangerous to begin believing that the loving act is to insulate our offspring from work rather than planning for the bumpy and unglamorous tasks of teaching them how to work hard.

Previous generations of Americans would regard our decision to raise the next generation largely free from toil as a destructive revolution. "Work," Albert Einstein wrote his son Hans, "is the only thing that gives substance to life." F. Scott Fitzgerald wrote his daughter,

Scottie: "Nothing any good isn't hard." Therefore, he explained, it was intentional that "you have never been brought up soft." Thomas Edison wanted to make sure the adolescents around him firmly understand that he "never did anything worth doing by accident, nor did any of my inventions come by accident . . . They came by work." Teddy Roosevelt exhorted railroad workers in Chattanooga: "Your work is hard. Do you suppose I mention that because I pity you? No; not a bit." For in work there is meaning. "I don't pity any man who does hard work worth doing. I admire him," for he is becoming something. Reserving his pity and contempt for the lazy, Roosevelt believed that the worker who put his play over his work could simply not be a good American.

Matthew Crawford shares Roosevelt's worry: "If the modern personality is being reorganized on a predicate of passive consumption," Crawford writes, "this is bound to affect our political culture." It's also bound to erode Americans' desire and ability to work hard, to atrophy our drive toward larger, common projects. Thinkers from Aristotle to Thomas Jefferson have wrestled deeply with the "republican virtues" that need to flow from our work. They have worried about jobs that lead us to become "too narrow in [our] concerns to be moved by the public good." They debated not just which employments would produce material wealth but also which would "in the end contribute most to real wealth, good morals and happiness." Our history has often romanticized farming because of its generalist nature, its necessity, and its demands on our character—consistent action and individual responsibility—for the livestock will ultimately die if they are not shepherded and fed, morning after morning after morning. Crawford notes that "the full flowering of mass communication and mass conformity [and mass work] pose a different set of problems for the republican character: enervation of judgment and erosion of the independent spirit."

The work-ethic tradition found its headwaters in Genesis, which itself begins with the creation of Adam to watch over and till the Garden of Eden. His work is not mindless but mindful, with his first task being taxonomy—categorizing and naming the animals. When Adam and Eve were expelled from Eden, they learned that their work would now be under the curse. The great core callings of farming and procreation would now, tragically, creak and ache. The field would be filled with weeds and thorns; the beauty of a baby's birth would now be painful and scary. We would now sadly "work by the sweat of our brows." Despite the horrors of the curse, however, work never becomes the core problem, but rather the thorns that plague the work do. Work itself remains a blessing—we work to survive, to eat, to have shelter, to protect our loved ones, to create. Even the curse does not undo Scripture's declaration that "in all labor there is profit." Solomon proclaimed, "To rejoice in his labor: this is the gift of God."

Work is poetry. Even humble work, Thomas Aquinas insisted, must be understood as more than just a means to bodily survival; it is noble and therefore a necessity for the soul: "To live well is to work well, to show a good activity," he wrote in his *Summa Theologica*. A job done well makes the world a better place. Thomas Carlyle, the Scottish philosopher, historian, and essayist, was one of the loudest and proudest evangelists for the work ethic that dominated nineteenth-century America: "Whatsoever of morality and intelligence; what of patience, perseverance, faithfulness, of method, insight, ingenuity, energy; in a word, whatsoever of Strength the man had in him will lie written in the Work he does . . . Produce! Produce! Were it but the pitifullest infinitesimal fraction of a Product, produce it, in God's name!" Now echoed by *Dirty Jobs* creator and host Mike Rowe, Carlyle preached that no job was too dirty if approached with the right attitude and proper spirit.

The work-ethic tradition looked back not just to Christian sermons but to Greek philosophy. Aristotle in his *Metaphysics* invented a word to define *who we are: energaea.* It means action. It also means "actuality." We cannot reach our full potential as human beings without taking action. The ancients that Americans have most cited knew that "[w]ork is not a disgrace at all"; rather, it is "not working [that] is a disgrace," wrote the Greek poet Hesiod. "And if you work, the man who does not work will quickly envy you when you are rich; excellence and fame attend upon riches. Whatever sort you are by fortune, working is better . . ." We are made to build, to create, to serve, to act, to do, to live.

None of this focus on work in the American tradition rejects the seriousness of needing balance in life. Rather, it reflects an awareness that balance ultimately comes from understanding the moral priority of neighbor-benefiting productive activities in the rhythm of a day and a week. Let's hope that, over time, we'll develop a bias, when we have an extra free hour, toward shoveling snow from the elderly neighbor lady's sidewalk over streaming another Netflix sitcom. Contrary to the dour stereotypes created by Mencken and other revisionists a century ago (Puritanism is "the haunting fear that someone, somewhere, might be happy"), Puritans were zealous about recreation as well—but they intentionally distinguished between "recreation" and "leisure." The latter tries to become the center of life; whereas the former is an exercise or escape used to restore people—to refresh and "re-create" them—*so that they can get back to being productive* for the glory of God and the good of their neighbor.

This long-held American ideal that work is a necessary component of becoming a fully formed adult, that a life well lived entails a forward-leaning embrace of responsibility, is part of what Elda and Elmer had so internalized that it flowed forth in their down-to-earth grandparenting, even though they didn't have the words to articulate it like a Teddy Roosevelt or a Frederick Douglass. They were reflecting the understanding of older Americans that, while recreation and play had their place, neither was possible without someone's work, and neither could make life complete, either physically or spiritually. But their storytelling—their passing on the simple ethic of work—was hugely important moral teaching. As odd as it might sound now, I remember my sister and me walking along the shore of a lake talking about whether we could have taught ourselves to farm, whether it was possible that we would grow up to be as tough as a ninety-nine-pound grandma. As I listened to my grandparents from the backseat of that Impala as a 10-year-old, I had already begun to internalize their ethic. I wanted—no, I *needed*—to become habituated to hard work.

THE DETASSELING ALARM
HURTS AT 4:30 A.M.

In the summer of 2016, the hashtag #firstsevenjobs began trending on Twitter. People from all walks of life started listing and celebrating their first seven jobs: "Assembly line worker; dishwasher; truck driver; editor; think tank fellow; author; professor." Another: "Burger King cashier; waitress at Poppin' Fresh Pies; filing clerk; cold caller for a stock broker; banker; director of credit; CFO." Not bad for an immigrant, she added. A professor notched a path from: "Burger flipper; bank teller; junkyard employee; stationery store clerk; LSAT instructor; attorney; adjunct."

Another: "Babysitter; messenger; mailroom flunky; receptionist; street ice cream vendor; manuscript reader; researcher." A beloved educator: "Milkman (for reals); green grocer; record store clerk; covers band; Santa Claus (seriously); video store clerk; pre-school teacher."

My wife thought I was perhaps a bit too excited about this trend, but I am a "first jobs" nerd. I ask friends and strangers, candidates interviewing for jobs and random Nebraskans at sporting events: What was your first job? What was the first hard thing you completed? What is the single hardest thing you've ever done?

Why do I ask these things? Two reasons: First, I've never met an interesting American who lacks an interesting and at least partially reflective answer to the question of how and when and where they learned a work ethic. Second, happily, many people quickly reveal their understanding that work is not narrowly about a job—about assignments that come with paychecks—but more fundamentally that we are built to be *creators*. Our work and our lives are an answer, an active response, to *a calling*. The great term for a job or for work broadly defined is "vocation." Vocation is a broadening of our conception of work beyond just tasks for which we are paid to include also obligations like parenting or comforting the sick or offering a hand to an unstable senior citizen crossing the street. The word comes from the Latin *vox,* meaning "voice"—as in something God "calls" you to do. Something is revealed about a person's character when they explain their understanding and ethic of work.

My first seven jobs were:

Ben Sasse ✔
@BenSasse   ⦿+ Follow   ∨

Bean walker
Lemonade sales
Stadium pop sales
Corn detasseler
Bike buyer-seller
Roguing (corn, AGAIN)
Lifeguard/swim lessons
#FirstSevenJobs

For those of us growing up in the breadbasket of the world, working in the field was just a natural part of growing up. Improvements in farming technologies have created a world with more bounty and a progressively reduced demand for farmers, but people from agricultural communities across the globe still tend to have had similar childhood upbringings where there was always work to be done and usually not enough adult hands to complete it all. I was 7 years old when my folks first sent me out into the fields to walk beans. "Walking beans" means weeding a soybean field, both of actual weeds and of volunteer corn that is sprouting. Back in the 1970s and 1980s, this was still done by hand, by hoe. (Today it is done almost entirely by spraying targeted chemicals.) It was hard but highly satisfying work, because you could see from the highway the marked progress of each day in the stark difference between a field still filled with weeds and one that has been walked and cleared (soybeans are short; weeds and unwanted corn are tall). Your parents could visually observe—and smile with great satisfaction at— the significant work that a 7-year-old had completed.

I graduated from walking beans to detasseling corn. Detasseling was a rite of passage for almost every Nebraskan when I was kid. Every summer for generations, near-teens and early teens have assembled at parks and playgrounds early each morning to be bused to the cornfields. Corn has both female parts (where the ear grows) and male parts (the pollen-producing tassel at the top). Detasseling involves removing the tassel of key rows to prevent self-pollination or pollination by the same breed in order to guarantee crossbreeding with another corn species from the neighboring "male"-designated rows, which are not detasseled. Such crossbreeding is essential for producing top-notch seed corn. (Seed corn is for planting next year and is too expensive to use for food or animal feed.) Although most large agricultural operations now use machines to detassel their corn, you still need kids to walk the field to look for any tassels the machines missed.

Even in the summer it is wet and chilly in the field at 5:00 a.m. because the irrigation systems have pumped and sprinkled cold groundwater overnight. Frequently center pivots (think: giant sprinklers) will have gotten stuck and flooded parts of the field with very cold water to a depth above your ankles in the uneven ground—making slipping and falling and getting soaked a common occurrence. We would thus begin the morning wearing sweatshirts underneath ponchos made from Hefty bags. By 10:00 a.m., though, as temperatures were arcing toward their hundred-degree destination, we would be hot and sometimes literally beginning to mold because of the damp sweatshirts now heating up under the plastic bags. Most boys would thus end up shirtless. One problem, though: The corn leaves that brush against you as you walk through the rows are sharp and give what amount to paper cuts about every five seconds for the entire day. They'd cut your chest and your neck and your cheeks, and we'd get home at the end of the day with big, nasty corn rashes. (One of my teenage daughters, who detasseled last summer, playfully designed a t-shirt for her friends that read: "These aren't zits. This is corn rash.")

Despite the suffering—the "hardest work I've ever done," almost all teenage detasselers will tell you—the money was great for a 13-year-old: minimum wage plus a retroactive bonus of 15 cents an hour if you never missed a day. In the early afternoon, we'd head home exhausted. We would be so caked in mud that mom insisted we strip down and hose off outside before entering the house for a second shower. I remember days when I'd come inside in the afternoon, fall asleep, and sleep straight through until the next morning when the alarm went off at 4:30 again.

The red numbers on the alarm clock still burn in my mind's eye as a horror—and yet even then it created a sense that hard-working people often begin their workdays in the wee hours. My grandfather had a saying when I was a boy that "every hour of sleep before midnight is worth two hours of sleep after midnight." It was of course absurd, and yet what he meant is that you should get up and out to work early enough that you're tired enough to prize being able to get to bed early again. Work first, play later; and limit your play as much as necessary to get back to bed to be able to work first thing again tomorrow. Super Bowl–winning coach Jon Gruden, a workaholic formerly known to friends by his regular wake-up time ("Jon 3:17"), once concluded after a painful loss that he needed more daily work time and thus permanently adjusted his alarm clock—and his nickname—to "3:11."

In my mid-twenties, I concluded that my grandfather was right: Early-morning hours, painful though they might be, that were set aside for work would ultimately prove more satisfying than late-night hours that could be squandered. I thus decided to permanently alter my wake-up time in life from about 7:30 a.m. to 4:00 or 4:30, a practice I continue to this day. It isn't accidental that this daily time mimics the red alarm clock numbers from the detasseling bell as I learned a preteen work ethic.

LESSONS FROM THE RANCH

Worried about the erosion of a shared sense in our culture of what hard work looks like, in March 2016 we sent our daughter Corrie to spend a month working on a cattle ranch in Holt County, about four hours northwest of where we live. She was 14 at the time and surprisingly eager to get her hands dirty. Thankfully, all of our kids are curious about how things work, and alongside that forward-leaning curiosity we're gratified to see budding in them a respect for work that matters and for the hands and souls that do it.

Still, we worry. Although our kids are obviously blessed to grow up in a free country where they don't have to worry about where their next meal will come from, we have the opposite problem of an entitlement bred by this surplus. "If you live today," Flannery O'Connor sagely observed, "you breathe in nihilism." It is the sea in which we swim. And she was writing half a century ago—today, we practically choke on the pathologies of our culture. Therefore, at our house we have come to conclude that building and strengthening character will require extreme measures and the intentional pursuit of gritty work experiences. To borrow another delightful O'Connorism, we believe that when the culture unhelpfully pushes hard against us, we are going to need to push back just as hard.

We believe that requires a healthy dose of inoculation against the bad effects of peer culture. Rousseau counsels in *Emile* to guard carefully a child's desires and sensibilities. But let's be honest: it's a nearly impossible task. Short of going off the grid entirely and retreating to a cabin in the wilderness, there is no way to protect your kids completely from the rot of celebrity-driven popular culture, secularism, consumerism, hypersexuality—you name it. So much of modern American life seems to be about finding more efficient ways of shirking responsibilities. Think of the young woman at Midland and her Pilates class. American teens hear plenty about their rights but correspondingly little about their duties. And when we as parents push duties that feel more onerous and burdensome than those faced by their friends, it can at first feel unfair or capricious.

We hear Teddy Roosevelt's admonition ringing in our ears—and we want them to hear it ringing in theirs: "Nothing in this world is worth having or worth doing unless it means effort, pain, difficulty." Inculcating the Rough Rider's sense of duty in others has been an overarching focus in the way we raise our kids. And so we have a shared understanding with our children that Melissa and I—as a core part of our calling as parents—aim not to coddle them but to see them toughened up.

We think it's important for our kids to *learn how to suffer*. Some might hear that phrase as unloving but it is actually the opposite. Because very simply, neither our children nor your children will grow up to be free, independent, self-respecting adults if we hand them everything without the expectation of something in return. It isn't the way the world works, and it is thus irresponsibly unkind. And so we need to be investing more of our time and energy in finding ways to help them learn the meaning of duty by going through little episodes of suffering—and emerging with more molded bits of scar tissue, also known as character.

The thought of sending Corrie to a ranch first came up in 2015. We got the idea after chatting with a member of our church who is a top cattle nutrition consultant to ranchers across our state. Nebraska is America's largest cattle state (by weight), and beef is a fascinating business. Getting a cow to gain an extra four hundred pounds in four months at the end of life is an engineering feat. If a cow doesn't gain the weight, the economics behind your delicious steak don't work. When that happens, ranchers call in experts. Our friend calls himself a "poopotologist," because he can determine whether an adolescent cow is getting the optimum amount of feed by scrutinizing bovine excrement. He explained to us in great detail how calves are weaned from their mothers and put out to graze. That's also called the fattening period. An adult cow weighs about 900 pounds when it's sent to a feedlot to be fattened up further. Ideally, you want a cow to weigh over 1,300 pounds when it gets to the slaughterhouse.

We thought it would be a special formative experience for Corrie to spend time working on a ranch. The rancher would get some free labor and our daughter would build some character by an unrelenting encounter with daily necessity. Our poopotologist helped us find a rancher who was willing to take on a teenage girl for a month. For obvious reasons we didn't want her to go to some remote cattle operation with a bunch of 20- and 21-year-old men working as hired hands. We were hoping for a family environment. We found just the place: a family-owned-and-operated ranch, where an earthy old rancher and his wife and three grown children and a new grandbaby lived and worked.

So on a March day still a long way from spring, we dropped her off at the ranch. She was nervous, but also eager. We left her with little advice other than to make us proud by working hard, to ask for coaching, and to never let her overseers hear her complain. March in Nebraska is calving season. That's when heifers give birth. It's one of the busiest times of a rancher's year—and a perfect time for a young girl to learn the ropes and add some genuine value.

Once she settled in, she would send me regular text messages about what she had done that day. Because many of her texts were funny, I began to tweet some of them out (my Twitter account is @bensasse) with #FromTheRanch. One of the obvious but recurring lessons was that calving is dirty, smelly, and wet work.

> got an orphaned heifer to take her whole bottle. (Also got tons of nose slime & snot on my jeans.)

> learned that artificial insemination works 60% of the time here. Then the 'clean-up bull' gets called to duty.

> today we checked to confirm some cows were pregnant— which Megan did by jamming her hand up their rectum. Eww.

Megan is the rancher's daughter. And it wasn't as if she stuck her bare hand up the heifer's rear end; she wore a long disposable glove. I mean they were really long: shoulder-length. And Corrie was told she would need one too. Megan showed her how to do it, then told her to do likewise. It was all of a sudden perfectly matter-of-fact. That was the work that needed to be done that day.

Poop turned out to be more prominent in the daily calendar, day after day after day, than Corrie had expected. But she soon realized that this was inevitable given a twenty-four-hour work clock that had feeding events as the most central schedule priority, ahead of even sleep. Hearing her readouts on her days, I was immediately reminded of how surprised Melissa and I were as first-time parents at how relentless breastfeeding can feel. My wife and I used to joke that each time it was time to nurse again, we could hear in our heads the train from Johnny Cash's "Folsom Prison Blues." We could hear that train relentlessly "a comin'"—it never stopped "rolling round the bend." Melissa was exhausted, yet she sang:

I'm stuck in Folsom prison, and time keeps draggin' on
But that train keeps a rollin' on down to San Antone.

It was a gift for her to feel that train-like relentlessness of work demands when she was only 14. And she would be able to come home to some "TLC" from her mom in just a few weeks.

> Am not going to call now. I need to get some sleep before checking cows—and feed the fats . . . By the way, Dad, the 'fats' are cows soon to be slaughtered.

> Set a new Personal-Record for dogs on the back of my four-wheeler: FOUR!

> It's been 2weeks since I learned the manual tractor & today I drove 1979 stick F-150. Can't wait to show u when u visit.

Learning to drive a manual transmission vehicle is a lost art nowadays. I learned to drive a "stick" when I was thirteen. My wife and I debated whether to buy an old junker just so Corrie could learn, too. Turns out, we didn't have to. That stoic rancher let her get behind the wheel and figure out for herself how to work the clutch and give it the gas. I was thrilled. Experience can be such a great teacher—and there wasn't too much to run into on the ranch.

> I've gone 4 days w/out a single 'electrifying experience' with a fence. I might not have electrocution in my future . . .

> Had a stillbirth last night. Sad—but I can hand off my bottle-heifer. We paired the newly babyless mama with my orphan.

> We had to use a feeding tube, but got baby warm/dry (& fed!). Mama getting the hang of it now

> We're also castrating bulls today. 50 so far. Ended up being 99 nuts. . . . Really weird [in 14y/o girl voice].

> My day: Learned to coil barbwire; backed trailer w/ 4wheeler; & dropped 2 cows for slaughter.

> To the cows we left for slaughter in Wausa I said: 'We are done feeding you. Now it's your turn to feed us.'

As the month wore on, my impromptu #FromTheRanch tweets attracted more attention. Hundreds of people began retweeting them. Before long, reporters took notice. My office began to get calls. The *Wall Street Journal* wrote a feature about Corrie's coming-of-age work experiences.

That story appeared in the midst of a heated presidential primary season. I had said a number of things critical of the honesty and trustworthiness of both major party presidential frontrunners that made headlines around the country. These comments were pretty controversial in my home state. Yet when word got out about Corrie's time on the ranch, politics became irrelevant. As I traveled Nebraska over the next couple months, just about everyone I met wanted to talk about my daughter's experiences on the ranch.

Parents wanted to know how they could make their kids suffer, too. I found this unexpected but repeated questioning strangely comforting. Lines would form and parent after parent wanted advice: How could their kid get a similar wake-up-call experience? In a culture with many problems, it felt like transmitting the work ethic was darn near the top of most parents' and grandparents' lists of concerns.

The lines and huddles of these anxious parents—repeated at scores of public events the last year—convinced me that there is a deep desire for a broader conversation about the cultural challenges of passing a meaningful work ethic on to the rising generation. Parents nobly yearn for their girls and boys to develop a strong, exploratory, "go-get-'em" spirit of adventure. They want them to become curious and service-minded. They want them to not be afraid of hard work.

MAKE GREAT SHOES
AT A FAIR PRICE

Many of our young people remain overachievers, of course—nothing here is meant to suggest that there are no hard workers among the rising generation. But even when we find hard work, I am not hearing a root sense of the shared purposes that drive the work, which need to be discussed together to advance a common culture. In his 2014 book *Excellent Sheep,* retiring Yale professor William Deresiewicz describes students at America's elite schools as "smart and talented and driven, yes, but also anxious, timid, and lost." He suggests that although many adolescents can fill page after page of a resume, they have "little intellectual curiosity and a stunted sense of purpose: trapped in a bubble of privilege, heading meekly in the same direction, great at what they're doing but with no idea why they're doing it." Bear in mind, Deresiewicz is talking about the supposed "cream of the crop," the undergraduates at Harvard and Yale, Stanford and Dartmouth—the likely leaders of tomorrow.

New York Times columnist David Brooks tells a similar tale of achiever culture in which many high schoolers and college students seek a never-ending series of experiences and "talents," but mostly for their college and job-application value. That's not enough. In our effort to develop our kids' talents, to provide them with a set of extracurricular experiences even more impressive than our own to help them stand out from the rest of the college-bound crowd, many of us might be unintentionally displacing lifelong "eulogy virtues" in favor of mere "resume virtues."

Reading Deresiewicz and Brooks on the regular shallowness of resume strengths, I couldn't help but think of the different kind of character visible in many kids who know the "gift of suffering" through having been compelled by necessity to work a good amount. One of the grittiest young women we had the privilege of hiring when I was at Midland keeps leaping back into my mind. Having grown up very poor and helping her dad in his mechanic shop, Haley's resume would not have turned heads in any elite college admissions office. Yet her gumption and perseverance suggested the kind of healthy core that will succeed in almost any environment. The pickup truck she drove—just shy of 450,000 miles on the odometer and literally held together with chicken wire and duct tape—was the kind of eyesore that would reveal the superficiality of many of us. But instead of being embarrassed by it, she named the old Ford "Jerry" and would invite friends to come out to the farm to watch her change its oil. Although she worked two jobs to help pay for school throughout her undergraduate years, we lobbied her regularly to adjust her schedule to find time to babysit our kids, even when we didn't really need any help, simply because we wanted our young children to be around more emerging adults like Haley. (Our one condition was that she couldn't shuttle our kids in rust-bucket Jerry. Fortunately, she's just the kind of woman to whom we were thrilled to loan our vehicles.)

Most of us will spend one-third of our lives and nearly half of our waking hours at work. This surely demands that we help our kids understand the *whys* of work and the meaning behind it. Yet, unwittingly, so much of our culture works against this intentional embrace of work. Soon after the *Wall Street Journal* piece on my re-tweets about Corrie's time at the ranch appeared, multiple lawyers contacted me to let me know that we had probably violated labor laws by allowing our 14-year-old to work on that cattle ranch. Please do not misunderstand: I'm not trying to pick a policy fight here. (Please see the postscript for why not.) I'm not in favor of repealing child labor laws. Our daughter's safety, long-term health, and well-being were and are at the forefront of our minds. But that focus on *long-term* health is precisely why a decision to shield our daughter from work—instead of intentionally introducing her into work—would be such a foolish decision. My wife and I hadn't thought for a moment that we might be running afoul of any Department of Labor edicts and mandates—nor had the ranchers or their grown children who have worked with cattle for decades. But upon further digging, it turns out that some existing state and federal laws make it very difficult for teens to develop good work habits and the beginner skills needed in the marketplace. In effect, the laws exist to do everything possible to prevent 15-, 16-, and 17-year-olds from working, whether it's limiting shifts to four hours or capping a teen's work week at three nonconsecutive days. Government policies presume the centrality—and almost exclusivity—of schooling in the upbringing of our adolescents. These well-meaning rules can thus unhelpfully exacerbate the challenge of intentional parenting by foreclosing the options available to parents and kids who aim to build character and hone their self-discipline through productive work experiences.

The older American ethic—of teaching kids why good work rather than the absence of work will make them happy—must be recovered in order to serve our kids better.

There is an oft-repeated story about Martin Luther that most Americans once knew that illustrates a deeper way of thinking about callings. During the intellectual and spiritual ferment of the Reformation, Luther met a man who announced that he'd just become a Christian, and was eager and anxious to now serve the Lord. So he asked Luther, "How can I be a good servant? What should I do?" He was clearly assuming that he should quit his job and become a minister. Or a monk, or a missionary.

Luther replied with a question: What do you do now?

I'm a cobbler. I make shoes, the man answered.

Then make great shoes, Luther replied, and sell them at a fair price—to the glory of God.

IN A GORGEOUS SCENE from the prison film *The Shawshank Redemption,* several inmates volunteer for a job resurfacing the roof of a local license-plate factory. The warden had asked for a dozen volunteers, but we are told that "more than a hundred men" volunteered for the job.

The men work hard on the roof and are finally each rewarded with a beer when their work is nearly completed. As Morgan Freeman's character notes in a powerful voiceover, "We sat and drank with the sun on our shoulders, and felt like *free men*. Hell, we could have been tarring the roof on one of our own houses. We were the lords of all creation."

It is the sort of feeling workers everywhere know. And I hope we can instill it in our own kids—without their having to go to prison to learn the freedom of escape into meaningful work. For there's no finer feeling on Earth than the sun shining on you as you look at your work, completed, after a long day of good pain.

STEPPING STONES TO IDENTITIES AS LITTLE WORKERS

Mom and Dad Must Plan Out Assignments

Many parents want to help their kids learn a work ethic but discover it's simply very hard to find them work. There is much less work around the house than at any point in history. Then, of the tasks that do exist, much of the time it actually takes longer to help your kids complete a task than to just do it yourself.

Shorter version: Yep, it's *work* to parent well with regard to work.

At our house, we have come to the realization that we must set aside time to plan work—and thus victories—for them. It is work to plan work, and we've had to resolve to do it, even when it feels artificial, and even when the kids think that this is borderline mean of us. (They don't actually think that. They've come to grasp that these planned exercises are for their character development, but it took work to teach them that this is what love sometimes looks like.)

A key breakthrough for us was realizing that much of the "work" we construct for them—from age 2 all the way until their teens—often doesn't look like "work." And that's okay. It often is better thought of as "callings" that are good for our family, or our neighbors, or their own self-control—and we try to create ways for these artificial tasks to become nearly a necessity. Some of our favorites:

- Start young. Send your 2-year-old to get your socks every morning. It creates a rhythm and pattern that can be easily and progressively upgraded to more complicated tasks and successes.

- Build toward "adult" work. Our 12-year-old buys many of our tickets, and our 15-year-old now conducts some of our financial transactions. If they do this stuff early, they won't be at sea when they first get out on their own.
- Reevaluate every service you're paying for at home and ask if your kids could do it. Mowing is a good example. (I actually wept when my brother gave us an old riding mower. I have my kids using the push mower on purpose.)
- Babysit together. Make your kids learn to change the diapers.
- Find shared exercise—from the jogger stroller when they're 1, to you running while they bike at 5, to joint running at 8, until you can no longer keep up with them. (I've just hit that last stage with mine. It hurts . . . and it's lovely.)
- Build a pet cemetery.
- Build a schedule to visit older relatives (or other senior citizens you know) more regularly than just holidays. Find tasks you can do to help out around their house or read to them from their old journals or keepsakes at the nursing home.
- When something goes wrong on a trip, or with a defective product that needs to be mailed back, don't just fix it. Ask your kids to assess the situation and propose a plan. Help create agency by asking them if and how they think they can fix various messes that life throws at us.
- Take them to your work, often.
- Take them to other people's work.
- Ask for plant tours.
- Learn to swim, young, almost as a job. We defined measurables on the way to learning to swim—chiefly involving me pushing our 12- to 15-month-olds through the water toward some handicapped entrance at a local pool. The girls were not quite doggy-paddling yet, but with partial propulsion from dad, they would bounce and crawl along the bottom and eventually up and out on the ramp. We referred to the learning stages as "their work"—and they came to love each step of the progressively longer climbs until they were swimming, young. They were beaming with pride about "their work."
- Find old people in airports and have your kids ask them about their first jobs.
- If there is a church or synagogue nearby, ask if your kids can volunteer to help serve the sandwiches in the fellowship hall after funeral services.
- Volunteer to help the less fortunate on a regular basis. (Our middle daughter reads to intellectually disabled folks on Thursday mornings through a wonderful organization called "Mosaic.")

- Make one holiday a year a family service opportunity. We have some friends who serve at a shelter every Thanksgiving—and the turkey they eat with the less fortunate ends up being some of the sweetest turkey they enjoy all year.

I would add "do forced marches" here . . . if I didn't worry it would appear to be too rigorously tough-love an approach. (But to be honest, my little ones loved the marches.)

The keys to all of these introductory work experiences for kids—young, preteen, and teen—is to build a shared sense of why you are urging them toward productivity, to plan the tasks together, and then to *praise them* to the skies for each win.

The younger they start, the more quickly they will proudly embrace their identities as workers.

SIX

CONSUME LESS

Things Won't Make You Happy * Millennials and the New Consumerist Captivity
Necessity Rightly Understood * The Story of How Humanity Conquered Necessity
From Farms to Factories to Faster * Fashion Comes to America
Our Postindustrial Age of Anxiety * A Dose of Stoicism for the Pampered Republic
Becoming Tough Enough to Be Uncomfortable

He who is not contented with what he has,
would not be contented with what he would like to have.

—Socrates

HARD WORK PRODUCES WEALTH, WHICH THEN PRO-
duces leisure. Over an individual lifetime, this seems both fair and good.
But across generations, it leads to people who know only the leisure and
not the work or character that created it.

Our young are more insulated from necessity, from the need to work
hard, from the obligation not to consume more than they produce than
any large community ever. Because we are the richest people the world
has ever known, our children know few limits. As a result, they breathe
the air of a culture that has transformed what used to be "wants" into
norms and therefore "needs." When all of your friends have an expensive
smartphone contract or video-gaming system, it's not surprising that

you come to feel these things are necessities. If everyone else has one, why shouldn't you?

We are unhelpfully allowing our kids to overlook the essential distinction between genuine needs—the things necessary to survive, to learn, and to live a fulfilling life—and those things that are merely wants. I'm not downplaying the challenge we all face as parents in successfully pointing out and reinforcing this distinction, but collectively we are doing a miserable job of explaining it to our children.

This chapter is a pitch for parents to develop a firm line between these things (just because your friends *have* it does not mean you *need* it), to model it personally (maybe I don't need to upgrade my phone this month just because the contract allows it, or buy a TV four inches wider when the old one still works, or lust after a new car just because I can afford one), and to start a conversation about how to resist the strong forces in our advertising and popular culture that push us mindlessly in this direction. It's a call to reemphasize core American traits—self-denial and deferred gratification—that will stand all of us well in the years to come.

The fear that our kids are getting soft, the haunting, aching suspicion that surplus creature comforts make a civilization fat and unambitious, is not new with us, of course. Parents and grandparents have worried about the virtue—literally, "the strength"—of rising generations in all times free of famine and war since the creation. The Spartans built an entire culture based on ensuring that their citizenry, and especially the young who would defend them in battle, would be physically and mentally tougher than their neighbors who were raised with greater material supports. But it is new for children to be tempted toward the soulless idea of limitless acquisition by the popular culture from before they are able to form even their first sentence. If we are going to protect our kids from "affluenza," from the historically bizarre inclination to view consumption as somehow their main occupation or "work," we are going to need to gently introduce them to the older notion that limits are real and often good.

THINGS WON'T MAKE YOU HAPPY

Arthur Brooks, the president of the American Enterprise Institute, is an odd bird: He started his career as a French horn player, later became probably the first professional wind musician to become a renowned economist, and is now making a third career as an expert in the science of happiness. Over the past decade Brooks has culled thousands of studies on what makes for a happy life, distilling the findings into a few basic precepts that can help us explain to our kids why consumption isn't a road to happiness.

Everyone should read Brooks directly, but here's the CliffsNotes version: It turns out that nearly half of our happiness is genetic, and another significant portion comes from having the good fortune to be born away from a definable universe of horrific events—war, famine, and epidemic. Much is thus predetermined, but of the portion of happiness somewhat within our control, there are four key drivers of what Brooks calls our "happiness portfolio." Somewhat surprisingly, none of the four are related to material abundance. These are the central variables that emerge from Brooks's research:

- **Faith:** Do you have a framework to make sense of death and suffering?
- **Family:** Do you have a home life with mutual affection, where the good of others is as important to you as your own happiness?
- **Community:** Do you have at least two real friends who feel pain when you suffer and share joy when you thrive?
- **Work:** Perhaps most fundamentally, when you leave home on Monday morning, do you believe that there are other people who genuinely benefit from the work you do? Is your calling meaningful? Not: "Is it fun or well-compensated?"—but rather, "Does it matter"?

The political scientist Charles Murray has studied "the kinds of accomplishments that . . . lead people to reach old age satisfied with who they have been and what they have done." Murray writes, you will find "that the accomplishments you have in mind have three things in common. First, the source of satisfaction involves something important . . . Second, the source of satisfaction has involved effort, probably over an extended period of time." You need to have invested your energy, worry, and time in it. "Third, some level of personal responsibility for the outcome is essential."

What sorts of accomplishments meet all three criteria? Like Brooks, Murray argues that people achieve the most happiness through their family, vocation, community, and faith. Murray emphasizes the old Latin term "vocation"—meaning "callings" from someone and to something larger than just our preferences. He is using "vocation" and "callings" in much the same way Brooks uses the term "meaningful work." This is not just about your paid employment. This "meaningful work" should not be conceived of as limited to the production or making of *things* for other people to consume, though of course it includes that. It is instead work or production more broadly, and it comes in many different forms, including the building of a good marriage or a healthy family. If you are doing something that benefits someone—from feeding your kids to washing dishes at a restaurant, from nursing the sick to teaching music lessons—the odds are that you will be happy. (We should hear this as pretty great news, because it means that lots of folks have more control over their happiness than we might have previously imagined.)

What is glaringly absent from either scholar's research? Any hint that higher earnings or more material goods translate into joy or fulfillment. Hence, unsurprisingly, data also suggests that the least happy people are lottery winners and folks with inherited money but no meaningful jobs. Does anyone think our culture is doing a good job of teaching those now coming of age—or *modeling* for them—the basic truths that television and movies are mostly misleading and that in the real world consumption is insufficient to make you happy?

Gretchen Rubin, author of the best sellers *Better than Before* and *The Happiness Project,* isn't quite as firm as Brooks and Murray. She believes that money can play a role in buying structure and support, which enable us to regain a sense of stability and control in an unstable world. But even so, the main thrust of her writing affirms the centrality of meaningful relationships and important causes to achieving happiness. Moreover, the self-described "happiness bully" teaches that it is our habits and our self-mastery that most determine whether we will build and strengthen those essential relationships with spouse, children, and neighbors.

Brooks recalls Aristotle's insight that it is not how much you possess that gives you control, but rather that you arrive at a state of self-sufficiency. We feel a sense of self-worth when we can meet our own basic needs. Brooks: The "deep truth" is that "work, not money, is the fundamental source of our dignity. Work is where we build character." It is not in our consumption, but in the "practice of offering up our talents for the service of others" that we find "value with our lives and [that we] lift up our own souls."

MILLENNIALS AND THE NEW CONSUMERIST CAPTIVITY

Christian Smith, a Notre Dame sociologist, focuses on the attitudes and, in particular, the moral beliefs of 18- to 23-year-olds. He and his colleagues surveyed and conducted extensive face-to-face interviews with "emerging adults" (Smith's preferred term). What the team learned led them to the distressing conclusion that the front edge of Generation Z (people born after 1995) and the bulk of millennials (roughly, those born between 1980 and 1995) are unreflectively materialistic and "captive to consumerism."

Of Smith's survey group, 65 percent said shopping and buying things "give them a lot of pleasure." And even though several of the questions that Smith asked seem to have been written to encourage answers that would avoid making the respondent sound shallow, nudging them toward spiritual, communal, and experiential values, the young adults returned continually to life's material pleasures. Well over half of the emerging adults agreed that their "well-being can be measured by what they own, that buying more things would make them happier, and that they get a lot of pleasure simply from shopping and buying things." For the growing share who have never been involved in productive work, the hunting-like act of shopping might actually substitute for the innate yearning to quest and venture.

The qualitative interviews that underpin Smith's book *Lost in Transition: The Dark Side of Emerging Adulthood* are as disheartening as the quantifiable results. His team expected to hear considered reflection on the dangers of overconsumption or the emptiness of mere acquisitiveness. They anticipated anguished talk about the value of the inner or spiritual life against the pressures of consumption. Perhaps a literary or poetic sense of the deeper things in life? Or at least maybe some discussion of how shared experiences are less shallow than mere material consumption? Smith offers little consolation to those of us worried about the rising generation's lack of seriousness or wisdom: "[W]e heard almost none of that" skepticism of money buying happiness.

So what did they hear instead? There were occasional misgivings about the danger our increasingly disposable society presents for a sustainable environment. But in almost every case, even among respondents who took a more negative view toward mindlessly using-and-discarding, the interviewers ultimately heard the same uncritical view of consumerism: "If you want something, you go get it." There was not a consideration of whether our affections are rightly ordered or whether all of our appetites are necessarily healthy. Rather, they heard: "Whatever makes you happy" and (what could be the motto of our era) "Who am I to judge?"

What about the concept of deferred gratification? Self-denial? These appear to be alien approaches.

One response in particular pained me: While being essentially asked if our age is becoming too obsessed with just getting more, one young man shrugged and said, "Um, it's capitalism." Now, I'm a big fan of capitalism. It allocates resources more efficiently than any other economic system in history, and has thereby yielded amazing fruit in lifting humanity out of poverty and suffering. But we should not confuse effective economic production and distribution with the whole of life and meaning.

To paraphrase Robin Williams's compelling teacher character in *Dead Poets Society:* We don't study poetry to get an "A," to graduate, to get a job, to make money, to meet material needs. Rather, "we read and write poetry because we are members of the human race. And the human race is filled with passion. So medicine, law, business, engineering . . . these are noble pursuits and necessary to sustain life. But poetry, beauty, romance, love . . . these are what we stay alive *for.*"

Sadly, Smith's interviewees appeared not to grasp any of this. Many went so far as to refer to consumerism as "kind of a way of life." They said that it is just "what America has evolved into. America sort of centers on it; it's necessary to survive."

What? Consumerism is *necessary to survive?*

No, it isn't. Not even close. If we wanted to get fussy and precise about it, we would say that human beings have a handful of survival needs: oxygen, water, food, shelter, sleep, and companionship. "Acquiring stuff" doesn't make the list. Neither does spending hours and hours online in daily virtual consumption.

NECESSITY RIGHTLY UNDERSTOOD

Where did we go wrong?

All of my grandparents, from the Krebs, Sasse, Laaker, and Dunklau families, as children of the Great Depression, would be thoroughly confused by an "I live to shop" sensibility. Mom has told me endless stories about the frugality of all of my great-grandparents: how they put prudential questions to themselves before each act of buying; how Grandpa tracked how many times he opened his wallet per week; how they cut twist-ties into thirds to use on plastic bags to maximize the refrigerated utility of leftovers, recombined the last fragments of nearly extinct bars of soap, calculated the driving distance and cents-per-gallon price differentials before deciding at which gas station to refill the truck, showered in cold water for as many months as possible annually, grew much of their own produce even in retirement when they had moved from the farm to town; and on and on. Remembrances of Dust Bowl habits can sound naively quaint, but it's also a fact that a stunning 30 percent of American adults today are not creditworthy. This hasn't happened in a vacuum; it is related to a culture that has abandoned older attitudes toward and practices of limited consumption.

Although we often fail at it, Melissa and I aim to imprint on our children the fact that *need* and *want* are words with particular and distinct meanings. When I'm accidentally wandering past the toy aisle at Target and my son points at something with the aggressive assertion of a 5-year-old, "I *need* that," I let him know that "need" actually has nothing to do with it. No amount of crying and whining will change the fact that their survival doesn't depend on securing that toy. Melissa and I have therefore resolved that our children should never see one of their wants met when they first misidentify that want as a "need."

America is, for better and for worse, a consumer's paradise. Almost all of us live within walking or short driving distance of a supermarket with two dozen brands of bread, twenty-six kinds of ham, thirty-one types of mustard, more than forty varieties of mayonnaise, and lettuce from multiple continents. Within minutes, we acquire the ingredients to return home and assemble the greatest sandwich the world has ever conceived. A sandwich that would have been beyond the reach of kings two centuries ago is now available to us by the push of a button on the Jimmy John's app—and the combination of artificial intelligence and drone delivery are about to make it even more seamless. This is a miracle of our modern global economy, of supply chains and logistics, of free trade and comparative advantage.

It is easy to see why some of us might have begun to confuse wants with needs and to mistake convenience and necessity. Smith and his team found that this generation of emerging adults might not merely be neglecting the distinction between *need* and *want;* they might, more tragically, have never learned this critical difference in the first place.

As recently as 1850, almost all of the world's 1 billion people lived in extreme poverty. A century later, in 1950, a stunning change had occurred, as only 75 percent of the world's then 2.5 billion people re-mained in extreme poverty (defined by demographers in inflation-adjusted terms as living on $1.90 or less per day in 2015 dollars). Today, less than seven decades later, almost unbelievably, less than 10 percent of the world's now 7 billion–plus people live in extreme poverty. More than 7 percent of folks (and almost 60 percent of Americans) now spend more than $50 a day. No one would have predicted either of these won-derful developments a century ago.

Where did this wealth come from? And why its recent arrival? We need to recover a little perspective on what "need" has almost always looked like if we are going to give our kids any chance of transcending entitlement attitudes and learning to live gratefully. Sadly, in our riches, we have stopped teaching our children. For those of us who should be passing along the most basic lessons of maturation to the rising genera-tion, some remedial history is in order.

THE STORY OF HOW HUMANITY CONQUERED NECESSITY

Most of the development of human civilization has been essentially the story of people learning to transcend scarcity, overcome necessity, and reduce the likelihood of near-term death. For the bulk of human history, mankind toiled and suffered to eke out a material living. Deprivation had always been a central fact of life. And thus overcoming deprivation has always been a central human aspiration.

For tens of thousands of years, our Neolithic forebears were abjectly poor—always less than one bad weather season from starvation. They "subsisted"—that is, they got by more than they ever really thrived—and physical life was indeed mostly as Thomas Hobbes famously described it: nasty, brutish, and short.

But then, 11,000 years ago, a game-changer: agriculture. Humans in Mesopotamia (Iraq today) discovered the possibility of cultivating and harvesting their own food. In the Fertile Crescent, and especially along the lush Tigris and Euphrates River valley, our great-great-grandparents began to notice the plants' cycles of growth and ripening, and soon they no longer had to move from place to place to find food. Conceptions of private property likely developed as people began to anticipate and rely on the eventual flowering of plants that were not yet fully ripe, resulting in both territorial sensibility and a willingness to invest effort in tending to and cultivating "their" plants. And as people moved around less, they began to invest more in creating permanent dwellings.

Most importantly, these itinerants-turned-farmers eventually produced more food than their clans needed, so they built both storehouses for surplus and markets for trade. As farming became more efficient, it required fewer hands, so people began to develop new areas of expertise in tasks such as carpentry and irrigation. This specialized division of labor promoted more joint projects and thus further increased the value of population density. Cities arose as excess agricultural goods needed commercial hubs for commerce. Permanent homes allowed religious groups to create permanent structures. Across different time periods, in emerging cities from Ur and Babylon to Jericho in the Middle East and from Tenochtitlán in Mexico to Cuzco in Peru, religious temples served not just as places of worship but also as marketplaces and civic centers. The combination of religious assemblies, commercial spaces, and longer-lasting housing became valuable enough to be worth investing labor and resources to protect. And so came the town walls.

Religion also helped spawn the rule of law, and about 6,000 years ago, alphabets appeared to aid in the clarification and perpetuation of both. As city-states and their merchants began to trade with one another, they saw more acutely the costs of arbitrary rule and wars of conquest, and so they formed leagues and alliances to combat certain kinds of piracy and war. In Greece particularly, the sprouts of Western civilization became visible.

There was surprisingly little economic progress in the thousand years after the fall of Rome in 476 CE (the so-called "Dark Ages"), but eventually the competition among European empires to conquer and colonize the New World—and the global race for gold, silver, spices, and other riches to send back to Europe—led to greater wealth back in many capital cities. Under mercantilism, the era's dominant economic theory, a nation would seek to acquire monetary wealth from other nations by selling more than it bought. This produced an ethic that discouraged mere consumption. The profits of trade with the colonies fueled growth generally, but most importantly they enabled and encouraged investment in the emerging manufacturing sector. The rising demand for skilled labor, combined with innovations in farming, accelerated the rise of the trades in these capitals.

London, for example, which had a population of only 50,000 as recently as 1500, boomed as the push of reduced farm labor needs from the countryside and the pull of markets to the city accelerated. By 1800, the British capital was teeming with a previously unimaginable 1 million residents. As cities grew, trees (England's primary fuel source) became scarcer and more expensive. Predictable economic pressures thus drove the disruptive search for cheaper and more plentiful alternatives. And so rose coal, the fuel of the coming era.

The rough outline of a very different economics was coming into focus—an era with which America's kids should become familiar not because of mere antiquarian curiosity, but because that age bequeathed to us our extraordinary material blessings and because it set the stage for the challenges into which we will soon enter.

FROM FARMS TO FACTORIES TO FASTER

The Industrial Revolution is one of the most important dividing lines in human history. Before the Industrial Revolution, life expectancy was about 30 years. These days, we're pushing 80 years. Before, average male height had been flat for centuries. After, it jumped by half a foot, to over five feet, seven inches. We could explore the rise of steam power and piston engines, pumps and railroads—and the rapid spread of running water and sanitation.

Before the Industrial Revolution, although specialization of high-end labor had been developing since the Renaissance in a few trading centers like Florence and the Netherlands, the vast majority of people were still generalists, producing most of their own food, making their own clothes, and building their own small shelters. After the Revolution, most of us became ever more specialized workers, for good and for ill.

These changes came faster than had any previous changes. After tens of thousands of years of hunting and gathering, each new stage of human experience has been shockingly shorter than the one before it. The dominance of agricultural economics was shorter than the hunter-gatherer stage. Then the dominance of the industrial stage was much shorter than the agricultural stage. The Industrial Revolution completely remade the entire material world, and yet that big tool, the factory-dominant era it birthed, lasted only about 150 years, compared to over 10,000 years for farming. And the global economy, powered by trillions of ones and zeroes moving at the speed of light, that we've just entered will put all past rates of change to shame. Each step of human civilization from immigrant to villager to city dweller to suburban commuter to global telecommuting knowledge worker is getting shorter.

The seventeenth-century migrants to New England and the mid-Atlantic would never have predicted that America would become a global economic powerhouse or that their descendants would become rich. The first settlers were not motivated by grand economic ambitions, but they were problem-solving entrepreneurs, establishing a moral template for Americans for centuries. When material possessions did become more common in the early eighteenth century, these frugal business builders drew an important distinction between investing more in production tools and deciding to simply consume more creature comforts. (In a way, this root distinction of tools versus disposables is at work in the "some technology but not other technology" attitudes of the Amish that most outsiders today find hard to comprehend.) By the mid-1750s, barely a century after the settlers' landing, amazingly, more than half of all estates in Plymouth County, Massachusetts, had spinning wheels, and one-third had looms.

Although the continuing economic growth of the colonies was cheered by many of the revolutionaries, other American Founders found themselves anxious about this emphasis on monetary progress championed by bankers and financiers. These moralist dissenters worried that material obsessions and more specialized jobs could undermine the virtuous labor base that would help parents pass along predictably character-developing work habits to their progeny. The Constitution provided an overdue framework for national political life, but there were many important cultural and economic fights yet to be had about the destiny of the country. The Federalists, led by Alexander Hamilton and George Washington, imagined the United States as a bustling commercial republic with a unified currency, easy flow of goods among the states along tax-funded roads and canals, and strong tariffs that would protect fledgling industries against foreign competitors. Democratic-Republicans, led by Thomas Jefferson and James Madison, wanted an agrarian republic populated with virtuous farmers and artisans, where state governments were preeminent and the national government was limited to a narrowly prescribed role.

Hamilton didn't live long enough to see it, but his vision was headed toward victory—and Jefferson and Madison's carefully crafted version of localist republican government would be swallowed up by the rising tide of commerce. The country was too big, and its economic engines too potent, for America to remain an agrarian republic for long. By the 1830s and 1840s, the American market revolution had finally and conclusively conquered necessity. From a global perspective, the history of humanity struggling against scarcity and trying to insulate themselves against the risk of calamity due to a bad harvest or a cold winter was over. Most Americans now had productive techniques and sufficiently large storehouses to ward off disaster.

As had happened in London over the previous decades, the Industrial Revolution had played a decisive role in the decline of country frugality and the rise of urban consumer values. The Industrial Revolution's explosion of productivity—and the much more bountiful world it birthed—had changed not just how Americans worked but also how much more fruit of our labor we began to expect to regularly consume.

FASHION COMES TO AMERICA

Every big change in the world—every innovative development and every market expansion—comes with trade-offs. Americans in the nineteenth century were getting wealthier, but their work roles were also becoming more specialized and less local. Boom-and-bust cycles in the economy ruined thousands of farmers, caused tremendous disruption, and fueled political unrest. The Jacksonians, like the Jeffersonians before them, were anxious about the economy's transformation from an agrarian experience, mostly with local people they knew (think: Saturday farmers' markets), into a placeless national market driven primarily by large manufacturing. The globalization we are experiencing today differs in significant ways from the antebellum experience with market disruption, but the feelings they had about the loss of local control parallel the way many Americans feel today about globalization and the shift toward a postindustrial economy. Free markets invariably disrupt and reshape cultures.

The explosion of surplus gave rise to what Charles Sellers in *The Market Revolution* calls a "fetishism of commodities." The ancient urge to keep up with the Joneses was married to this new, much more plentiful kind of consumerism. By 1830, "many a reluctant Illinois patriarch felt . . . pressures, as neighborhood after neighborhood abandoned buckskin, homespun, and moccasins in favor of cloth coats, calico dresses, and shoes." Everyone felt they "needed" the latest goods and clothes. Then as now, the younger generation disproportionately drove changes in style. Illinois governor Thomas Ford observed at the time that "the young ladies," instead of walking to church barefoot, "now came forth arrayed complete in all the pride of dress, mounted on fine horses and attended by their male admirers."

The clothes they made at home no longer seemed sufficient. Old-timers didn't like the shift toward showy consumption one bit. They complained, the governor recounted, that the basic "spinning wheel and the loom were neglected and that all the earnings of the young people were expended in the purchase of finery." Old agrarian republicans denounced "luxury" as immoral, but the pressure to conform was too much to resist. As one British visitor noted, American women increasingly desire the latest fashionable "dress not only because it is becoming, but because they revolt from sinking, even outwardly, into a lower station of life than they once held." A farmer who formerly deferred consumption to save up for more tools would now instead sometimes go into debt, even at the risk of foreclosure, "in order that his wife and daughters may dress like the ladies of Boston."

Sociologist Thorstein Veblen, in his 1899 tome *The Theory of the Leisure Class,* coined a new term for this kind of behavior: "conspicuous consumption." But the insecurity behind the idea is as old as civilization itself. Wherever there is wealth, there will always be wealthy people looking to show off their riches. It's about power and status-seeking— the ultimate example of *want* triumphing over *need.*

What was new in nineteenth-century America was the convergence of mass conspicuous consumption and mass governance, since in a republic the average folk are supposed to be the rulers. Free-market forces were making America rich and, many believed, were likely to make the middle class soft. As Jefferson had warned, increased leisure and consumption of the conspicuous kind undermines republican virtues—virtues like public-spiritedness, self-sufficiency, self-sacrifice and duty. Luxury, as one newspaper tartly put it, is "the bane of republics." The eighteenth-century French political theorist Montesquieu, whose *Spirit of the Laws* and *Considerations on the Causes of the Greatness of the Romans and Their Decline* greatly influenced the Founding Fathers, described virtue in a republic as "a most simple thing: it is love of the republic . . . The love of our country is conducive to a purity of morals . . . The less we are able to satisfy our private passions, the more we must abandon ourselves to those of a general nature." Love of the republic in a democracy, Montesquieu went so far as to say, requires a love of frugality.

Shorter version: It is very difficult for a rich republic to remain virtuous.

OUR POSTINDUSTRIAL
AGE OF ANXIETY

Today, we are wealthy—extremely wealthy. But something dispiriting happened along the way: Despite all the expansion of wealth and leisure time, Americans report being less happy than we were fifty-plus years ago.

Political scientist Francis Fukuyama unpacked the complicated back-story in an *Atlantic* essay (and subsequent book) called "The Great Disruption." First, the good news: A society built around knowledge tends to produce more freedom and equality. We have much more choice now, in consumption options, educational pathways, job opportunities, social networks, and so on. As information becomes freer, large and cumbersome institutions give way to smaller, more flexible ones. Computing power is no longer just for large companies with established connections to a gymnasium-sized mainframe at MIT, but rather for everyone in their pocket. There isn't one Ma Bell phone company; there are mobile phones for almost everyone. We replaced $175 stock transaction fees on 100-unit blocks for those whose calls the stockbrokers return first with $7 instant options for everyone with Wi-Fi. From your pocket you can book a flight to anywhere in the world, order and direct private cars, rent short-term lodging, and watch your favorite shows from your favorite networks. The knowledge-based economy is empowering individuals at the expense of formerly impenetrable government and corporate bureaucracies. So far so good.

But somehow, even though everything material is closer to perfection than ever before in human history, we aren't any happier. Fukuyama also explained how the rise of the modern information-based economy—which began not with the rise of the internet in the early 1990s, but rather in the 1960s—drove the decline of heavy industry and manufacturing, and a large number of so-called "rust-belt" communities as well. Jobs necessarily became less permanent, and consumption easier and cheaper. People were decreasingly part of shared projects, including the epic human adventure to overcome scarcity and necessity. Most of us became more absorbed with private acquisition. All of these developments produced bigger homes but also bigger loneliness. And it turns out that more stuff is an insufficient salve for feelings of isolation.

Not surprisingly, "trust and confidence in institutions went into a deep, forty-year decline . . . The nature of people's involvement with one another changed as well. Although there is no evidence that people associated with each other less, their mutual ties tended to be less permanent, less engaged, and in smaller groups of people." Necessity is the mother of invention, and shared suffering is an occasion for human bonding—so when we conquered so much necessity and suffering so quickly, an unanticipated casualty was a decline in large shared projects and thus a decline of neighborly bonding in the America in which our young people have been coming of age in recent decades.

Fukuyama was not the first to observe that the conquest of necessity could cut in two directions at once—that material abundance could make us freer and less dependent, but simultaneously more lonely and isolated. There has always been a wisely skeptical strain of stoicism in American thought. Those who take the long view have worried about the negative effects of easy creature comforts on the vigor and vitality of our adolescents.

Those fears reached a fever pitch in the United States as the economy boomed in the years following World War II. Books like David Riesman's *The Lonely Crowd,* John Kenneth Galbraith's *The Affluent Society,* C. Wright Mills's *White Collar,* Paul Goodman's *Growing Up Absurd,* and Vance Packard's *The Waste Makers* sounded an alarm about abandoning an older ethic that frugality and deferred gratification produce shared experience and shared virtue. (Anecdotally, it is almost impossible to get our 13- and 15-year-old daughters to make music together . . . until they realize that we are serious that no TVs or other screens are coming on at our house on a given night. Then, almost like magic, within ninety minutes they are spontaneously gathered around the piano with a guitar or a violin composing and singing. They are producing rather than consuming—and we're all more satisfied.)

Critics of the cultural consequences of consumerism were often suspicious of the broader capitalist order as well, and a few of them were bona fide socialists. But one not need share their skepticism of a market-oriented system of production (I don't) to nonetheless worry deeply about a collective decision to fan the flames of appetite rather than self-restraint (I do). They offered an important line of questioning: What happens when the peddling of more goods becomes a larger societal riddle to solve than the making of goods? What happens when the brightest brains become invested in stimulating demand rather than either fulfilling or restraining it? What happens when our most talented poets find their highest calling in advertising? What happens when people stop saving and turn their "labors" to spending? Is it possible to be a nation that exists on an installment plan?

These worriers had an abiding contempt for salesmen who used marketing tricks and techniques derived from psychology and propaganda to persuade a generation of Americans to lust for more. They disdained advertisers who argued that limitless consumption was practically a patriotic duty. Packard decried the push toward "forced consumption." Foreshadowing the millennials we met earlier who assume consumerism as a fact of life, marketing consultants in the mid-1950s began extolling consumption in quasi-religious terms: "Our enormously productive economy . . . demands that we make consumption our way of life, that we convert the buying and use of goods into rituals, that we seek our spiritual satisfactions, our ego satisfactions, in consumption," wrote one. The model year, it is a-turning. "We need things consumed, burned up, worn out, replaced, and discarded at an ever increasing rate." This was a remarkable change coming just a decade after war rationing and only two decades after the Great Depression. It also represented a profound shift in the American attitude toward commercialism.

We have now completely entered this fourth economic age in human history (following the hunter-gatherer, agricultural, and industrial ages). We're so confused by it that we can't even settle on its name. Sometimes we call it the information economy, or the knowledge economy, or the IT economy. Fukuyama refers to it simply as the "post-industrial" economy—which is really just another way to say that we don't know what to name it, so we'll call it the "after-the-last-economy" economy. A "great disruption" is an apt description of this new, digital, rapidly dislocating economy that first appeared after World War II when IBM began making advances in commercial computing. It took flight with the beginning of deindustrialization in the 1960s, reaching stratospheric heights with the personal computer and the internet in the 1980s and 1990s, and it has now taken it up another level with mobile telecom networks. "Dizzying" is an overused term in business literature, but in this rare instance it probably understates the pace of what will come next with more widespread automation and artificial intelligence.

As the economy gets faster and faster, the future becomes more unpredictable in ways both fascinating and horrifying. There is an obvious tension between the great benefits of globalization and free markets at the macro level and the disruption they cause so many at the individual level. In times of rapid economic and cultural change, democracies become vulnerable, because people with easy answers prey on our fears and our anger at losing out.

Our emerging adults are unlikely to demonstrate the resilience and flexibility that the ever more rapidly changing digital economy will demand without a more nuanced understanding than they now have about the recency of current baseline assumptions of material "needs." If we let them remain so historically ignorant as to believe that the upgrade from the iPhone 5 to the iPhone 6 is a great divide in human happiness, they are probably going to have a tough time navigating the coming years.

A DOSE OF STOICISM FOR THE PAMPERED REPUBLIC

The generation coming of age has little sense that our walk-in closets are now bigger than the entire dwellings of many of the earliest American arrivers. Most of them do not know that the average new home today is more than three times larger than the average new home in 1950. Our kids are often so needy, so "wanty," so rich—both in absolute historical terms and relative to the rest of the world today—that they aren't fully equipped to confront the stark challenges ahead of them. Being subconsciously insulated from necessity and transforming more wants into needs hasn't made us happier. And it certainly hasn't made us stronger. We have instead a generation drifting into adulthood that has been reared with an entitled and false sense of both how much material comfort they need, and how easily it should come to them. Behind them, there is a generation in waiting that shares the immersion in these problems but overlays a second reality of supposed "digital needs."

Here's the question Baxter, or Jefferson, or Roosevelt, or Postman would be asking: Could we perhaps be rearing a generation that might not be tough enough to be good Americans? For a good American needs to be *tough*. We believe in the independence not just of rugged individuals but of persevering families. If a family—the most basic unit of community—is going to survive, it has to be able to get through hard times. The republican old-timers of Jacksonian America were not wrong to regard luxury as the "bane of republics." And Teddy Roosevelt's extolling of "the strenuous life" helped shape a generation. Life in the twenty-first century is anything but strenuous. Much of our stress now flows not from deprivation but, oddly, from surplus. It's too easy to be pampered, and being pampered is the opposite of growing muscle—and character. Both of these come from scar tissue.

One antidote for the pampered life is a taste of stoicism. We often think of a "stoic" disposition via a caricature—maybe a passionless old man, indifferent to the world around him. Our teens probably know Webster's definition of a stoic as "one apparently or professedly indifferent to pleasure or pain; one not easily excited or upset." I reject the notion that stoic is "indifferent"; rather, the stoic is strong enough and long-term-focused enough to not be tossed about by short-term changes beyond his or her control. Someone who is stoic appears calm under stressful circumstances—the man or woman whose internal equipoise is not dominated by external conditions.

Stoicism, which is experiencing a small revival today thanks to Ryan Holiday and Stephen Hanselman's best-selling *The Daily Stoic,* is a practical wisdom tradition with roots reaching back to Socrates. Zeno of Citium founded his philosophical school in Athens around 300 BCE. His students would gather to hear him lecture under a painted *stoa*—a kind of portico—and so they became known as "the Stoics." Stoicism influenced the Romans, notably among them Emperor Marcus Aurelius, whose *Meditations* have been widely read for centuries. Without getting themselves tangled in abstract fights about epistemology and ontology, the Stoics taught that self-improvement is possible only through training, habits, and the cultivation of self-discipline, both physical and mental. You've heard the adage "You are what you eat"? A Stoic would say, "You are what you think." As bad thoughts precede bad actions, so too does good thinking precede good action and the cultivation of honorable habits.

The old Stoics were among the first to teach that experiences are more valuable than possessions. Stoics don't care about fashion. They have no use for the "cult" of youthful physique whereby one vainly comes to care more about one's physical appearance than about the strength of one's mind. Health and wealth are not *goods* in themselves, but natural pursuits. The point is to develop habits or skills to "live in agreement with nature," which leads to happiness, rationality, and right living.

Epictetus, an emancipated slave, wrote in his famous *Enchiridion* (a Latin word for "handbook"), "Some things are under our control,

while others are not under our control." Under our control: "conception, choice, desire, aversion, and . . . everything that is our own doing."
Not under our control: the inevitable decline of our body, most of what
happens to "our property, reputation, office, and . . . everything that is
not our own doing." If your life is focused on acquiring *things*, "you will
be hampered, will grieve, will be in turmoil, will blame both gods and
men." If you desire things beyond your control, "you are bound to be
unfortunate" and disappointed.

Here's the important thing: he is saying our desires can be brought
within our control. To achieve that would require a complete reordering
of most of our lives, to reshape our affections. Conversely, and again
contrary to how we usually think, he teaches that a focus on acquiring
things will not really ever yield enough products to produce happiness.
Rather, it will invariably end in grief and disappointment.

Stoics are patient with everything—except their own negative emotions like envy, fear, anger, and avarice. It's really no surprise that modern psychology has picked up on much of what the Stoics grasped 2,000
years ago: you cannot control everything in your life. In fact, you cannot
control most things. You don't even have full control over the core reality of your body—your mortality. *But you can control* your judgments,
and your responses to events, both good and bad. Today's buzzword
"mindfulness" is really just a new gloss on Stoicism.

We have not explored here the religious discipline of fasting, but it
is worth noting that many traditions have long encouraged intentionally
abstaining from food or drink (or sex or other delights) for a period of
time, obviously to focus the mind and to contemplate eternity, but also
to subdue the flesh and to heighten one's gratitude for daily bread and
provisions. And even amid the trivialities of pop culture, there is often a
recognition that pausing to return to basics is in order:

> *How 'bout stopping eating when I'm full up . . .*
> *How 'bout me not blaming you for everything*
> *How 'bout me enjoying the moment for once . . .*

Alanis Morissette's "Thank You" gives repeated shout-outs to the gifts
of silence, disillusionment, frailty, and consequence—and urges a reconsideration of not just over-medication, but also the assumption that

privation is always bad. She climaxes with the insight that the "moment I let go of it was the moment I got more than I could handle."

BECOMING TOUGH ENOUGH
TO BE UNCOMFORTABLE

To make ourselves more useful in the world, we can become lower-maintenance—we can free ourselves from needless consumption. If our older daughters want to help get their little brother out the door in the morning, then they must either have tended to themselves first, or have reduced the amount of self-tending that is "necessary."

Rousseau—who wanted to keep natural man free from God, from duty, from family, and from other relational obligations—was wrong about so much, but he was right on this score: People living life well want to be free from the shackles of society's demands of fashion and fad. The need to conform to social convention might be part of the human condition, but that doesn't make it one of our finer traits. Rousseau's romantic idea of the noble savage is sometimes worth emulating. "The savage lives within himself," he wrote, "while social man lives constantly outside himself." Rousseau's whole-man is governed by his own choices of how and toward what ends he should live. The society man, by contrast, lives the hamster-wheel tyranny of keeping up with the Joneses.

Emile's education begins at birth: "before speaking, before understanding. He is already learning." And the core lesson Rousseau wants to teach first is freedom from man-made constraints, prejudices, and social pressure. He wants the natural man to conform only to the true dictates of nature, not the whimsical and artificial dictates of culture. Wealthy society decides that the luxury of hot water is somehow necessary, that life cannot be lived without it. Not Emile. He is immediately desensitized to heat and cold as a baby, for example, by being bathed in hot and cold water. "Thus after being habituated to bear the various temperatures of water . . . one would become almost insensitive to the various temperatures of the air." (Unsurprising side point: after living abroad and rarely having hot water for half a year, upon returning home I found myself simultaneously lower-maintenance in my expectations and also more appreciative of a hot shower whenever I got one.)

In another lesson, Jean-Jacques teaches Emile to be comfortable with being uncomfortable. "It is important in the first instance to get used to being ill bedded," Rousseau writes. "This is the way never again to find an uncomfortable bed. In general, the hard life, once turned into habit, multiplies agreeable sensations; the soft life prepares for an infinity of unpleasant ones." If a child is tough, and his consumption expectations are intentionally chosen and constrained rather than expanded, his or her denominator of expectations is easy to satisfy: "People raised too delicately no longer find sleep elsewhere than on down; people accustomed to sleep on boards find it everywhere." Emile is taught to draw conclusions from hard-won experience. Rousseau warned him not to play ball in the house, because he might break a window. And when he does, his tutor dispassionately announces: When the boy breaks "the windows of his room, let the wind blow on him night and day, without caring for the cold he may take; for it is much better for him to have a cold than to be a fool" for the rest of his manhood.

Living the good life doesn't require the budding adult to live without goods, without things, without stuff. But a truly good life is incompatible with a *dependency* on such things. At the very least, maturation requires imagining life without material wealth, resolving that we could be happy in such a state, and actually experiencing what mild deprivation is like from time to time. We have some friends who camp occasionally not because they like it, but so that they appreciate their home even more.

When my family gathers at the table for supper, we each give thanks to the Lord for the blessings we've received that day. I don't want my kids to spend a lot of time being grateful for things that don't matter very much, like a new video game. Thank God for shelter. Thank God for safe travels, for protection from violence. Thank God for good health. But for those prayers to make much sense, my children need to have experienced the rugged outdoors, the lack of shelter. They need to grasp that in this fallen world there is regularly violence, deprivation, and sickness.

Our children will be ennobled by learning to aspire to free themselves from pointless convention; to recover something simpler and more meaningful; to love your peers but also to stop worrying what any of them think about silly fashion. One of our daughters is a serious runner, so we purchase high-quality shoes to protect her developing bones—but we buy lots of her other clothes at Goodwill and second-hand shops. We believe you're most fully alive when you distill things to the essentials of life—and then learn the habit of finding great pleasure and great gratitude in those essentials. It's the kind of life that recognizes and seeks out the fulfillment of production and avoids the lethargic unfulfillment of restless consumption.

If the unexamined life is not worth living, neither is a life of passive material appetites. My wife regularly quotes Margaret Thatcher to our children to the effect that, unless we're talking about actual capacities humans lack (for example, the ability to fly), the word "can't" will not come out their mouths in her presence. Don't announce that you're the kind of person who cannot do X or Y or who cannot sleep easily out of your own bed. Rather, resolve to *become* the kind of person who *can* do X and Y, and can sleep easily, flexibly, wherever the opportunity arises—and who can awake refreshed and grateful for the rest that came to body and mind.

THIS CHAPTER IS NOT a zealous pitch for stoicism or the frugal life. It is, rather, an assertion that anyone who swims so completely in a sea of material surplus as to be unaware of the virtues of the simple life is flirting with great moral risk. In an age in which false prophets are everywhere announcing that consuming the best, the prettiest, the most will finally satisfy you, the true adult will humbly but skeptically ask questions informed by the wisdom of earlier ages. He or she will reaffirm the older American traits of self-denial and deferred gratification.

At one level, happiness is an equation that has "needs met" as the numerator and "presumed total needs" as the denominator. One way to achieve temporary happiness is to invest more energy seeking to fill up the numerator. But another way, a more stable way, is to reflectively guard against the growth of one's denominator of needs, and to cultivate the habit of gratitude at the satisfaction of real and basic needs.

The challenge of raising thoughtful and grateful teens is not merely an individual family's problem. It is a broader, shared quest. And if we cease to discuss together and wrestle over the national dangers of wealth and limitless want, that is itself a choice—and a bad one for the preservation of a virtuous republic.

To become adults, and indeed to be fully human, we need a vision and an awareness that is bigger than just the set of peers marketers see us as when they pitch new trinkets to us. One of the best ways to become secure in your adulthood, in your independence and self-assertiveness, is to learn to disentangle nature from culture. The culture you live in may be more or less healthy. But how will you really know until you've experienced cultures other than your own?

Knowing the history of how humankind overcame brutal necessity in order to forge civilization, as we unpacked in this chapter, is important. We need to grasp that material abundance is a very recent development, and we need the wisdom to understand how and why so many of our ancestors achieved happiness even without walk-in closets and storage units of consumer goods. But to internalize the difference between *need* and *want,* there is no substitute for actually experiencing subsistence. The best way to do that is to get out of a you-centric world and into the larger world.

To do that, one must travel. As the next chapter will show us, you must travel far and wide—and especially, you must travel light.

STEPPING STONES TO CONSUMING LESS

Make Logs and Lists

If you want to consume less (less junk food, for example), it is helpful—before you try to change your behavior—to first know what your behavior actually is.

 One baby step is to write down every single bit of junk food you eat every single day for a month (or for whatever time period you choose). Even without resolving yet to change your junk-food intake, the act of being honest with yourself usually leads to improved behavior. Typically, we have been fooling ourselves into pretending that our habits are not as bad as they really are. Beginning to create a full record for ourselves—and perhaps to share with an accountability partner—compels a new level of honesty with ourselves, and thus a new seriousness about changing our behavior. Step two is then the concrete goal-setting (for example, a maximum of three servings of dessert per week for the next month). Step three is . . . the willpower.

This simple strategy can be useful for a broad range of behavior you want to reduce, such as:

- hours spent playing video games
- dollars spent on nonessential items
- glasses of alcohol consumed
- hours spent watching screens
- words spoken in anger or impatience to your spouse or kids

Perhaps even more important than habits you want to limit are the habits you want to expand and regularize. For example:

- Waking up by 6:00 a.m.
- Working out five days per week
- Going to bed by 10:00 p.m.
- Spending more hours each day on your main work priority for the week
- Reading one book per month
- Investing more hours on your preferred volunteer activity

There is no magic technique for *how* to log your time or document your behaviors. The important point is that you are true to yourself for your month (or two weeks, or whatever initial period you set) to *record every single instance.* My technique is to put little stacks of 3x5 index cards and pens everywhere—in the car, by the bed, on my desk, by the shower, in my briefcase, in my locker at the gym, everywhere. I keep a little box on my desk and transfer each index card that ends up with a note and a date on it into the box. Then once per week, I sort and tally the index cards and email myself a summary of what I did—for example, six desserts and only two workouts this week (versus my stated goal of five workouts and only three desserts).

Keeping a log or a timesheet—that my wife or a buddy knows I am keeping, and that they might ask to see—quickly alters my behavior . . . even before I have intentionally moved on to the next step of setting a precise goal.

SEVEN

TRAVEL TO SEE

*Black Leeches, Duck Eggs, and New Eyes * Travel versus Tourism*
*Seeing Contrasts for the First Time * Exploration as a Liberal Art*
*Sucking the Marrow * Packing My Mental Suitcase * Breaking Bread with Widows*

A man who has been through bitter experiences and travelled far
enjoys even his sufferings after a time.

—Homer

CHEVY CHASE IN *EUROPEAN VACATION* SMILE-YELLS:
Look, kids! Big Ben! Parliament! Let's go.

Mark Twain in *Innocents Abroad* teases such harried tourists and our
supposed "business of sight-seeing," in which everyone is in a hurry to
see without looking. He ridicules the scavenger-hunt mentality common
to tourists. "I cannot think of half the places we went to, or what we particularly saw; we had no disposition to examine carefully into anything
at all—we only wanted to glance and go—to move, keep moving!" We
have another sight to see, another box to check. If we hurry, there's time
before sundown to use one more timeless monument as the backdrop
for one more selfie.

There is, of course, a more satisfying approach to traveling, one that
provides valuable perspective on one's own life and the lives of others.

Like hard work, it challenges us. When we travel, we subject ourselves to the vertigo that accompanies leaving familiar surroundings, customs, language, and food, while diving headlong into a different world. Like reading a wide and varied array of books, it arouses our curiosity to learn the perspectives of other people and cultures—it creates empathy. It also heightens our appreciation of the great benefits we have as Americans.

Of course, foreign travel is expensive and not within everyone's means. The good news is that the *habit* of traveling well doesn't require a ton of money or even necessarily going that far from home. The goal here is *discovery*—which can be accomplished with just big curiosity, a good chunk of time, a little money for transport, and one organized backpack. The friends I will introduce here came invariably from humble beginnings, as do most of the literary figures mentioned below. But they do bring a couple characteristics often in short supply: resilience and a low-maintenance attitude for the journey.

BLACK LEECHES,
DUCK EGGS, AND NEW EYES

From the time I was 7, my dad took me fishing scores of times every summer—usually to the lakes west of town, sometimes along the Platte River, often in Cutoff Creek, occasionally at Branched Oak near my grandparents' house. But the most memorable place involved a nine-hour drive to Leech Lake in northern Minnesota, where my uncle Roger (the one whose bassinet grandma attached to the tractor) had a small cabin near Walker Bay. The lake—which is the third largest of Minnesota's 10,000 lakes and is located entirely in the beautiful Chippewa National Forest—derives its name from being, in fact, full of leeches. It was exhilarating and terrifying to see the worm-sized leeches floating toward you. We didn't really need the frequent reminders from Aunt Fran to check our privates after swimming, in case one of those little bloodsuckers attached under your swimsuit. Think ticks, but the size of nightcrawlers.

We had a blast in Minnesota. This was before cell phones and we had no television, so evenings centered on cards, board games, baseball on the radio, and longer-form stories from grandma about the Depression than I could ever get in a house where TV was an ever-present alternative. It wasn't exactly Johnny Cash in rural Arkansas listening to the Grand Ole Opry on WSM 650 AM from Nashville, but you felt like you could hear it from there. From the daylight hours around the lake, many memories remain imprinted on my brain: the frigid water when Uncle Rog would dare the kids to dive in at dawn as we'd head out on the boat; the biggest fish I've ever caught—a walleye that I described as "fish story long" throughout my teens; the endless theoretical argument about how many hours you should stay at a spot when nothing is biting ("theoretical" because grandpa wasn't moving regardless); my first jet-skiing experience; and being allowed to walk to the general store and buy ice cream on a tab. But by far the most vivid memory is how dad and his brother would talk about being "spoiled for fish." We made some great hauls, at least in my youthful estimation. But no, no, dad would say. Nothing could compare to the fishing they and their buddies did in Canada when they were young.

As they reminisced, these fortysomething men were transformed back into teenage boys, discovering the world anew. Every spring in the late 1960s, my dad and three of his pals would compare final-exam schedules. The poor guy who had the last final of the semester would be roundly mocked. When the appointed day and time arrived, the three friends whose semester was completed would pack the aging light blue Chevy convertible with supplies and idle in front of the building where the fourth was finishing his test. When he finally emerged from Swanson Hall, the car would begin to pull away—forcing him to run and leap into the back of the moving convertible.

The quartet would head up Highway 77 from Fremont, Nebraska, through South and North Dakota, ultimately making their way to a lake on the border between Minnesota and Manitoba. There they ditched the car. The boys packed light—bringing only sleeping bags, a box of matches, a can opener, and a few emergency cans of beans. Otherwise, they would nourish themselves on the walleye and northern lake trout they caught. Over the course of a week, the fellas would cover a 110-mile loop canoeing and portaging.

At dusk, they would find two islands close together—one for sleeping, the other for keeping their food elevated. It was a doubly cautious way of protecting themselves against bears. On the island where they camped, they would tie pots and pans to ropes they would hang around a perimeter. That way if a bear happened to swim ashore, they would have warning.

I loved hearing about these four kids from small-town Nebraska, in the north woods, all alone, without power, decades before GPS or cell phones, with little food. The only heat they had came from a campfire; their nightlight was the moon. Living on bare necessities for a week yielded glorious memories. Once they stumbled upon a nest of duck eggs. My dad today still describes that surprise breakfast cooked over a campfire as the best meal he's ever had. Not all the stories were heart-warming, of course. There was the time dad was the first to look in the window of a car that had wrecked into a bridge abutment. Both guys inside were dead, and from the faded color of their skin, dad concluded that they had been there undiscovered for quite a while.

Compared to the remoteness of the primitive Canadian wilderness and the bounty of eating so much fish from unfished waters, our week-long outing at a rustic cabin in Minnesota, while memorable, was al-most too civilized. Some of my dad's tales were probably embellished, but at their core, they pass along something enduring: The world these boys had inherited in rural America was good, but it was a world built for them by someone else. It was received rather than discovered. They had neither created it nor chosen it. And to embrace something fully, you need agency. You need to be making choices. You need to have more than one option on the menu in life. The wilds of Canada without chaperones provided them with an alternate choice, a new vantage point on the world, so that they were now involved in the choice to continue living in—even to fall in love with—their inherited life in their own hometown of Fremont. That is what their early adventures were about at their core: They were learning a new way of seeing.

Obviously they needed some technical skills to survive—like fish-ing, canoeing, building a fire, deterring bears, and avoiding poisonous plants—but the main takeaway from these trips thirty years later for them was not this or that skill, all of which could be learned; rather, the critical fact was that they had done it alone. They had not been passengers on someone else's trip. They were the actors. They were the planners. They were the decision makers and the risk calculators.

TRAVEL VERSUS TOURISM

Sometime around the middle of the last century, we forgot how to travel. Commercial tourism as we know it took off during the economic boom years after World War II. More people could travel, yes, but in the way they started doing it, they were often missing out on the most important parts of the experience. Historian Daniel Boorstin wrote at the time that "the tourist sees less of the country than of its tourist attractions. Today what he sees is seldom the living culture, but usually specimens collected and embalmed especially for him, or attractions specially staged for him: proved specimens of the artificial."

That's not how it used to be done. We remember Edward Gibbon as an eighteenth-century member of parliament and as the historian who authored *The History of the Decline and Fall of the Roman Empire,* but before all that, he had another interesting job. Gibbon worked early in his career as a consultant to would-be travelers. These were the days of the Grand Tour, when a traveler—usually young and wealthy—would embark on a journey of months or even years through all the major European capitals. In addition to wanting to know what the visitor to Paris or Geneva or Rome needed to pack, many wondered what it took to travel successfully. Gibbon's response offers a helpful start on the habits of the good explorer:

> He should be endowed with an active, indefatigable vigour of mind and body, which can seize every mode of conveyance, and support with a careless smile every hardship of the road, the weather or the inn. It must stimulate him with a restless curiosity, impatient of ease, covetous of time and fearless of danger; which drives him forth at any hour of the day or night, to brave the flood, to climb the mountain, or to fathom the mine, on the most doubtful promise of entertainment or instruction . . . I have reserved for the last a virtue which borders on a vice: the flexible temper which can assimilate itself to every tone of society, from the court to the cottage; the happy flow of spirits which can amuse and be amused in every company and situation.

This is a pretty stout list of attributes for someone one might recommend as a fellow traveler. Frankly it's a pretty great list of attributes for a spouse—as a lifelong travel partner as well: physical and mental energy; an easy smile; untamable curiosity; obsessive about stewarding time well; fearless; driven to climb mountains and brave floods; a flexible temperament; and a desire to amuse and to be amused, all the time. Sign me up to travel with that friend!

Notice what isn't here: Although the travel of Gibbon's era was limited to the richest 1 percent, there is actually nothing here requiring one to be a wealthy scion of European aristocracy to take advantage of Gibbon's suggestions. Indeed, in our increasingly connected and democratized world, it is possible for more people to travel to more places more economically than ever before. It can become an essential part of growing up for people of all income levels—and so we should be teaching all of our kids how to do it actively and thoughtfully.

America's next generation will be our next generation of rulers—that's how a republic works. Just as a liberal arts education—which should be a radical act *against* dependency and *for* self-sufficiency—was once conceived of, wrongly, as a luxury that only the rich needed, so too have we tended to think of intentional travel as something for only the elite. But if earlier generations were correct in their judgment that travel was helpful for the budding aristocrat in the eighteenth century, then I submit that we should be thinking of it as helpful for *all* of our kids coming of age today.

But first we need them to understand that we don't mean consumer tourism. Almost everyone has fond memories of their first trip across the state to a mass amusement park. Millions of people annually marvel at the view from the observation decks of the Space Needle in Seattle and Sears Tower in Chicago. Cruises and package tours are as popular as ever, and they're nothing if not convenient. You buy a ticket; you stay at a resort; you take a bus tour to get efficiently in and out of the most visited attractions. When in London, everyone goes to Trafalgar Square to take pictures of the statues and to Buckingham Palace to watch the changing of the guard. In Paris, the Eiffel Tower and the Arc de Triomphe are must-sees. In New York, by all means visit the Statue of Liberty and the lights of Times Square. But . . . please understand this kind of tourism is essentially consumption. Nobody's life was ever greatly changed by spending a week on the beach in Cancun (except for the accidental pregnancy or the drunk and disorderly arrest).

We mean something different here. The key distinction here is between *active seeking* and venturing and learning on the one hand, and *passively taking* in the sights on the other hand. Boorstin, formerly the Librarian of Congress, drew a distinction between the nobility of travel and what he saw as the boredom of touring. What's the distinction? In an elegy for what he called "the lost art of travel," Boorstin explained that the traveler is fundamentally "active; he is strenuously in search of people, of adventure, of experience." The old English noun "travel" is the same as "travail"—which means "trouble," "work," "torment." "To journey—to 'travail,' or (later) to travel—then was to do something laborious or troublesome," but meaningful. It is hard—and that is to be cherished. "The traveler [is] an *active man at work.*"

By contrast, "the tourist is passive; he expects interesting things to happen to him. He goes 'sight-seeing.'" Tourism is becoming more common simply because it is becoming cheaper, but the idea behind it isn't new. In fact, it's as old as the newly moneyed classes of the Roman Empire. A tourist was "a person who makes a pleasure trip." Boorstin noted that "tour" comes from the Latin word *tornus,* which itself came from a Greek word for "a tool describing a circle." Upper-class Romans would take holidays during which they would be transported through a predetermined set of ruins in Greece, and then to the pyramids of Egypt, and then back again. It was a sanitized, predictable circle.

Whether communicating in a foreign language, adjusting to the pace of a new place, or eating strange food, travel done right is a kind of work that takes you out of the familiar—out of your comfort zone— and offers the chance to see the world through fresh eyes. It forces you to look at the material nature of how you live. Do I really need so much stuff when I seem to be freer when I'm away from it? It can make you broaden the horizons of your diet. It can help you evaluate whether you've conceived of your sleep environment too rigidly. (After a few camping adventures in our teens, my little brother and I decided to sleep outside more often, even at home. I ended up spending most of 1988 sleeping outside, and fairly accidentally came to know the lunar phase—and the slightly different sleep rhythms I'd experience under a full, versus partial, versus limited moon.) You certainly think differently about technology after traveling to places where the necessary signals cannot penetrate. What tools do others depend on that have been hidden behind the grocery stores and supply chains in our experience? You will find that other people organize their lives around technology much differently than you do.

Children will obviously not all have the same experiences as they learn about travel from their parents. Some of us come from more out-doorsy families—I learned to fish from my father, who learned from his father, and so on. Others will come from wealthy families that can afford the airfare to fly overseas. But the *where* isn't nearly as important as the *how*. What is key, though, in terms of making travel a formative experience for your kids, is to put them into situations where they are out of their comfort zone and seeing things they don't ordinarily see. And then, force them to help plan, to make decisions, to reflect and summarize, *to discover*. If your children embark on a trip without any idea of where they're going, without having played any role in deciding what to visit, or if they return from a trip and immediately return to their devices and routines without actively reflecting on their experience, we will have sacrificed an opportunity for them to grow.

My dad and his friends were traveling not just *to* someplace unfa-miliar; they were traveling *away* from somewhere too familiar. They were leaving not just *their* built environment, but all built environments. They would later say that only then did they really see their own homes for the first time. Just as Canada was the needed contrast that allowed those boys to discover home, everyone coming of age needs multiple experiences that enable seeing back to home from outside. C. S. Lewis's go-to description of a sheltered life and an impoverished future is "an ignorant child who wants to go on making mud pies in a slum because he cannot imagine what is meant by the offer of a holiday at the sea." The teenage homebody is indeed worthy of pity, but the problem of his truncated vision cannot be solved just by notching a few stops at tourist attractions in his belt. For the point of important traveling is not some atypical moment at a famous place that you will repeat only a handful of times in life; instead, the point is the mental impressions and reflective experiences that give you new eyes and lasting comparative perspectives.

The significance of first travel—the way life is changed by travel—is that it offers the young person a broader menu of choices for how to think about life, and then for how to build better habits of living. When that happens, we are taking concrete steps toward adulthood.

SEEING CONTRASTS FOR
THE FIRST TIME

Early in my business career, I noticed that people who talked about travel in meaningful ways tended to be the same people who excelled at complicated work projects. Sometimes this was simply because they had specific experiences that shed useful light on an analogous riddle our team was trying to solve. (For example, a colleague at the Boston Consulting Group who had just worked on a technology solution to a supply chain management problem for a consumer goods company in Sweden ended up having breakthrough insights for a U.S. airline figuring out how to predict where more than 2 million airplane parts would be needed across 250 cities.) More often, though, the well-traveled just tend to be mentally flexible—not tied to one approach or solution, calm under pressure, and thus able problem solvers. They can process present experiences and challenges by comparing them with other experiences and challenges. It is a bit like being bilingual—where the benefit is not merely getting to know the second language but also having a new vantage point from which to look back on the grammar and the vocabulary, the strengths and weaknesses, of your native tongue.

Over time, I started to collect stories from such folks and intentionally to ask questions of other mentors and friends about their first formative travel experiences: How old were you when you first ventured out on your own? Where did you go and why? Did your parents encourage the trip or resist the idea? Tell me one of your big "Aha!" moments. How was the world different after the trip? How did the experience change your parenting? Did it inspire you to encourage your children to venture out younger than most other parents would be comfortable suggesting?

The destinations to which these folks have traveled differ widely, covering the far corners of the earth, but their takeaways are remarkably similar—and often similar as well to the insights of great American literature on travel. I have changed names to protect people's privacy, but I suspect that most of them wouldn't mind being named, because the nuggets they impart suggest a shared reservoir of wisdom. From their experiences, from my own, and from those others have recorded, I began to notice some overarching themes: conquering your fear of being alone; seeing beyond instinctive prejudice; looking more deeply; eliminating low priorities; doubting social convention; learning to sleep anywhere; and so on.

In 1960 novelist John Steinbeck wrestled with all of these as he set out "to rediscover this monster land." Equipped with only a pickup and a custom-made camper top—and his French poodle, Charley—the author of *East of Eden* headed out for three months to the four corners of the lower 48 because "I had not heard the speech of America, smelled the grass and trees and sewage, seen its hills and water, its color and quality of light." The result was *Travels with Charley in Search of America,* a semifictional travelogue. Among the many reasons it is still worth reading is the way Steinbeck captures the anxiety leading up to solo travel: "There was some genuine worry about my traveling alone, open to attack, robbery, assault," he wrote. "And here I admit I had senseless qualms. It is some years since I have been alone, nameless, friendless, without any of the safety one gets from family, friends and accomplices. There is no reality in the danger. It's just a very lonely, helpless feeling at first—a kind of desolate feeling."

My friend Martin built a shorter but similar cross-country experience and came to a similar conclusion. "When I was about 24, I moved from Georgia to Florida, so I decided to hit California on the way," he recalled. Traveling alone for the better part of a month, Martin budgeted exactly $0 for lodging. He stayed at friends' houses along the way on three different nights, but all of the "other nights I slept in my sleeping bag on top of my Ford Explorer." As you might imagine, the first few nights sleeping under the stars in a parking lot or on the side of a road took some getting used to, but soon enough, he was comfortable.

Martin was truly scared only one night. "I was about to run out of gas at 2 a.m. on a long stretch of road between Phoenix and L.A. Someone had carved 'gas' into a sign with a map at a rest stop. I drove to that spot, where I found a doublewide with a bell. I rang the bell." Two Dobermans started barking. Then a man appeared in the door of the trailer with a shotgun. "I really thought he might shoot me and collect my car," Martin said. "Instead he sold me five gallons of gas for $20—back when gas was a dollar a gallon." It was a bargain.

For Martin, no night since that night has been the same. He now consciously appreciates every setting that allows safe, secure sleep. On a long trip, especially overseas, you might go weeks without talking to anyone back home. For Martin, this solitude turned into a fear of the abyss, and then a religious experience. As he traveled—"By myself in the car for hours. Seeing no one I knew for days. Alone with my thoughts. Away from the expectations and demands of others. No one to judge me but myself"—he came to the obvious conclusion that he was smaller than he thought. It wasn't just the sky above him that was big; it was also the awareness that he wasn't self-sufficient even to keep his own heart beating. He says that up until that point, he had observed religion "only in a cultural sense," not a personal sense. Now, he wanted to change that. So each day he began reading Scripture and attempting to pray. These two habits endure today, and he marks their origin at "the awareness of God" that struck him during his month alone.

If you have companions, you have conversation and fellowship. But if you travel solo, Steinbeck observed, you have your thoughts, and they grow bigger. "When the quality of aloneness settles down, past, present, and future all flow together. A memory, a present event, and a forecast all equally present." In other words, traveling alone forces you out of your comfort zone, turns off much of the noise we use to distract ourselves from the lonely worries we try to deny we even have. For me, images outside the window from solo train rides on my college visits in the summer of 1989 and while studying abroad in 1992–93 are still present in my mind's eye as if they were last night. I can see specific parts of the Bronx under the tracks as I was deciding where I would go to college, and then I turn on the mental video of the Dutch countryside as I was reaching resolve about the woman to whom I would likely propose.

Martin and his wife are now trying to impart the value of active travel to their girls. On trips to different cities, they have started a new routine of sending their preteen daughter to scout the day's sightseeing. She is given "a Metro card, a phone, and $20. Even those little trips out into the world alone make a difference to her," the proud father told me. "Without adults around she becomes a better observer." She's a storyteller when she returns, and it has "boosted her confidence and sense of independence." The habit of scouting is increasingly a part of her identity, and her younger siblings think she's courageous and have an emerging appetite to follow her path-finding.

My friend Sean took his first solo trip at the age of 18, flying to Chicago from his hometown of Philadelphia to visit colleges. He'd been in the air only once before, a thirty-minute ride in a single-engine prop plane for his tenth birthday. "The big thing I remember is taking the train downtown and just walking all over—probably unwise in 1984, as the un-coolest kid (I was no doubt wearing my treasured velour shirt, feathered hair parted in the middle—a real lady killer). But I just walked around the Randolph Street station up by the Chicago River." Even though Philadelphia also has its skyscrapers, the high rises and "the fake Gothic" of Chicago seemed so different—not least because Sean was the one deciding where to walk, what to do, and how long to gaze up.

More than the physical differences between the cities, though, was the social difference: here his identity would not be predetermined by the line between Irish Catholic and non–Irish Catholic. His uncles, policemen and union workers, thought it was "crazy" to go to Chicago. Every one of his cousins who had gone to college "went to a 'Big Five' Philly school," so when he got a scholarship to St. Joe's, the family believed it was done; there was no decision to be made. (When Sean later won a scholarship to attend graduate school at Oxford, the same uncles told him it was "disloyal to go to school in a country that had oppressed the Irish.") Despite the fact that "my parents thought I was out of my mind," he concluded that Chicago "was exactly the break I so wanted from my family, from Philadelphia, to have my own life." He had dreams that were bigger than that neighborhood. He needed some space.

It was a decision that he couldn't have seen clearly enough to make in Philadelphia. Like Tom Petty "Runnin' Down a Dream," Sean was "goin' wherever it leads," convinced now that everything was possible. He would know a fresh start:

> *There's something good waitin' down this road*
> *I'm pickin' up whatever's mine*
> *Yeah runnin' down a dream*
> *That never would come to me*

EXPLORATION AS A LIBERAL ART: LEARNING HOW TO SEE

How many times have you been surprised by how different a place looks in person from what you saw in a book or on the web? Many places are bigger. No photograph can capture the vastness of the Grand Canyon or the majesty of the Nile. But the western end of the Mediterranean is actually much smaller than you imagine—the Strait of Gibraltar that separates Africa and Europe is only nine miles wide. Thus the relationship between the two continents—and between Morocco and Spain, Libya and France today, or Hippo and Rome in Augustine's day—became very different to me when I explored many different ports around the Mediterranean (some by train, some by ferry) at age 20. I finally started to see the sea in my mind's eye as the horizontal oval-shaped body of water that it is, rather than merely as an eastern cove off of the Atlantic as I'd incorrectly imagined it. A sunset looks different in Nice than it does in Tel Aviv or Rome or Athens—or Fremont, for that matter. Venice smells like stagnant water. Addis Ababa smells like an endless campfire. But you won't know until you go and experience those things with your senses.

Travel at its most enchanting is exploration and, as landscape historian John Stilgoe puts it, "exploration is a liberal art." What does that mean? That exploration is on the same plane as literature and philosophy? No—it's more fundamental than that. Exploration is "an art that liberates, that frees, that opens away from narrowness." Imagine that you're blind but like to take walks. Surely your sense of smell is more refined than most other people's. Now, imagine you gain sight for the first time. That's what all new exploring should be like.

I took Stilgoe's class on the history of the built environment in college. Imagine not just architecture or the history of buildings but the history of all material things and the layering up of them over time. With a bowtie and a Boston accent that made him the quintessential representative of New England professors to me, this award-winning historian and photographer had something of a cult following. His lectures were always packed. Though his courses were nominally about how people have shaped and built up their physical surroundings over time (think: time-lapsed photography of a city from before it was founded until it was fully built), Stilgoe maintained that he was really offering an education in *learning how to see*. And indeed, he would alternately whisper and shout to a completely dark classroom for ninety minutes as images of the built landscape flashed across a movie-theater-sized screen, keeping all three hundred of his students entranced twice a week. (Six years later in New Haven, I had the privilege of listening to another great historian of built American landscapes, Vincent Scully, give similar lectures for a semester. Their approaches are very different, so I recommend reading at least one book by each of them.) Buildings that I walked by thirty times a week suddenly came alive, fighting with their neighbors. (Along the same line, the enclosed parts of the car frame right behind the rear passenger windows suddenly made sense, recalling the design of horse-drawn carriages more than a century ago.) In a similar way, Stilgoe's books call inanimate objects to life, announcing their history to those with eyes to see. "History is on the wall," he writes in *Outside Lies Magic,* "but only those willing to look up from newspaper or laptop computer glimpse it and ponder."

Stilgoe encourages his students to explore their surroundings slowly and with "deliberate absence of mind," by which he means not bringing what we know or assume of the world. Things are not always as they seem. Exploring the landscape in this manner "first awakens the dormant resiliency of youth, the easy willingness to admit to making a wrong turn and go back a block, the comfortable understanding that some explorations take more than an afternoon, the certain knowledge that lots of things in the wide world just down the street make no immediate sense."

A "palimpsest" is a piece of paper that has had most or all of its writing scraped off, to be replaced by other writing—sometimes many times over. Stilgoe says that the human landscape is like that. "An acute, mindful explorer who holds up the palimpsest to the light sees something of the earlier message," and the "careful, confident explorer of the built environment soon sees all sorts of traces of past generations." Look up! Look around.

None of my friends and coworkers put it quite this poetically, but it is what many of them told me less eloquently: Once they saw something new about the world, they could not unsee it. It was like going from two-dimensional to three-dimensional sight. It was like how Michael Jordan in his heyday in the 1990s, when he would put up fifty or sixty points per game on consecutive nights, would say that it was sometimes too easy—that when his "vision of the hoop was on," the hoop seemed gigantic, like he was throwing the ball off the edge of the Grand Canyon. It just wasn't possible to miss.

Once you can see a distinction, the vision to see it goes with you. Eskimos have more than fifty different words for snow, some of them the result of linguistic differences across geography, but mostly the result of people who know snow so well and who experience it so often that they are able to recognize many differences in snow density and texture. Someone living in Houston who sees it only on television just observes "snow," but he would be changed by spending a winter in Juneau. *Seeing distinctions is a learned habit.* When you travel to another continent and study new forms of vegetation, it increases your awareness of differences in vegetation in your own country once you return home. When you go on a safari, you think about cats' differences differently when you return to suburbia. When you buy a new vehicle, you tend to notice many more of your make and model on the road than you observed the day before you made the purchase.

Fine-tune your eyes. Ditch as much of the demanding immediacy as possible while traveling, so that you can be fully present where you are. You're not going to have the same experience if you are in part of the developing world that has cell service and you're constantly checking the scores or whiling away your time "liking" the Instagram pics your friends posted of *their* trips.

When Steinbeck left New York for his early 1960s voyage, he was trying to cure a "virus of restlessness" that had come over him. He had come to see cities as highly similar everywhere and not nearly as diverse as the local cultures outside them: "New York is no more America than Paris is France or London is England." Most urban places have some habits of life that are roughly the same in Los Angeles or New York or London or Bangkok. People may look different and speak different languages, climates may vary, topography changes, but a city is mostly a city. So he struck out to see the variety of rural America, where life was defined by the kind of crops or livestock raised on a particular stretch of land. Traveling 10,000 miles over eleven weeks, Steinbeck and Charley discovered new places and rediscovered familiar ones from New York to Maine, to Oregon, to California, to Texas, to the Deep South, and then back to the Northeast. "I discovered that I did not know my own country" anymore, Steinbeck confessed. "I, an American writer, writing about America, was working from memory, and the memory is at best a faulty warpy reservoir." But what he rediscovered was not always encouraging. The country was losing some of its regional distinctiveness. Food, he noticed, was beginning to taste blandly similar everywhere he went. He was prescient: a flattening homogenization of the nation was coming quickly.

A decade later in 1971, my friend Marcus, then age 11, and his family took a three-month journey similar to the one Steinbeck had taken. After spending a year retrofitting an old school bus over evenings and weekends, the family set out to discover their continent. They crossed the width of Canada, made a sharp left in Vancouver down the West Coast through Washington, Oregon, and California into Mexico, then back up across the United States. "I slept in a tent every day for sixty-two days and got to see how people lived in very different situations, even within North America," he said. The transformative event led to a replay in Europe four years later, as they spent another summer traveling when he was 15. The campground in Holland where they learned that Nixon had resigned is still vivid in his mind's eye. And the "passing through Checkpoint Charlie from West Berlin into East Germany" is still among the "most compelling" and life-orienting experiences of his youth. "First time I ever saw soldiers with guns walking the streets. Creeped me out to no end," and it drove his decision to become politically active.

The exposure to and "zest for travel" that his parents inculcated has now profoundly shaped the way Marcus is raising his own children. He has worked in many countries and visited forty-seven and counting. He and his wife also resolved that they would "make sure our kids visited a new country for every year of their life," including places where they didn't feel like they could possibly fit in. Spring breaks in China, Colombia, Vietnam, Argentina, Russia, and Italy are obviously not the norm for their peers, but it led to a confidence in going anywhere and conquering the logistical challenges; their three children have all subsequently studied and worked abroad. They are all hooked in getting to know their world better, and they "understand that the world is not flat—that there are very different ways of living and looking at the world, different value constructs and means of social organization that are as legitimate as those they grew up in."

SUCKING THE MARROW

Leaving home for the first time, without parents looking over your shoulder, is a rite of passage, a thrill. Dan recalls a two-month excursion through Western Europe and (accidentally) a bit of Eastern Europe during the Cold War. He budgeted $12 a day and mostly stuck to it. As a 21-year-old trying to find his way in the world, Dan called the experience "liberation from the shackles of daily life." His parents were the resident managers at a poor nursing home in inland northern California. Rules required that residents "be ambulatory, but some weren't," so in practice it was his job to help them navigate. His official job as a kid was as a janitor. "It was a real job. My mom was psycho about everything being clean *every day*. I also did most of the dish-washing and, when I could drive, transporting to doctor's appointments." Because times were tight, his dad always had a side project "as a builder or razing some structure." Although Dan looks back now at that period as having taught him discipline and kept him from the drugs that many of his friends ended up addicted to, he also recalls that his "father's assumption was that I should always be working in the nursing home" or helping "clear yards, dig ditches, etc."

Dan was curious about the broader world, but his father considered formal education a distraction. When "I'd be reading another book, that tended to piss him off." It was on the train a continent away that Dan, in his early twenties, first had the liberty to make his own choices and to follow his curiosity—and to read on his own schedule.

Travel as an escape, especially from a stifling, oppressive home, in search of freedom has been a staple of coming-of-age literature for generations. "We gotta get out of this place, if it's the last thing we ever do" has also been a centerpiece of rock and roll since the genre began. Even the celebration of roots (think: Springsteen, and half of all country music) is framed against the backdrop of first needing to doubt and rebel against the initially stifling nature of the small town. Even if you'll "prob'ly die in a small town," you first need a contrast with some other big towns, as John Mellencamp tells us.

The greatest novel in American literature, Mark Twain's *Adventures of Huckleberry Finn,* is about this escape. Huck flees his drunken, abusive father and Jim steals away from a life of bondage. Together they escape down the Mississippi River on a makeshift raft, where they are beholden to no one—at least for a while. "It's lovely to live on a raft," Huck explains.

> We had the sky, up there, all speckled with stars, and we used to lay
> on our backs and look up at them, and discuss about whether they was

made, or only just happened—Jim he allowed they was made, but I allowed they happened; I judged it would have took too long to make so
many . . . We catched fish, and talked, and we took a swim now and then
to keep off sleepiness.

Even when they were merely "drifting down the big still river, laying
on our backs looking up at the stars," with little urge to converse, even
then they remained free from the slave master and from the father's
rage.

Travel compels the reconsideration of the world free of many social
conventions. The more time you spend in other cultures, the clearer it
becomes that almost every fad, every passing phase you thought important isn't terribly important after all. When you leave on a trip, you
are forced to unclutter yourself not just from unimportant stuff to pack
but also from low-priority tasks and stresses. Something happens when
you're packing late the night before a scheduled 5:00 a.m. flight and you
still have materials for twenty-seven tasks to pack and complete. You can
take only five; you have to abandon twenty-two. And once you set sail or
get in the air, the five tasks you brought with you to finish weren't nearly
as vital as you thought. You never touch three of the supposed priority
five. The world doesn't end.

When you arrive wherever you're going, you learn that people in
other places don't have the same stresses you have. And you don't have
the same stresses they do. Everyone's rat race is different. Theirs isn't that
compelling to you—and once you grasp that, much of yours then becomes less compelling to you as well. There's nothing like a few miles—
or a few hundred, or a few thousand—to help you gain some perspective
on what's really important. And here's the trick—it's similar to the kind
of perspective that you gain over the course of years and decades as you
grow older. Traveling helps condition you to look for it.

Poet-statesman Johann Wolfgang von Goethe traveled through Italy
in the mid-eighteenth century, seeking to escape the rat race of genteel
court society in Germany. Upon crossing the Alps into Italy, Goethe felt
relief flood over him. In Naples, he wrote back to a confidante, "here I
only want to *live*, forgetting myself and the world." The euphoric freedom continued for weeks: "Naples is a paradise; everyone lives in a state

of intoxicated self-forgetfulness, myself included. I seem to be a completely different person whom I hardly recognize. Yesterday I thought to myself: Either you were mad before, or you are mad now." One of them had to be true, because the two lives were so divergent.

The most brilliant American chronicling of this desire to live, to forget both oneself and the social demands of the world, was given to us by Henry David Thoreau. Needing to explain his 1845 move to the woods near Walden Pond, he evangelized for simpler living: "I went into the woods because I wished to live deliberately, to front only the essential facts of life, and see if I could not learn what it had to teach, and not, when I came to die, discover that I had not lived." To live deliberately is to live with intent, to use your brain, to take nothing for granted, and to decide what is necessary for living and what isn't. To choose. At a time in American history when the country was rapidly expanding, when people were connecting as never before by rail and telegraph, Thoreau took pains not to be too attached to the immediacy of material things. "Our inventions," he wrote, "are wont to be pretty toys, which distract our attention from serious things."

Thoreau yearned to squeeze out the trivial and the distracting and to double down on the substantive: "I did not wish to live what was not life, living is so dear; nor did I wish to practice resignation, unless it was quite necessary. I wanted to live deep and suck out all the marrow of life." He wanted to reclaim his days, "to live so sturdily and Spartan-like as to put to rout all that was not life, to cut a broad swath and shave close, to drive life into a corner, and reduce it to its lowest terms, and, if it proved to be mean, why then to get the whole and genuine meanness of it." But if he found something that proved to be tender, then he wanted "to know it by experience, and be able to give a true account of it in my next excursion."

Many of those I've questioned about youthful travel ended up going through a sort of "prioritization conversion," attempting to reorder their lives after experiencing extreme poverty—and contrasting the deprivation with our excess. Again Steinbeck, traveling America: Our cities are now "like badger holes, ringed with trash—all of them—surrounded by piles of wrecked and rusting automobiles, and almost smothered in rubbish. Everything we use comes in boxes, cartons, bins, the so-called packaging we love so much. The mountain of things we throw away is much greater than the things we use."

My friend Victor went to Ecuador twenty-five years ago, supposedly for the purpose of improving his Spanish. And he still lobbies every high school senior he meets to commit to at least one semester abroad, both to become bilingual and simply because our "cookie-cutter educational system leaves most of us clueless about the rest of the world—geographies, people, groups, history, and so on." His life-changing learning, though, was ultimately not grammar and vocabulary, but rather seeing for the first time what living day to day looked like. A few of the families he met literally did not know where their next meal would come from. It is one thing to have data on a page describing a poverty rate or an infant mortality rate, he told me, but it's another matter altogether "when you see it up close, meet some actual people, and really realize the human experience of mass poverty." Not to mention your own prosperity: "It made me realize that America's poor are rich by comparison and that my middle-class life was one of immense privilege" from the vantage point of history. Americans at that time earned $65 a day on average; the typical Ecuadorian earned more like $5 a day. Victor didn't come home from Quito with a t-shirt, but instead with a lifelong realization that there "are few things that will force you to work through your own belief system better than being in the midst of a different culture."

These friends' learnings—about necessity, about meaning, about what is essential versus what is accidental—echo Mark Twain: "Broad, wholesome, charitable views of men and things cannot be acquired by vegetating in one little corner of the earth all one's lifetime." Thoughtful travel is an obligatory part of education because travel "is fatal to prejudice, bigotry and narrow-mindedness, and many of our people need it sorely on these accounts." It is somewhat like the exercise of assigning a student in a debate the task of arguing for the position that they reject. Articulating both sides of an issue doesn't just broaden your mind—and strengthen your own argument, if it survives the scrutiny—it also treats your interlocutor with dignity.

Shorter version: Walking a mile in another man's shoes, in his country, produces understanding, empathy, and healthy doses of self-reflection, self-criticism, and gratitude.

PACKING MY MENTAL SUITCASE

There is not any one place your kids must go. Nor is there any one particular moment at which it must happen. The central goal to have in mind for your budding travelers isn't complicated: acquiring vivid contrasts. We are trying to help adolescent eyes focus for the first time on the sea of assumptions in which they swim at home.

In my eclectic work history as a business strategist, college president, and now senator, I've met plenty of kings, presidents, prime ministers, and global CEOs. Many of these have been fascinating people, and all of them have been powerful, but when I talk with high school and college kids they tend to badly overvalue these somewhat unique trips. In reality, none of these journeys mattered a fraction as much or were nearly as transformative as a series of trips I took before my twenty-first birthday.

Four adventures—at ages 8, 15, 17, and 20—changed my life permanently. First, I will never forget the first time I saw the ocean. It was February of 1980, and I was turning 8. My parents decided the family would take a trip to Florida. This was delightfully shocking (we had little money) and scary. Today I board a dozen planes every month as I commute weekly between my home in Nebraska and my job in Washington, DC. But that was the first time I'd ever set foot on an aircraft, and I was terrified we would crash. My dad, ever entrepreneurial, couldn't have cared less about my fear of flying. In fact, he happily announced that he had found a way to intentionally book us on a double-connection in order to get us first-time fliers an extra takeoff and landing under our belts. Fears are to be conquered. And so the five of us flew from Omaha to Kansas City, to St. Louis, to Orlando.

For a boy of 8, the world looms large—and in hindsight, strangely deformed. My early sense of geography was anchored around eight cities in six states, all but one of them adjacent to Nebraska: Ames, Columbia, Stillwater and Norman, Manhattan and Lawrence, Boulder, and, far, far to the southeast—like a lodestar—Miami. Practically every child raised on Cornhusker football immediately knows the meaning of those cities: they were the home campuses of the (now defunct) Big Eight Conference. Every kid knew the eight schools: two Oklahomas, two Kansases, Missouri, Iowa State, Colorado, and Nebraska. And Miami was the site of the most important game of the year: the Orange Bowl, where for three decades it was a decent bet that Nebraska or Oklahoma would face off against some squad to battle for the national championship at 8:00 p.m. on January 1 on NBC with Don Criqui in the booth.

On a map, Miami is practically a foreign country to a kid in a land-locked state with neither beaches nor mountains. It sits near the end of a jutting mass surrounded on almost every side by *so . . . much . . . blue.* I had seen pictures in books and the stage-setting imagery for the Orange Bowl on television, but the vision in my head was much different than the reality of it. Naturally, we did the things tourists in Florida do—Disneyworld and Epcot Center, Busch Gardens, and the Daytona Speedway. We went to a water park called Wet and Wild, where I stood on my tiptoes to illicitly clear the height bar for the big-kid waterslides. But the main thing—the memory that sticks—is seeing the Atlantic and marveling at how vast it was. And then driving west across the state and wondering at the seemingly endless Gulf of Mexico too.

That was the first time in my life I began to get a sense of topography as diverse—that the flat, grain elevator–punctuated expanses of my county that seemed like the default norm were actually not the norm anyplace else in the world. Part of travel is simply that: leaving your native geography and topography, experiencing those differences, and expanding your mental suitcase.

My second formative trip was closer to home—about fifty miles away in a neighboring town. I had grown up with dad driving me every week of my life to some sporting event—big or small, high school or college, near or far. Sometimes dad was working—as a coach, or scout, or referee—but often we just watched and diagrammed plays, and he taught me by ex-plaining what he'd be telling the team if he were on the football sidelines or wrestling mat edge. (To this day, my dream is still to be the offensive coordinator for the Huskers, the same job I've wanted since 1979—and surely my dad's diagramming of football plays is much of why.) But when I was 15, somehow these long-familiar sporting events became new and textured when I became the one driving my friends (at that time you could get your driver's license when you were 14 in Nebraska). I asked my parents for permission to submit a note to skip school to take my buddies to the state track meet. Incredibly, they said yes—telling me that I had been responsible in driving near town so I could now venture farther.

Incidentally, Sarah, a friend I didn't meet until a decade after college, tells virtually the exact same story of her high school coming-of-age trip: she and three friends were allowed to travel from home, unsupervised—to a state basketball tournament. A similar road trip had been an annual tradition for the girls since they were 10, but always with their fathers. When they turned 17, their parents agreed to let them make the 150-mile drive on their own. "Our parents let us ditch school," she told me, "and we were there Thursday through Sunday." Sarah has since worked abroad a fair amount—in France, Italy, Israel, Saudi Arabia, Kenya, and Australia. Undaunted now by travel, she believes her self-confidence is rooted in that first parental decision to let her take that 150-mile baby step. Her view of the world is heavily shaped by conversations and meals with "the Israeli mom living in Sderot whose bus stop has been outfitted as a bomb shelter and who is just trying to keep her children safe" and the "college president in Kenya trying to make sure there is enough potable water for his students." The seeds of how to plan today's 15,000-mile treks were sown by a mom's decision to let her plan her initial voyage. She knew her parents would have been able to cover the 150 miles quickly to help out, but it was a training-wheels-off dry run at "taking ownership" and "fending for herself." As soon as it worked, she was no longer "intimidated about the logistics or worried that something would go wrong." Of course "stuff goes wrong, and of course there are disappointments, but you adjust."

Two weeks after my voyage to the state track meet, I made the request again, this time to attend the state tennis tournament. None of us cared about tennis, mind you (although watching Mary Jane Manhart play added to the experience). It was mainly just a way to skip school and drive to Omaha, which wasn't actually a hundred times the size of our farm-dependent town but seemed to be. Once we had driven to another town by ourselves and met kids from other schools, a new slate of possibilities opened up. Before long, my friends and I were attending every state championship—and occasionally dating girls who lived fifty miles away.

It was then a much smaller step two years later when my parents consented to another set of transformative trips: they allowed me to travel alone to the East Coast to visit the colleges that were recruiting me for wrestling. I took three trips by plane, train, and bus, from Nebraska to Virginia to Massachusetts and many places in between. These voyages in 1989 were my first time feeling alone for an extended period. I could get myself into trouble if I chose to—and it was immediately apparent that making the right choice while alone was different than submitting to a physically present parent or other external constraint.

When the Berlin Wall fell in November 1989, I felt the itch to go abroad for the first time. Growing up just fifty miles from the U.S. Strategic Air Command in Omaha, one of the prime targets for the Soviet Union's nuclear missiles, meant that the Cold War had been very much alive in the minds of my classmates and me. We had regular emergency drills at my elementary school, not only for tornados but also for bombs. The experience left a lasting impression, creating an early curiosity to see East and West Berlin, East and West Germany, Eastern and Western Europe.

In 1992 and 1993, I spent most of a year in Europe—a few months of it in the east, where half of the population had only recently escaped decades of Soviet domination, and where the steel cases in the grocery stores were still shockingly empty. A friend, Scott, had just moved to East Berlin, and we decided to travel together for a month, mostly by train. As we embarked on our cash-strapped tour, we relied on train schedules and used travel books and intelligence from other travelers— including the oddly cautious Americans who would sew Canadian flags on their packs to discourage attention—to get around. I read plenty of those "dollar-a-day" books that provided tips and tricks for making your deutsche mark or franc or lira stretch. And we learned to take overnight trains to cities eight to ten hours away. That way we could sleep on the train instead of paying for a hostel. Instead of spending money on meals at cafés, we would keep jars of peanut butter and mustard in our backpacks and buy fresh loaves of bread in whatever town we arrived. It wasn't Canadian duck egg quality, but I can still almost taste a specific sweet loaf in Monte Carlo, memorable not least because I had seen the movie *Dirty Rotten Scoundrels* a couple months before and kept expecting Michael Caine to emerge to evict vagrants like us from Beaumont-sur-Mer.

We learned to be skeptical of vendors and especially hoteliers. In the days before Yelp and TripAdvisor, finding a decent hostel or cheap hotel was generally a matter of word of mouth and good luck near the train station. Once, when Scott and I arrived in Athens at midnight, we found what we thought was an adequate hotel. We asked the clerk to show us the room before agreeing to pay for the night. He showed us a room that looked clean enough, so we said yes. But after we paid, the key he gave us turned out not to work in that door when we got back to it. Instead, it opened the door across the hall—to a much shabbier room with an open drain on the floor between the two beds as the only toilet. We were never physically threatened in Greece (as we had been by zealous rug salesmen in North Africa), but this kind of lodging bait-and-switch was a common scheme that took time to sniff out.

The best lesson for learning gratitude on this European tour was ultimately not the hunger pangs until we finally found bread on the Riviera, nor was it the grumpy cop enforcing a no sleeping rule in the Amsterdam train station, but rather a frigid January night. Nearly out of money and needing to cross the Adriatic Sea off of Albania, we economized by booking an outdoor passage on an overnight, cruise-ship-sized ferry boat. It was below freezing, and we slept on deck chairs after putting on every article of clothing in our backpacks. My view of how to prioritize in future packing was forever changed that night. (See the Stepping Stone on packing at the end of this chapter.)

All of these experiences, whether good or bad—from the delightful nights of guitar-singing on the Charles River Bridge in Prague to the miserable robbery outside Rome (fortunately our cash and passports were hidden away from the electronics and batteries that the thieves seized)—ultimately contributed to a year that was far more transformative and educational than any year of my college classes.

BREAKING BREAD WITH WIDOWS

But one event towers above all the others from that year—an event that could never have been planned. It was the Sunday before Christmas 1992, and a group of older widows in Berlin invited Scott and me for lunch after church in one of their apartments. One thing led to another, and we began talking about World War II. I come from a part of Nebraska heavily settled by German immigrants between 1885 and 1910. Many of the people in these communities had taught school and conducted civic business in German until World War I, when concern with immigrant communities and skeptical non-Germans drove them to convert to English. My conversation with these widows began with their remembrances of Germans who had migrated to America, but it quickly turned to Hitler's rise to power and sensitive debates about what responsibility ordinary Germans bore for what transpired. It was heavy stuff and the long conversation, combined with heavy German food, led to bonding among five people divided by generations and language, who hadn't previously known each other.

Eventually, when the host said she wanted to change the subject, I assumed it would be to something less emotionally burdensome. Instead, she asked Scott and me to come to the window. She pointed to the yard behind her building. "We all hoped we would be liberated by your grandfathers, by Americans." (Both of my grandfathers had in fact gotten the call from Uncle Sam to fight in the war.) She paused and looked us both in the eye. "Unfortunately, the Russians got to this part of Berlin first." Another pause, and then: "My rapist is buried back there," pointing to a corner of the yard.

As we let this sink in, she described in gruesome detail being raped by two soldiers at the age of 15, and how she grieved and bonded with the other women in her family and in her building (the men were all away fighting) while the Russians were "liberating" them. She then explained how her mother and aunt took matters into their own hands, including not just the shooting but also the clean-up—and then the role she played assisting in the burial.

These women at lunch had had experiences that were so different from mine, and yet our conversations over a meal quickly revealed our common humanity and set the stage for the decades of unanticipated bonding that I've had while traveling. It "rebooted" my sense of priorities, my sense of what we all share.

My current job as a senator from Nebraska has brought me to war zones in Iraq and Afghanistan and allowed me to see firsthand the cascading Syrian refugee crises. I've met with foreign military leaders and intelligence officers in many countries where distinguishing the good guys and the bad guys is harder than it should be. After one such meeting with Pakistani leaders about their war against jihadists in central Asia, I remember concluding that in the face of particularly grotesque threat, a provisional alliance—though very hard to explain—was clearly the least bad option of a bunch of bad options, at least for a time. Those of us in this particular (classified) meeting did not agree on much, and certainly didn't agree on what the bounds of ethical action by a government might look like, but we still shared a common goal of disrupting a particular network of folks who engaged in human trafficking and killing in the name of religion.

Joe Donnelly, a Democratic senator from Indiana, was with me at these meetings in the northwest tribal region of Pakistan, and I cannot recall a single issue on which we differed there. To hear the national media talk about it, Republicans and Democrats never agree on anything. Now, to be sure, Joe and I differ on a broad range of domestic and economic policy matters. But in the face of these jihadi suicide bombings, Republican and Democratic labels didn't mean much; you couldn't find an inch of daylight between these two Americans. Travel to Pakistan had been a kind of "rebooting" of what was most important, much like my trip to East Germany had been for me a quarter century earlier.

TOURISM NOT TRAVEL is the default mode of travel in our culture of cheap amusements. My guess is that for most of us, our kids show up on day one of any trip we take as a family having done little more than show up. Like much of what I discuss in this book, teaching your kids the right way to do something will require some effort. If you really want your kids to become explorers, to experience the growth that traveling can bring, you have to (1) encourage them to travel alone, even if it means having to overcome your own fears of what might happen; and (2) offer them a philosophy of travel that goes against the consumerist grain.

With regard to point one, we can start by removing the bubble wrap and encouraging those first ventures out on their own, however small the baby steps—even having your 8-year-old plan and map the family's urban hike. Eventually your 12-year-old's solo daytrip to a nearby city might progress to your teen's extended visit to a culture thousands of miles away. Some kids don't need encouragement to explore; others have to be pushed to overcome fear of the new and different.

The philosophy of travel starts with the important lesson that travel is an *active* pursuit that requires preparation (actually "work" if you want to call it what it really is) and openness. If you don't know the language, you can certainly learn basic travel phrases and muster up the courage to use them. I can't tell you how many wonderful serendipitous encounters I had simply because I made the effort to greet people in their own language, though of course that required enduring a few awkward moments of people who didn't want to talk to a foreigner. Read about the history and culture of a place *before* you go. If you're visiting Normandy, you shouldn't be learning about its role in World War II from a brochure the day you arrive. Watch a dozen documentary movies about it. Then, follow through by learning more about things that piqued your interest on your trip when you return. Try new things, even if they seem uncomfortably different. It's okay to make mistakes and get lost. The more you try new things—eat the local food, drink the local drink—the more you'll feel you've actually visited rather than just passed through a place.

Exploration should awaken an insatiable desire to read as you "travail." As my train rolled out of Berlin just before Christmas 1992, my head was spinning, and I had the deep urge to study the history of Russian conduct in World War II. This wasn't homework mandated by some teacher with power over my transcript; this was an internally motivated need to know more. Done right, travel should awaken a desire to read history and geography and comparative economics. Read religious pilgrimage logs. Read about explorers who sought new trade routes and blazed trails for new settlements. Read about itinerant Americans seeking fame and fortune who set out west and didn't stop until they reached the Pacific. Travel is a way to experience history. Reading Thucydides's *History of the Peloponnesian War* for an ancient history course can be edifying . . . but dry. Now read him while hiking the hills along the coast of the Aegean Sea. Half a dozen of my friends offered some version of this comment: "My young experiences abroad gave me time to reflect, and to mature, and they made me yearn to read." We travel across not just place but also time to have the experience of wrestling with different ways of living. And when we return, nothing is ever the same. For our eyes have been changed.

And so we need more travel companions, both embodied and—as we'll find in the next chapter—in literature.

STEPPING STONES TO AWAKEN TRAVEL APPETITES

Walk More, Pack Lighter, and Fill Your Home with Maps

The best way to inspire curiosity in your kids about other places is, first, to take them other places and, second, to let them help plan the family's treks. The challenge isn't hard intellectually; it just requires planning and forethought:

- Start with the mundane when they're young. Print out a big map of the roads to grandma's house, highlight the path you will take, and hang the map on the back of the front seat so your child can follow it on the drive. Reverse the highlighting of the course on the way home. Talk about it a lot.
- Let your 6-year-old order the pizza, let her pay the delivery person, and make her ask how he or she got to your house. Then go get the maps out again.
- Take your kids on work travel. My last two jobs (college president and senator) have both required many nights per month away from home. People at my meetings might find it odd to have a 5-, 10-, or 15-year-old along and reading in the back of the room. So what? My kids' time with dad, and my introducing them to geographies and cultures, is far more important than submitting to our social norms about age segregation. My kids have traveled with me for work for years—and it not only has created a wonderful set of memories and shared experiences; it has also driven us to read books together in ways that classroom instruction alone would not have.
- Stop at roadside historical markers.
- Assign your kids the task of planning family vacations. Start by giving them a day to fill—perhaps just one urban hike. Then let them plan a whole trip. Let them make mistakes—that's the best part and where they'll learn the most.
- If you're from the city, take your family and go live (not vacation) in the country for weeks. If you're from the country, go live in a city. This won't work for some jobs with set schedules and set geographies, but fewer and fewer of us will be working in such jobs without interruption for our whole lives going forward. I've discussed this "go live somewhere else for sixty days" idea with dozens of folks who initially thought it could never work for them, but then a review of their family's calendar over the last five years revealed that in almost every case there had been a window of time when it could have worked if they had been searching for the opportunity. It'll change your family forever.

- Read the journals of great explorers. I live outside a town named for John C. Fremont, an abolitionist senator and the first presidential nominee from the Republican Party (1856). "The Pathfinder," as he was known, became an object of fascination for me as a boy, because I live on one of his famous routes westward, along the north bank of the Platte River. Fremont led four large expeditions into the frontier, established the Bear Flag Republic in California, and united the North and West in popular imagination. There are still times on this big river with my kids, three or four hours after I've left my cell phone behind, when we get lost in both nature and time, perhaps closer to his 1840s voyages than to our twenty-first-century frenzy.

- Let them take a semester-long pause in high school and go live with a relative far away, working a job, preferably something with their hands.

- Watch documentaries about the great explorers. Trace the paths of Leif Erickson and Vasco da Gama and Columbus, who wondered if fortune was just beyond the horizon and went looking. Watch the Ken Burns film on Thomas Jefferson dispatching Meriwether Lewis and William Clark to map and explore the Louisiana Territory and cross the continental divide to the Pacific Northwest before Britain or Spain might have a chance to claim it.

- Become obsessed with lean packing—truly obsessed. Some travelers have perfected the art of packing the bare minimum. Travel writer Susan Heller offers a classic piece of advice: "When preparing to travel, lay out all your clothes and all your money. Then take half the clothes and twice the money." Good rule—you cannot possibly pack for every contingency, so don't try.

- Step one in becoming a lighter packer and better traveler: Buy a good backpack that can hold no more than eighteen or twenty pounds, and for some of your trips, take only what you can easily carry on your back. (Obey the "rule of three": one shirt to wear, one to wash, one to dry.) Take a long trip by train and bus, and learn to love walking . . . Now make your kids each carry all their own gear too—and some of the common materials or food. It will change all of your lives.

EIGHT

BUILD A BOOKSHELF

*Digital Distractions and the Habit of Reading * The Bloodless Revolution*
*From Reading to the Marketplace of Ideas * America the Debate Club*
*Jefferson's Syllabus for Citizenship—and Its Atrophy * The Canon Wars*
*Personal Canon versus National Canon * The Argument for Your Canon, Now*
*My Priority Five-Foot Shelf * Raise Them as If They'll Rule Someday*

Europe was created by history. America was created by philosophy.
—Margaret Thatcher

AMERICA IS A DIFFERENT KIND OF PLACE. IT WAS founded *deliberately,* by people with strong *ideas* about heaven and hell, about rights and responsibilities, about public and private—and about the kind of society that would promote virtuous living and serious thinking.

And it has therefore always been a magnet for the intense.

Our settlers and founders were an opinionated lot—people of controversial ideas, life-and-death ideas. They wanted the liberty to worship and to argue freely, and to not be subject to a Church of England they considered decadent. The Puritans who left the Old World for the New brought with them a particular piety and a strain of democratic civic-mindedness that would eventually give birth to modern constitutional self-government.

We cannot understand them, or this nation of theirs we've inherited, without grasping that one crucial—and at the time radically new—element that made possible the widespread dissemination of the religious and political ideas they carried with them: the printed word.

The men and women who founded our nation did so by riding the wave of the print revolution. Their moment was historically unprecedented, and our failure to remember this neglects the related truth that what we read, or don't read, still drives not only what we believe but also how we engage with each other and how we make decisions about our future. As has been noted often in this book, living in a republic demands a great deal of us. Among the responsibilities of each citizen in a participatory democracy is keeping ourselves sufficiently informed so that we can participate effectively, argue our positions honorably, and, hopefully, forge sufficient consensus to understand each other and then to govern. To this end, our critical faculties must be in top condition—the ability not just to evaluate sources, weigh evidence, and check facts, but also to understand motivations, resolve apparent contradictions, cut through ambiguities, and maybe even discover truths. These skills and habits are in ill repair, and the informed contentiousness that a free republic demands is beleaguered and fraying.

On the way to adulthood, young Americans must develop these skills, for themselves and for us. If they don't, we're all in big trouble. The proliferation of distractions and misdirections is growing worse by the day. As "fake news" stories spreading on social media demonstrate, we all have to be skeptical of things passed along as news. The digital communications revolution will continue to democratize people's access to information in ways that are both healthy and unhealthy. Critical, engaged reading skills are not a luxury, but rather a necessity for responsible adults and responsible citizens.

America's future depends on the kind of thinking that reading presupposes and nourishes—and such thinking demands a rebirth of reading.

DIGITAL DISTRACTIONS AND THE HABIT OF READING

You met my buddy Scott briefly in the last chapter, as the guy with whom I spent the winter of 1992–93 traveling abroad. In the two decades since,

he's spent most of his time back home in Pittsburgh prosecuting crimi-
nals and coaching his five rowdy sons in Little League. As fathers, we
compare notes about parenting—our joy in our kids' development, our
worries about cultural gales threatening to blow them off course, and
our uncertainty about whether we're doing a good enough job toughening them up for the future. Scott is endearingly quirky: When we graduated from Harvard, he had bills to pay and was worried about his own
work ethic; so—without really telling anyone—he went and worked
in an iron foundry for the better part of a year before starting his first
permanent job.

Last year, Scott took a similar lean-in approach to his parenting
when he posed what at first seemed like a simple question, but one that
ended up consuming weeks of my life: "Carrie and I worry that our kids
don't understand the glories of books enough—they don't love them
enough. What books do you want your kids to have read by the time
they leave home?"

Melissa and I work hard to shape our kids toward reading well,
and loving reading, and embracing and really knowing a bunch of good
books, but we'd never put it quite like this. That *end date* on Scott's
query—"by the time they leave home"—nudged us to a new urgency
about our calling to have them be not just functionally literate but fully
habituated to reading important things by the time they depart from
under our roof. We realized that for them to claim their full inheritance
as Americans, they need to read and to understand the role of reading in
our republic. They need to feel a desire in their chests to become people
of the book, even amid the seductive lure of the screen. And this won't
happen without a program for what to read. We aim for our kids to leave
home for college or work, not necessarily having *finished* a great reading
list but definitely having *built* and begun to get to know their own great
starter reading lists.

And so we direct and encourage them: to build their own long-term
reading list, to persuade others to read their favorites, to be humble and
curious in accepting the recommendations of others, and to actively adjust their list as they wrestle with and learn from others. This process
we've created is not the same as claiming that they can develop one fixed
canon of what to read that is right for everyone, but rather that they
should have an evolving list of their own that they will use in prioritizing
their reading of fifty or sixty key books. The primary goal is premised

on the idea that there are only so many hours in a day. This makes it essential that they become stewards of their limited time as they fall in love with reading particular books. The second goal is to encourage them to engage with friends and neighbors and in the process develop a kind of list of "water cooler books" instead of just TV shows. It's fun that my kids can quote some old *Seinfeld* episodes with their cousins, but it's far more meaningful for them to be able to quote some Shakespeare together.

Becoming truly literate is a choice. Reading done well is *not* a passive activity like sitting in front of a screen. It requires a degree of attention, engagement, and active questioning of which most of our children currently have a deficit. The core question is not whether you hold in your hand an old-fashioned paper book or a new electronic book, but rather that even when you read from a screen, you develop the self-discipline to ignore the temptation to check email or scores or social media every few minutes. Reading done well requires a forward-leaning brain. Our culture's ever-present distractions—the obsessive appeals to immediacy ("What 'news' might I be missing?")—conspire to blunt our curiosity and distract us from sustained thought. The relentless pull of the digital world, with its demands that our kids submit to the shiny and the immediate, threatens to make them not just less literate but also more like subjects than citizens. At our house we challenge ourselves to read for sixty minutes without looking at smartphones, televisions, or computers.

Tragically, according to the Bureau of Labor Statistics, the average American now reads only nineteen minutes per day. And younger Americans are reading far less than the national average. That our emerging adults take so little interest in reading today is not just sad for them, it's also a threat to the idea of democracy, which has long assumed the ability to read—and a desire to read. It is not only the content of a book that changes you but the shared community with those who have read it, discussed it, argued about it. Books create communities here and now, as well as across space and time.

Obviously movies and television shows can also create a shared experience of a story, but a culture ruled by print is very different from one ruled by images. Print shapes the way we write, speak, think, and remember. Every presidential election year, people lament the shallow, soundbite-driven spectacles that pass for debates and pine nostalgically for the depth and honest substance that Lincoln and Douglas brought to their encounters. But few Americans would have the patience or the endurance for a Lincoln-Douglas-style debate today. When the two men met on stage in Ottawa, Illinois, on August 21, 1858, they agreed to a format that would have multiple hour-long speeches and rebuttals. At one debate, Douglas spoke three hours uninterrupted. In another forum, Lincoln suggested a break so the audience could "go home, eat dinner, and return refreshed for four more hours of talk."

We aren't wired that way anymore. Or, more accurately, we no longer have the habits—the attention span that comes with concentrated and uninterrupted reading—that would make debates like that conceivable, let alone pleasurable. But a republic's survival still depends on an informed and engaged citizenry. Conscientious reading—and therefore dispassionate deliberation—remains the key to grappling honestly with the pressing issues of time.

The good news is that these skills can be self-taught. And our unique history has much to offer in our quest to revive a love of reading among the rising generation.

THE BLOODLESS REVOLUTION

For our emerging adults to understand America's place in world history—and to participate fully as inheritors in this project of self-government and resilient citizenship—they must first comprehend what an outlier it is, across the sweep of human experience, for every single one of us to have cheap and easy access to books. The origins and perpetuation of this experiment in self-rule are simply not understandable without grasping how unprecedented it was for our Founders to be able to make the argument for the *universal engagement of a people in deliberation* about their own self-governance.

Many of us have played the New Year's Eve games "Who was the most influential person on the globe last year?" or "What was the feel-good recovery story of the year?" or "Which athlete had the best season in sport X?" History professors sometimes have a similar final-exam question: "Which leader had the biggest impact on event Y or cause Z? Who, if he or she didn't exist, would have rendered a certain outcome impossible?" For our purposes, consider this thought experiment: Who is the single most influential maker of the modern world? Who is your man or woman of the millennium?

Some might argue Isaac Newton, whose universal laws of motion and gravity revolutionized the study of physics—or Albert Einstein, who rocked the foundations of Newtonian physics with his theory of relativity and changed the way we look at space and time. Some might say Washington, Jefferson, or Madison. Or Darwin with the theory of evolution. Or Thomas Edison and his lightbulb. Christopher Columbus. Galileo. Da Vinci. Or the inventor of the transistor, the integrated circuit, or ARPANET?

Underneath all of these sectors, one inventor's contribution was foundational for all of the others. If you want to live a free and prosperous life, you need to be literate. If you want a free and prosperous citizenry—or if you want a creative and broadly innovative economy—you need broad literacy. And if you want a literate populace, you need a large supply of reading material. For that, you need a cheap way to produce books, pamphlets, newspapers, journals, and anything else worth reading. For hundreds of years, until the recent arrival of the digital age, you needed a printing press.

It's hard to exaggerate how transformative the move was from a preliterate to a mass-literate culture—and that shift was enabled by one man's invention. For that we owe our thanks to Johannes Gutenberg, my "man of the millennium."

The debut of this historically unique tool in 1454, in the words of one scholar, "heralded nothing less than a *bloodless revolution*. New dimensions of knowledge, its dissemination and networking were opened up by the media revolution that was set in motion," first in Germany, and eventually everywhere. The printing press took the production of books out of the hands of scribes meticulously copying manuscripts for years and gave it instead to typesetters who could produce hundreds of copies of a book in a matter of days. Gutenberg's invention quickly supplanted the old, inefficient way of preserving and transmitting knowledge. "Learning became book-learning," as Lewis Mumford observed, and anybody could acquire it.

In arguably the most radical leveling event in history, the poor suddenly became near equals of the rich in terms of access to information. Almost every other step of inclusion of the previously economically marginalized over the coming centuries depends on this first step of inclusion into the community of those with access to knowledge. Printing democratized reading and fertilized the cultural soil that produced the Renaissance, the Reformation, and the Enlightenment, along with the political, scientific, and industrial revolutions that sprouted in the seventeenth century and reached full flower two centuries later. "More than a triumph of technical ingenuity," the printing press was "one of the most potent agents at the disposal of western civilization" in bringing together scattered ideas of thinkers across time and geography and then spreading those ideas far and wide. And its number-one product—the book—was "one of the most effective means of mastery over the whole world."

Printing had existed before Gutenberg came along, but the process was so grossly inefficient as to not matter much. The prior measure of productivity was that one monk could reproduce, on average, just over one, nearly error-free, handwritten manuscript page per day. Gutenberg's innovations, which eventually produced presses literally millions of times as efficient as monks copying by hand, remade the world overnight—and there was unimaginable demand for the broadsheets and books he made possible. People wanted knowledge. There was insatiable appetite for old wisdom and new information, from near and far, on every subject under the sun. Within fifty years, more than 1,000 printers had set up shop in 350 cities and towns throughout Europe, publishing 30,000 to 35,000 different titles with a total output between 9 and 20 million books.

Unsurprisingly, the first book Gutenberg printed was the Bible. Until about the year 1000, the most literate men in Europe belonged to the clergy, which had a monopoly on this book. Almost everybody else learned through icons and images. Before Gutenberg, churches chained down their Bibles, in part because they were so expensive and difficult to produce, but also to limit their circulation and who was permitted to read them. The cheap and quick production afforded by Gutenberg's press democratized and universalized reading, transforming hierarchies of knowledge and ultimately all of society. The shift from a manuscript culture to a print culture was radical. With manuscripts, the emphasis was on preservation. If you had the only existing copies of Cicero's *Letters* or Euclid's *Geometry*, you weren't likely to share these rare, fragile artifacts. Instead, you kept them safe from vandalism and decay. The physical book was often more important to its owner than the ideas therein. You would want to ensure the survival of those manuscripts for subsequent generations of elite, full-time scholars.

After Gutenberg, print culture made copying simple. If you were a printer, you had different incentives: to see your work spread far and wide. Preservation became less of a concern than *propagation*. Books were transformed from heirlooms to *tools*. And ideas were freed to become viruses, for good and for ill.

FROM READING TO THE MARKETPLACE OF IDEAS

Before Gutenberg, books were printed in Latin, the language of scholars, and thus accessible only to the elites. With the advent of the printing press, it became profitable to bring books to the masses in their own languages. Translating boomed. A new German translation of the Bible arrived in the late 1460s. Then an Italian one in 1471; then "Dutch in 1477, Spanish in 1478, Czech around the same time and Catalan in 1492"; then many French innovations with abridged Bibles; then dozens of competing German editions in the early 1500s. It is impossible to understand the Protestant Reformation of 1517 and beyond without seeing it against the backdrop of frenzied translation activity that created so many more conversations about this book. More translations inevitably meant more competing views, more debate.

This new intellectual stew would not stop at Bibles, of course. Printers soon came out with thousands of tracts, catechisms, and spiritual guides. Then they added math and science titles. Then law books, then reprints of works by ancient Latin and Greek writers, then poetry, and more. This new wealth of literature opened people's minds and changed the way they looked at the world. No longer did everything seem settled. Now that printed copies of texts were available, there "was less hand-copying to do, and there was more time to devote to thinking for oneself."

Uh oh.

Not everyone thought this freer press was a positive development, as printing necessarily upset the status quo. The Catholic Church had initially welcomed the appearance of Gutenberg's Latin Bible, but authorities were less enthusiastic about competing *commentaries* on the Bible. Church officials preferred to have a monopoly on deciding what texts meant. The Vatican would establish its Index of Prohibited Books in the 1550s and update it for the next four hundred years. Governments felt similar angst about debate, and about the problem of organized dissemination of competing views. England made private ownership of presses illegal, because they could be used to publish pamphlets that would incite people. Blasphemy, libel, sedition—even "imagining the king's death"—were all crimes in Britain that were vigorously enforced from the sixteenth century through the end of the eighteenth century.

History textbooks remember Martin Luther, on October 31, 1517, nailing to the church door a letter he wrote to his archbishop disputing the Church's sale of indulgences for the forgiveness of sins. This popular picture of the German monk rattling the world with his little hammer is a fine starting mental image—except if we miss that the ripples of Luther's pebble became a wave not that month in the little town of Wittenberg but rather a year later when printers across the Holy Roman Empire printed and began selling copies of the *95 Theses* everywhere. This was not a typical theological dispute siloed in scholarly circles. Atypically and much more disruptively, Luther's objections to church doctrine were spilling over to regular folks.

It is perhaps more useful to conceive of Luther as becoming the head of a multilevel marketing organization than as exclusively an academic theologian. Church authorities warned Luther about his "heresy" right away in 1517, but people hadn't really paid attention then. It wasn't until the laity had cheap printings of his arguments in 1519 that Rome panicked. He was declared a wanted man, and by 1521, this formerly irrelevant, small-town ranter would be standing before the emperor. He was ordered to recant. His refusal at the Diet of Worms changed the course of history—partly by awakening greater demand for his now widely available writings. Citing *sola scriptura*—the Book alone—Luther was embracing not only the doctrine of salvation by faith alone; he was also explicitly rejecting the pope's claim to be infallible interpreter of what this book meant. Luther aligned himself with printers and with translators—who could get his writings into vernacular languages across the continent—to challenge not just the religious but the social, political, and intellectual orders of his era. It is no accident that Luther later described "printing" as "God's highest and extremest act of Grace."

Gutenberg's "bloodless revolution" would not remain bloodless for long. He was disrupting too much, revealing the brittleness of old institutions. Religious warfare convulsed Europe for more than a century following Luther's protest. Eventually, killing in the name of religion gave way to the new concept of religious toleration and, ultimately, to religious and political liberty.

A rudimentary distinction between "false" or "bad" ideas on the one hand and "illegal" ideas on the other began to bud. It wasn't until the mid-seventeenth century that writers began making a case for religious and press freedom, noting that ideas cannot be extinguished by force; ideas can be countered only by better ideas. But even before it was safe to be controversial, the marketplace of ideas had been born, and the most influential thinkers almost inevitably became marketers.

AMERICA THE DEBATE CLUB

The European settlement of North America in the 1600s is a direct fruit of the more pluralistic world Gutenberg birthed. There is simply no way to understand the 150 years culminating in 1776, and more precisely the 1787 Constitutional Convention in Philadelphia, without understanding how religious conflict—and the conscious, historically rare choice to tolerate this kind of conflict going forward—created this nation. The north star of the American idea is the First Amendment, where freedom of religion, assembly, press, speech, and protest embody our core sense of liberty and how to protect it. All five of these freedoms flow from Gutenberg's revolution and the culture of competing presses it fostered.

The settlers from Massachusetts to Virginia would eventually cease to think of themselves as temporary voyagers away from their old lands, and the first representative of their new shared identity—the "First American"—was Benjamin Franklin. Schoolchildren know him as a signer of the Declaration of Independence and a framer of the Constitution, an inventor, diplomat, meteorologist, scientist, early abolitionist, philanthropist, and raconteur. All these are true, but the beating heart of young Ben Franklin thumps from an earlier experience.

To understand Franklin, we must see first the runaway boy who came of age as a start-up publisher. "Printers are educated in the belief that when men differ in opinion, both sides ought equally to have the advantage of being heard by the publick," he wrote as a young man. Franklin the breadwinner would eventually become wealthy as a pamphleteer and newspaper owner. He was crafty, recognizing that it was wise for a printer in the early 1700s to accommodate a wide-ranging clientele and advocates. Think of him as hosting the *Crossfire* of his day. While he was also figuring out how to make a fortune publishing *Poor Richard's Almanack,* one of the best-selling books of all time, a significant part of his business was printing pamphlets and self-help treatises. Franklin in 1734 published *Every Man His Own Doctor.* Two years later, he followed up with *Every Man His Own Lawyer.* He then published an announcement—sort of joking, sort of not—that the third in the series would be titled *Every Man His Own Priest.* These were practical works with an underlying political purpose: to teach readers how to govern themselves without needing to defer to faraway experts.

There are many crucial debates to be had about gender and race in patriarchal colonial America, but at the level of nonslave households, early America probably set a high-water mark as *the most broadly literate place in human history* to date. These colonists were "as committed to the printed word as any group of people who have ever lived." They braved the ocean with their books as key cargo. Historians estimate that white male literacy ran between 89 and 95 percent, based on written records.

Before a single shot was fired in the Revolutionary War, thousands of pamphlets, tracts, and broadsides had provided intellectual ammunition for the cause of liberty and independence. Thomas Paine's *Common Sense* was "the first American best-seller" and perhaps "one of the best-selling publications of all time," according to literary historian Emily Garcia. The earliest settlers did not take ideas for granted, and they understood the power of the printed word to keep them alive—and eventually the power to start a revolution. Near the end of his life, John Adams told a prominent newspaper editor that "the revolution was effected before the war commenced. The revolution was in the minds and hearts of the people, a change in their religious sentiments of their duties and obligations." Because of Americans' shared reading and thus shared ideas, "this radical change in the principles, opinions, sentiments, and affections of the people was the real American Revolution."

JEFFERSON'S SYLLABUS FOR CITIZENSHIP—AND ITS ATROPHY

How could the atypical engagement of that unique founding moment be sustained? Few of the revolutionaries spent as much time as Thomas Jefferson worrying about the challenge of perpetuating a free, self-governing republic. Born in Shadwell, Virginia, in 1743, the author of the Declaration of Independence was among the most educated of the Founding Fathers. He began French, Latin, and Greek when he was 9, and entered William and Mary at 16. He was a voracious reader, and 6,400 volumes from his personal library served as the starting collection of the rebuilt Library of Congress, which the British had burned in the War of 1812. Earlier in his life, he had sold off much of his library to pay off debts, but he ended up quickly buying more because, as he famously wrote to his friend and rival John Adams, "I cannot live without books."

Jefferson matters to our purposes here not because of his personal learning or his efforts to build the University of Virginia after his presidency, but because he was—despite epic moral contradictions—a democrat at heart. He believed it would take the whole people, not a small governing class, to preserve individual liberty. He wanted "all free children, male and female" to learn the basics of reading, writing, and history. Literacy was at the heart of Jefferson's mission, for he believed it was a precondition of freedom.

"The Sage of Monticello" took a significant role in the education of his nephew, Peter Carr. When he left the country to become U.S. minister to France in 1785, Jefferson continued to write back with advice, giving us a window into his ideal curriculum for a 15-year-old. "It is time for you now to begin to be choice in your reading; to begin to pursue a regular course in it; and not to suffer yourself to be turned to the right or left by reading any thing out of that course." Uncle Thomas provided a plan heavy on Greek and Roman history ("reading everything in the original and not in translations"), beginning with a survey and leading into detailed biographies and histories: "Herodotus, Thucydides, Xenophontis *Hellenica,* Xenophontis *Anabasis,* Arrian, Quintus Curtius,

Diodorus Siculus, Justin." Then there was Greek and Latin poetry, where he listed Virgil, Terence, Homer, Euripides, and Sophocles, among others. Then in English, Milton's *Paradise Lost,* Shakespeare, as well as Alexander Pope's and Jonathan Swift's works, "in order to form your style and your own language." In morality, Jefferson piled on the Stoic philosophers Epictetus and Seneca, Plato's dialogues (all of them), and Cicero's philosophical works (ditto). Although nephew Peter was the age of today's high school sophomore, Jefferson was building a program for him that looks like the reading list of a graduate student in classics.

Why do we care about Jefferson's prescribed curriculum? When we look at his daunting list, most of us first likely feel a bit of guilt that we don't have either the "buns of steel" or the attention to sit that long reading. But then we move to a second feeling of bafflement that they would have read this way for this long. To be clear, Melissa and I do not recommend a program this ruthless or exhaustive for your kids, or ours. Nonetheless, it's useful to understand why Americans abandoned this older program—and whether we might have departed too far from it.

It is beyond our purposes here to delve fully into why Jefferson's canon of Greek and Latin classics was eventually abandoned, but a handful of contributing factors are worth noting briefly. Rapid population growth, and especially the waves of immigrants after the 1820s, left most educators yearning for a simpler and more practical curriculum to help the new arrivals assimilate into American life and jobs. Then, beyond the sheer numerical growth, the greater cultural diversity of the nation produced increased skepticism of classical programs. Third, many developing sciences made demands for time and space in the curriculum—and also produced greater religious doubt, which diminished the shared interest in many texts. Fourth, twentieth-century changes in how reading was taught, and particularly the sidelining of phonics by the "whole language" approach, played a major role in displacing traditional texts.

Perhaps most significantly, in the middle of the twentieth century, television replaced papers and magazines as Americans' primary source for information—and news evolved toward entertainment. Newspaper circulation per capita in the United States declined steadily over the last seventy-five years, from 35 percent of the public just after World War II to well under 15 percent by 2010. Newspapers have further been consolidating and shedding personnel as people are flocking online for their news. During the divisive presidential election of 2016, for example, 44 percent of U.S. adults got much of their news from Facebook. This has many complicated consequences, not least that fake news becomes more prevalent in a world without editors.

In our era of supercharged cultural warring, both traditionalists and progressives often wrongly assume there was one crystal-clear moment where intentionally reading enduring texts was rejected in some final, deliberate choice. But this isn't what happened. Perhaps no one better embodies the complexities of how Americans abandoned shared readings than Charles W. Eliot, who took the helm at Harvard at age 35 in 1869 as the youngest president in the university's four-century history. Eliot, who set out to transform the continent's oldest university from a ministerial training college into a world-class research institution, broke apart the old classics curriculum to make room for more science, math, modern languages, and applied disciplines like engineering. Because of this practical focus, he has often been presumed skeptical of any need for broadly shared books and readings.

This wasn't so. In fact, as he approached retirement in 1909, President Eliot clarified his views, arguing vigorously for "great books" as a democratic means of social mobility. Not everyone could go to Harvard, he told a group of working-class men, but everyone could read like "a Harvard man." A "five-foot shelf" of books, Eliot said, could provide "a good substitute for a liberal education in youth to anyone who would read them with devotion, even if he could spare but fifteen minutes a day for reading." Nationwide, disciplines were being rapidly professionalized and narrowed. But Eliot, who had become a national celebrity-intellectual, remained a zealous advocate for broad reading and the notion of a "common culture."

Editors at Collier, one of the largest publishing houses of the day, were moved by Eliot's crusading and spotted a profit opportunity. They made this pitch: Assemble that "five-foot shelf" you have been referencing in your speeches and we'll market it. The result was the *Harvard Classics,* a fifty-one-volume anthology of works first published in 1909 that aspired to offer "the progress of man . . . from the earliest historical times to the close of the nineteenth century." The anthology was broken down into the following topics: "The History of Civilization," "Religion and Philosophy," "Education," "Science," "Politics," and "Criticism of Literature and the Fine Arts."

In the first twenty years of publication, Collier and Eliot sold an astounding 350,000 sets of the *Harvard Classics.* It turned out this literate nation still had a big appetite for great books.

THE CANON WARS

Many other national leaders attempted to revive and recover a set of books that Americans would share in common as well. Most notably, Robert Maynard Hutchins, president of the University of Chicago from 1929 to 1945, and Mortimer Adler, philosopher and popular author, worried that businesspeople were becoming so specialized in their crafts and thus their training that they were decreasingly well educated. So they set out to develop a set of evening classes for adults, first in Chicago but then in many cities, with the aim of helping thoughtful Americans who wished to fill gaps in their education with critical reading of important books. One of their early students was an executive at Encyclopædia Britannica, Inc., who recognized a business opportunity. He commissioned Hutchins and Adler to identify the most important writings of Western civilization.

But what constitutes a "great book"? Historically a canon has been used to say, definitely read this, but not necessarily that—and the "not necessarily that" portion of the equation has often generated significant fireworks. Hutchins and Adler identified three criteria they used in deciding whether or not to include a work in their fifty-four-volume set: First, it had to be relevant to contemporary times. Second, it had to be worth reading more than once. Third, it had to be a part of what they called "the great conversation about the great ideas." Adler oversaw a staff of more than a hundred researchers, investing an estimated 400,000 hours. The project took eight years and cost Encyclopædia Britannica $2 million, culminating in 1952 with *A Syntopicon,* a two-volume index of thirty-page articles on 102 "Great Ideas," like "Being," "Chance," "Habit," "Happiness," "Revolution," "Time," and "Tyranny." Hutchins wasn't modest about the aims of his publishing effort: "This is more than a set of books, and more than a liberal education," he proclaimed at the series' launch at the Waldorf-Astoria Hotel in New York

City in April 1952. "Great Books of the Western World is an act of piety. Here are the sources of our being. Here is our heritage. This is the West. This is its meaning for mankind."

Many individuals and families purchased the series and were enriched by wrestling with big ideas, but on net, the Adler and Hutchins project failed: it did nothing to slow the long and steady decline of American familiarity with a shared set of classic works in school curricula or the public square. From the 1960s to the 1990s, colleges and universities increasingly did away with required humanities courses. The belief that there should be a "core curriculum," that students should read the same books, fell into disrepute and was entirely expunged by most schools.

At Columbia University, for instance, where generations of students had been molded by the prestigious Core Curriculum, the reading list was assailed for being comprised of mainly "DOWGs"—dead old white guys. Are we indifferent, asked the canon's detractors, to the lived experiences of women, racial minorities, and the poor who often didn't write, and when they did, rarely had their writings preserved? Most importantly, the critics pressed: Who decides which books are in and which are out? Isn't "classic" just another way of saying "what the powerful want you to read" to reinforce the biases that led to their hegemony? Isn't judgment itself discriminatory? Isn't truth what each of us makes of it? To advocates for multiculturalism, any attempt to create a definitive list of what to read was attacked as provincial, ethnocentric, or guilty of reinforcing privilege.

By the late 1980s, the critics had won. *Cultural Literacy* by literary critic E. D. Hirsch and *The Closing of the American Mind* by philosopher and classicist Allan Bloom were published within months of each other, both mourning the decline of any shared reading list for an educated public. Both would quickly become best sellers, but they were basically the laments of the losing side in the curriculum wars. Hirsch regretted that he was often written off as a reactionary, but he actually defined himself as "a political liberal" who simply believed he was "compelled [to] the conclusion that achieving the democratic goal of high universal literacy would require schools to practice a large measure of educational traditionalism." Bloom similarly concluded that the "failure to read good books . . . both enfeebles the vision and strengthens our most fatal tendency—the belief that the here and now is all there is."

Nonetheless, he resigned himself to a mere reclamation effort, believing that the larger quest for a common culture was doomed.

I will argue later in this chapter that E. D. Hirsch was right. In a world in which the media we consume are increasingly tailored to our individual tastes, and in which economic pressures are significant and arguably getting worse, it's essential that we have some common ground, some starting points, for remembering—and for debating. Because the business of picking individual books is so difficult, I'll suggest first that we start by identifying some top-line categories in our personal canons or our prioritized reading and re-reading lists.

But for the broader public, the apparent permanent marginalization of the old Western canon was most vividly highlighted by developments at Stanford in 1987. Democratic presidential candidate Jesse Jackson led five hundred students in a Palo Alto march attacking the "Western Culture" requirement for Stanford freshmen. Newspapers and the evening news across the country seized on the protestors' chants of: "Hey, hey, ho, ho, Western culture's got to go!" When the university decided to abandon the older curriculum, it signaled to many the definitive end of an era.

PERSONAL CANON VERSUS NATIONAL CANON

The main focus of this chapter—and this book—is on rebuilding a culture comprised of resilient, literate, thoughtful *individuals.* This chapter is not chiefly a lament about the decline of the *national* canon. But . . .

The individual is always part of a community, and the literate individual is reading someone else's work, and reading it alongside others. We must tend to that togetherness or we will inevitably spin apart. I think we've made some big wrong turns in abandoning a consensus set of readings. For reading is *not only about individuals* deciding what we do and don't believe; it is also always about the preservation and cultivation of a *shared* heritage. Only with some common points of departure can we find sufficient room for healthy debate about inherited beliefs and possible alternate futures.

Meaningful engagement requires a certain amount of basic common knowledge. The repudiation of a shared canon thus wasn't just about the marginalization of certain *content;* it also necessarily reduced shared *experience.* Our national abandonment of a shared set of readings has harmed us not just individually—it has also damaged our community and exacerbated polarization.

When I was president of Midland, it was obvious that the college's decision two decades earlier to abandon a rich core curriculum had made the student experience hollower, shallower. Even if someone had big and legitimate objections to parts of the old core curriculum—either what it included or what it omitted—there was still great value in students, faculty, and alumni at least having some books in common, even if only as a point of departure from which to argue. When previous generations of students had been in the dining hall, or after they had lost a big game, or when they were wrestling with ethical questions in the dorm late at night, or they were thinking through a broken relationship, or when a student was killed in an accident or diagnosed with cancer, there had been common language for approaching problems. No more. Having shared intellectual traditions glues us together, helps newcomers assimilate, and allows us to take active roles in our shared community.

In a republic, there is a perpetual danger that citizens will neglect our responsibilities and take our liberties for granted—or that the up-and-coming generation of Americans won't even understand why these freedoms exist or the purposes they serve. There is a danger that we will forget our history, our shared story.

I believe we are failing our young people. The ideas we desperately need to pass on in order to ensure the survival of our great experiment are not getting through to them (as the next chapter will explore in detail). If we cannot successfully transmit even the basics of our democratic and republican system they stand to inherit, how will they be able to pilot it when their time comes? We need a baseline of knowledge, a launching pad of common values and sentiments. If the next generation takes power with a firm grasp of the underpinnings of our system, they will be able not only to maintain it but even to improve it. The American experiment is ongoing. It has been adjusted over time, most successfully in ways that made our nation freer. When we insisted once and for all—nearly a hundred years after our nation's founding—that slavery had no place within our borders, we expanded the universe of what it means to be free.

But that expansion of freedom—the turning from America's original sin of slavery—did not spring from the forehead of Zeus completely absent any history or roots in our national tradition. Rather, Abraham Lincoln, arguably our most eloquent president, preached the new black American *citizens* into existence by reweaving our national tapestry. The author of many of the most powerful phrases in our history, from "a House Divided against itself cannot stand" to "new birth of freedom" to "malice toward none," Lincoln had an inspired knack for revivifying American ideals.

Yet this same man—born into poverty in frontier Kentucky soon after America's birth (1803)—didn't go to high school, didn't go to college, and only apprenticed his way into a law practice. The Great Emancipator estimated that he spent less than one year in school in total across his lifetime—but he possessed something greater: he had an inheritance in the American literary tradition. The seeds of Lincoln's great speeches and writings were planted by his and his mother's childhood reading. He loved Shakespeare and quoted often from *Hamlet* and *Macbeth*. He relished the poetry of Lord Byron, William Cowper, Edgar Allan Poe, and Alexander Pope, and he committed many of Robert Burns's verses to memory and would recite them with a Scottish accent in performances for his family. He knew both the substance and cadence (King James Version) of the Bible backward and forward because as a boy his mother had spent so many evenings by the fire reading it aloud to him.

Lincoln drank deeply from the headwaters of the old canon—and these sources changed not only him, but us. A national canon of shared great works—focusing first on what unites us as Americans rather than what divides us—could help us recover a sense of shared meaning and shared purpose today.

This is not to suggest that the bounds of any canon would be easy to reconstruct. Critics of the old canon have rightly argued that it overemphasized the perspectives of the powerful and excluded much of the experience of others. Nor is this chapter an argument for a governmental process to decree a shared reading list for a nation. In public life, I have long tried to push back against presumptuous, one-size-fits-all solutions from the federal government. In short, what business does some U.S. senator have telling anyone else what they should read?

Two responses: First, I don't write primarily as a senator, but rather as a citizen, as a dad, as a reader, and as a former college president who has closely and painfully observed how little our kids have read of our tradition. Second, I am talking about persuasion and debate. I do not write with any proposal to use government power in the forming or reforming of a list of readings. I am not here suggesting any kind of compulsion. Teaching history does not mean accepting our history uncritically, nor does it mean simply going along to get along. Rather, living in a constitutional republic means that we fight, we argue, and we debate. But we will fail to have meaningful debates if we are not building on a shared history and on common points of departure.

My hopes are thus twofold: individual reading habits and progress toward a broader shared reading list. We need to begin again the great conversation about what ideas—and debates—unite us. To do that, we obviously need to stimulate prior appetites in our kids to become serious readers. And they need to be introduced to enough of the menu of great readings out there to be able even to comprehend the riches of the tradition they're inheriting.

A deeper sense of our common human history becomes even more important in an era where constant gushers of information flow so quickly over social media and other channels, and where even "news" is suspect. Indeed, in an age where we now have the ability to choose our own news, and firmly confine ourselves to echo chambers filled only with those who already think like we do, cultivating anew a national knowledge base of the shared is all the more urgent. For only such cultivation and preservation will allow us to cut away individual differences and get to the core ideas of our nation. From there, we can craft a clear vision of what we want our shared future to be.

THE ARGUMENT FOR
YOUR CANON, NOW

If my children are going to become addicted to reading—if they are going to develop the lifelong habit of reading—Melissa and I think they probably need to be hooked by their late teens or early twenties. For that to happen, they need to fall in love not just with the idea of reading in the abstract but with some particular books. For that love to be sparked, they surely need to follow their noses and explore widely, but they also need a plan to ensure they are drinking deeply from some enduring, truly great works.

I have concluded that I need to better model for them a life saturated by a stack of truly life-changing books. I thus resolved not to let bookcase after bookcase of the rarely opened volumes sit indistinguishably in our home office and living room—but rather that our kids should be able to perceive by our habits that there is one special bookshelf of more life-changing works to which we return again and again. The main problem behind our insufficient deep reading is a frenzied pace and boundless digital distractions, but we have also passively let the potential for reading quantity undermine the habit of repeatedly reading quality—of returning again and again to a small number of important texts until they are shaping our family's shared grammar and vocabulary.

So, taking a cue from Charles Eliot's "five feet" of books, I decided, admittedly somewhat arbitrarily, to set aside sixty inches of a single shelf next to my desk to build a list that would be limited to only sixty books. This isn't exactly my friend Scott's question of "what books . . . by the time they leave home," but his fixed constraint of their departure time from home did lead us eventually to the somewhat related constraining limit of "only sixty books" on my own life-changing shelf.

I set out to build a starter list both for my own good and to model the habit.

It's up to us as parents. Schools and public libraries can give us lists of approved or recommended books, and they can make a useful starting point, but I find they tend to be too long to be meaningful, and they also tend to feature books with easy narratives and overly simplified looks at politically charged issues.

There is no disputing that we have many different communities and subcultures in this nation, or that such diversity presents both risks and opportunities. But the way to something common from our broad diversity is through more thoughtful and principled pluralism, rather than through unquestioned cultural atomization and disintegration. The path to finding overlap is for individual families and neighborhoods and religious groups to first be reading and knowing and loving their own traditions—and then to also be wanting to listen to and learn from other families and neighborhoods and groups.

Melissa and I thus resolved to want to show our kids sixty books that we judged important. We set out to build our own short "family canon."

MY PRIORITY FIVE-FOOT SHELF

The process of building our list was both delightful and embarrassing. I spent much time pulling books from my shelves, creating index cards, talking to friends, re-sorting my piles, arguing with myself—and finding vast new gaps in my knowledge and my reading. I considered carefully whether a book was important and interesting enough that I would likely read it more than one more time in my life. In the end, I chose books that represent a wide range of genres, that provide a good return on investment in terms of time and an idiosyncratic but helpful filter for me: Would I likely have or have I already purchased additional copies to give to family members or close friends?

A few qualifications are in order. Let's be clear about what my evolving list is and what it isn't. First, although the classics of Western civilization are well represented, I reject the absurd idea that only white males had big and durable ideas. There can be no doubt there were brilliant thinkers and poets who lived in bondage and submission and who also promulgated great ideas that have sadly been lost. But we end up talking a lot about Greece and Rome because we're talking about the artifacts we have, not the artifacts we wish we had. Second, there is no reason to read old books simply because they've managed to survive intact for hundreds or even thousands of years. Unless we're professional antiquarians, a book's simply being old doesn't satisfy any of our core criteria. Study Aristotle's ethics and Homer's epics not because they're old but because they impart lasting truths. Read Augustine and Chaucer to learn something about your soul and your world. Examine St. Paul and Martin Luther King Jr., who both wrote from jail cells, to discover something about humility and perseverance. Third, my personal list is quite heavy on theology. That is partly the product of my having written both a master's thesis and doctoral dissertation on religious-historical topics. But more importantly, it's because I'm someone who finds the center of his identity in the Christian understanding of union with Adam in sin and then union with Christ in redemption.

(The argument about Genesis 3 found in Romans 5 is by itself worth a lifetime of contemplation.)

There are no "bad" books on my list—that is, I'm convinced my kids wouldn't be wasting any time by getting lost for days or weeks in any of them. Importantly, though, there are a few *wrong* ones, in my humble opinion—and there should be. There is material out there worthy of disagreement in profound ways. Not every book below is good, or true, or beautiful—that is, I disagree with some of them and am frightened by others. But each and every book on my shelf of sixty is *important.* We must be able to grapple with ideas we don't like, and internalize the distinction between a *bad* book and a *wrong* book. In life, hopefully many ideas will unsettle you, spurring you to grow strong enough to push through.

As a decision-making device as I considered thousands of candidate books for my personal list of sixty, I decided that no category should be allowed more than five books. So I kept sorting books and creating new categories until I finally neared twelve categories of five books each. Many of the categories are nothing like what I envisioned when I began my wrestling and sorting. And, importantly, I'm not really done yet. But here's where I am right now heading toward twelve categories:

1. God
2. Greek Roots
3. Homesick Souls (or, Fundamental Anthropology)
4. Shakespeare
5. The American Idea
6. Markets
7. Tyrants
8. The Nature of Things (or, a Humanistic Perspective on Science)
9. American Fiction
10. ?
11. ?
12. ?

Around category ten, things started getting tricky . . . and a bit embarrassing.

Some of the most powerful literature I devoured as a college student involved the uncommon theme (for most of us) of *captivity*. But "prison literature" seems like an odd category. Still, Nelson Mandela's landmark memoir **Long Walk to Freedom** and Nazi victim **Dietrich Bonhoeffer's** poignant *Letters and Papers from Prison* and **Martin Luther King Jr.'s** powerful **"Letter from a Birmingham Jail"** all shaped me in profound—and in some surprising senses, similar—ways. For these writers, it wasn't being confined behind bars itself that mattered. They were interested in freedom writ large. They were writing from a place in which they had no control, and it spoke to the existential truth that none of us has total control over our lives. The context barely matters. You may be in prison, you may have a gravely ill child or spouse, or you might be stuck in an airplane on the tarmac in Omaha waiting for the weather to clear. For the vast majority of your life, you are restricted by external constraints. We always try to romanticize the "totally free" way of living, but that is not real. That's not how people live. Prison literature offers a different way of looking at all the limits in our lives. And the best of those who write from prison here are not writing primarily about their own freedom. Self-pity is not the focus of any of these works. For ultimately, life isn't about *freedom from* constraint. Life is about the *freedom to* act courageously within limits.

Another stack of works that had shaped me most fundamentally involved conversion narratives. Beginning in college, I noticed that many of the most persuasive friends and conversationalists I knew were people who had changed their positions on big matters—folks who had gone through conversions, whether religious or otherwise. I soon realized that similar people tended to make the best authors. People who merely advocate but never get persuaded of anything new themselves seem two-dimensional rather than fully alive and truly struggling with hard things. **C. S. Lewis** wrestled and rebelled into his thirties, but then ultimately converted to Christianity and explained his reasoning in **Mere Christianity.** Lewis attributed his conversion partly to his "dangerous encounters" with friends and writers J. R. R. Tolkien and G. K. Chesterton. According to Lewis, their books—like **Chesterton's** *Orthodoxy*—left "traps everywhere" for the unsuspecting. Even highly polemical works like **J. Gresham Machen's** *Christianity and Liberalism* allow you to fall in love with them, even if you sometimes hate the core argument. This is because big polemics tackle something important head-on. They force the intellectually honest to assent or to dissent; there is a time for deliberating and then also a time for deciding. I suspect there is a similar set of works for Jewish Americans, and I am certain that American discourse would be better off if some Muslim Americans would advocate for a set of conversion-to-Islam narratives with which a broad range of non-Muslims could argue and wrestle.

Then there is the fact that I had almost nothing from the last thirty years. How could I possibly leave off **Nicholas Negroponte's** *Being Digital,* with its nice introductory steps into the IT revolution that is going to upend ever more sectors? And it's insane to overlook **Michael Lewis's** fascinating case study of the transformation of baseball scouting in *Moneyball.* (Uber and Lyft's triumphing over the old taxi industry provides an illustration of what will happen in more and more parts of our life as digital technologies offer us a glimpse into what the guy two floors up who we don't know is about to make for dinner and whether we want to buy two servings of the dish.)

And then I have no poetry section. This is shameful. Yes, along the way I include some Homer, Chaucer, and Shakespeare. But still, it's a tiny slice of a huge genre. And I'm constantly pushing my kids to memorize more. How can I overlook poetry?

And then there is the absence of any explicit history section. I'm a historian, for goodness' sake!

I finally realized that the path forward here is not to lament the unfinished and important debates around the periphery of my sixty, but rather to first charge zealously and happily into the core of my list. The works below should be considered only as guideposts in the categories they represent. They are far from the only books worth reading in these subjects, but each of them offers lessons that all of us—Americans from every race, creed, and background—can appreciate. They challenge us. They make us think. They help us prepare for this precious experiment in self-governance that our children will soon inherit.

With so many great ideas to engage and consider, where better to start than at the beginning . . .

Category 1: God

Who are you? Where did you come from? What is our place in the universe? These questions lead directly to God. There are certain books of the Bible that every educated person should know, whether or not you believe in a higher power. The first eleven chapters of **Genesis** alone—that is, before we even get to Abraham—are worthy of a year of sustained reading. Among the Gospels, **Matthew** is the grittiest, placing Jesus against the backdrop of Jewish history and hopes. And **Romans** is the systematic theology of the whole Bible.

If we're going to consider the nature of God, we must also consider how we relate to Him. **Martin Luther** was shaken to the core about our guilt before a demanding God, and explains this in his ***Commentary on Galatians.*** Similarly, **John Calvin** in ***The Institutes of the Christian Religion*** says that if you begin with questions about human fallenness, they will lead inevitably to the contrast between our brokenness and the idea of a righteous standard, namely the holiness of God. Conversely, if you begin more philosophically with the nature of God and the infinite, you start to realize how finite—how small—we and the troubles of our world are. Any honest accounting of either human fallibility or divine perfection immediately demands the other. God is something prior to and different from who we are. And the honest person cowers at our crookedness.

The Judeo-Christian tradition proclaims that the most primal need we all have—alongside food, shelter, and sex—is relationship with the divine. We sense a longing, gaping vacuum in the soul that can't be filled by anything smaller. Even if you don't share these beliefs, you will gain a better understanding of the billions who do.

Adherents of Judaism, Islam, and other religions should also be joining in the conversation, arguing for the most important theological works from their traditions.

Category 2: Greek Roots

No matter where your ancestors hail from, grappling with the broadest, deepest, and oldest questions requires a literary trek back to ancient Greece. But this is about more than just appreciating the influence of

Plato, Aristotle, and their contemporaries on other writers, thinkers, and statesmen from Augustine and Shakespeare to the American Founders. Greek thinkers effectively *created entire categories* of art, literature, and philosophy.

When you start reading the Greeks, you soon stumble onto the origins of arguably the longest-running philosophical divide in history: Are you with Plato or Aristotle? To get a good understanding of each, start with **Aristotle's *Ethics*** and **Plato's *Crito.*** If you find you love the body and love freedom, then you're on the side of Aristotle. If you're attracted to the proto-totalitarian, overly spiritual Plato, or if you're skeptical of the value of blood, sweat, and tears, then I recommend reading more Aristotle. (If the Greeks did emojis, I'd put one here.)

But the Greeks are not only valuable for their philosophy. They also wrote some of the greatest adventures stories ever told, like **Homer's *Odyssey.*** They also advanced the art of chronicling history, with **Thucydides's *History of the Peloponnesian War,*** the story of a conflict between the two great states of Athens and Sparta, remaining an incisive look at the nature of war. The Greeks knew how to entertain, too— ***Three Theban Plays*** by **Sophocles** represent some great work by the world's first tragic playwright. Today we'd call them downright Freudian.

Thanks to the Greeks' wide-ranging influence, many of the world's insights over the last two and half millennia begin with them.

Category 3: Homesick Souls (or, Fundamental Anthropology)

We've now moved from the ancient and the pagan to the medieval and the Christian. In the older stories, like the *Odyssey,* struggle is external, with deities and monsters. But now we move to writers like **Augustine,** in whose ***Confessions*** the struggle is internal, with his own demons and untamable desire to be god. His wrestling with his carnal desires and his troubled relationship with God is probably the oldest coming-of-age story we can read.

Other early Christian thinkers wrote about the frailty and fallibility of souls. They wrote stories of *weak* souls, *wandering* souls—searchers, wayfarers, and wrestlers with Truth. **Anselm of Canterbury,** for instance, in ***Why God Became Man,*** builds on Augustine's aching about the paradox that we do not do what we *want* to do—and therefore the revealed contradictions of the human soul—to reflect on what it means that humans are unable to reform ourselves. He arrives at the profound mysteries of the doctrines of incarnation and atonement. **Martin Luther,** in ***Bondage of the Will,*** concludes that only monergistic grace can save Adam's selfish great-grandchildren from a self-centric bent. Another example is ***Summa Theologica,*** in which **Thomas Aquinas** labors to reconcile Aristotle's philosophy with Christian theology.

But not all of these medieval works about lessons learned from wanderings are exclusively religious. **Geoffrey Chaucer's *Canterbury Tales*** is ostensibly about religious pilgrimage, but underneath it tackles the complexities of humanity and the soul—the lusts and jealousies and worldly confusion that we all encounter along the road, regardless of creed.

As with the theology category above, Americans from different traditions should argue for non-Christian and competing perspectives. As we explored in the introduction, besides the Bible, I cannot think of a single book that I carried around, wrestled with, worried about, or cared about more than **Jean-Jacques Rousseau's *Emile.*** I lived with that book for the better part of eighteen months once. At his core, Rousseau is confused about how best to raise children. He abandoned his own children at an orphanage to write the book. (What does that tell you?) But *Emile* is a good argument for a more romantic anthropology than I have for my children. I think he's dangerous and very wrong in the end. But he's wrong in weighty and fascinating ways, and I continue to learn from him. Platonists tend to love Rousseau. I dislike Plato and I dislike Rousseau. But someone should be arguing that *Emile* is a book worth grappling with. Indeed, the book you're reading now would not have been possible if I had not seriously confronted Rousseau and other thinkers like him.

Category 4: Shakespeare

When we get to literature written in English, American schoolchildren are usually forced to read Beowulf and other excerpts in Old and Middle English. I'm not convinced this awakens their appetites. Instead, I would propose lots more Shakespeare.

Dana Dusbiber, a high school English teacher in Sacramento, took to the pages of the *Washington Post* a few years ago to announce that she detests teaching Shakespeare. "There is a *world* of really exciting literature out there," she remarked, "that better speaks to the needs of my very ethnically diverse and wonderfully curious modern-day students." She even griped that Shakespeare wrote "in an early form of the English language I cannot always easily navigate."

We should pity Dusbiber's students. If she believes her charges cannot relate to love, betrayal, self-sacrifice, mistaken identities, angst, revenge, and redemption, she's in the wrong line of work. Shakespeare covers the gamut of human emotions—and even the broader set of teen emotions. As for his language, the "Bard of Avon" created literally thousands of new words that remain in use to this day, such as "addiction," "cold-blooded," "swagger," and "uncomfortable."

Shakespeare's catalog is so rich and wide-ranging it's hard to pick just a handful of plays. So, assuming everyone already knows **Romeo and Juliet,** let's drink deeply of his historical and political plays. **Hamlet** and **King Lear** look at the far-reaching consequences of complex family dynamics. **Julius Caesar** and **Macbeth** examine how far humans will go when power hangs in the balance. Aside from drama, the **Sonnets** offer thoughts on love that haven't lost their charm over the centuries.

A final word on Shakespeare's works: don't read them only in your head but read them aloud, for his cadence and meter need to echo in your ear.

Category 5: The American Idea

The American Founding made the bold claim that most peoples and most governments throughout history had been wrong about the nature of power and the nature of freedom. Our Declaration of Independence was more than just an announcement to King George III that "Americans" and Britons would go separate ways. More lastingly, it articulates "self-evident truths" applicable to "all men at all times" about justice, liberty, and equality.

To understand what Lincoln was wrestling with during the Civil War when he called the **Declaration of Independence** an "Apple of Gold" and the **Constitution** a "Frame of Silver," we should first be familiar with the original documents themselves. Beyond that, *The Federalist Papers* help expand on the Constitution's meaning and scope, while showcasing the great minds of their authors, **Alexander Hamilton, James Madison,** and **John Jay.**

An early visitor to our new Constitutional Republic, **Alexis de Tocqueville,** provided an essential fresh pair of eyes through which to view this new experiment. His *Democracy in America* is mentioned at length elsewhere, but it is worth suggesting once again that it be read in its entirety.

To see the founding vision expressed in a more perfect union, no one is more necessary to read than Frederick Douglass, the former slave and arguably our greatest abolitionist leader. His autobiography, *Narrative of the Life of Frederick Douglass, an American Slave,* became a national best seller and helped shift public opinion toward true freedom. The **Lincoln-Douglas Debates of 1858** also provide excellent context to the political issues surrounding slavery in the run-up to the Civil War. But to understand the American idea, with all its imperfections, I recommend starting with Frederick Douglass.

Category 6: Markets

From before the year 1000 until almost 1800, economic growth was practically nonexistent. Then every indicator from population growth to productivity began to skyrocket. Why? The Industrial Revolution, obviously. Technological innovation, certainly. But the development of free markets, above all.

The overarching story of the last two hundred years isn't chiefly about the expansion of human liberty, though that's obviously a wonderful part of it. It's really a story about why we have so much more material prosperity today than our ancestors ever dreamt possible. The question is how to keep the economy free and dynamic in an age of increasing uncertainty—and how to keep the blessings of material prosperity without reducing human existence to mere materialism.

It might be helpful to begin even further back, with the ancient roots of modern market economic theory. The first book of *Politics* by **Aristotle** is all about home economics. Aristotle understood that the family is the basis of civil society and the home is the basic building block of a political economy. In wisdom that is truly timeless, he teaches that vibrant economies flow from free societies, which themselves require worldly institutions that are voluntary and rooted in the heart.

From that grounding, you can move on to the classic work on the free market: **Adam Smith's** *Wealth of Nations,* which tells us that enlightened self-interest is what makes the world go round. For a look at how this kind of thinking took root in early America, consider **Charles Sellers's** *The Market Revolution: Jacksonian America, 1815–1846.* For a more modern perspective on the free market in the post–World War II world, **Milton and Rose Friedman's** *Free to Choose* is great. **Jared Diamond's** *Guns, Germs, and Steel* examines how early ideas about innovation were essential to the economic growth that built the world as we know it today.

Category 7: Tyrants

This is one of the most important, yet painful, parts of the list. Any education in freedom demands a thorough understanding of freedom's enemies. Our Founders immersed themselves in ancient and modern history because they desperately wanted to avoid repeating the mistakes of failed governments. Jefferson's history syllabus for nephew Peter is largely a literary tour through the wreckage of dictators, despots, and tyrants. But even though tyranny is the theme, a particular species of tyranny—twentieth-century totalitarianism—overshadows other readings in this category on my list.

The newfound popularity of socialism among millennials is an alarming trend. This generation has no clue what it's embracing. Thankfully, a wide range of works exist that can serve as an antidote to a very bad idea.

With the *Communist Manifesto,* **Karl Marx and Friedrich Engels** laid the intellectual foundation for communism and, hence, the murder of more than 100 million people. **Hannah Arendt's** *Origins of Totalitarianism* is the best analysis of the rise of scientific racism and anti-Semitism in nineteenth-century Europe, which led directly to the Holocaust. **F. A. Hayek** was one of the first to see that fascism and communism were closely related, and he explains this in *The Road to Serfdom.*

Fiction and the power of imagination can be weapons against tyranny as well. *Animal Farm,* **George Orwell's** allegorical fable about Stalinist Russia set on an English country farm, lays bare the brutality of socialism. Though Orwell called himself a socialist, the most famous line from the novel is a devastatingly succinct indictment of the injustice inherent in socialist government: "All animals are equal, but some animals are more equal than others." A worthy alternative option, of course, is Orwell's *1984.* While I find *Animal Farm* a more lively read, especially for younger folks, both works have merit, and comparing the two could be helpful.

One of the most frightening forms of tyranny may be the one presented in **Aldous Huxley's** dystopian novel, *Brave New World,* in which people are kept passive and "happy" by limitless drugs and sex provided by the state. Most of the characters don't even realize they're slaves. A *Brave New World* is what you get when a republic loses its virtue and vigor.

Category 8: The Nature of Things
(or, a Humanistic Perspective on Science)

No liberal education is complete without the sciences—but that doesn't necessarily require technical proficiency in the Science, Technology, Engineering, and Mathematics (STEM) program. Even for the nontechnical among us, a *humanistic* appreciation of science—which is even scarcer than technical skill—can be appreciated by delving into the classics of the field. Natural sciences should not be a separate field of study, but rather a coherent whole, where philosophy meets hands-on observation, experimentation, and analysis.

This approach is especially useful in an age when appeals to science are intended to shut down debate rather than spur further questioning—a tyranny of a different kind. Our students rarely understand what science really is, as appeals to authority now regularly undermine rather than advance the broad dissemination of scientific perspectives. We get a caricature of science from television personalities like Bill Nye and Neil deGrasse Tyson.

If science and data are going to shape politics and policy, then you should have a sound grasp of the scientific method. The thoughts of

Lucretius in his work *On the Nature of Things* are helpful as well. Students who have drunk deeply from **Thomas Kuhn**—especially his *Structure of Scientific Revolutions*—find that his paradigms and paradigm shifts will reorient how you think about the relationship between facts and narrative in every debate in every field.

Finally, **Euclid** and his *Elements of Geometry* changed my life. While he was probably the author I was least interested in reading when I began my master's program in the "great books" curriculum at St. John's Annapolis in the 1990s, he ended up opening new worlds for me, so that I almost understand today when I hear a math or science geek say that they "need to do some math" almost as a kind of therapy or synthetic escape.

Category 9: American Fiction

The idea that any handful of suggested novels can capture more than two centuries of American fiction is ludicrous. But given that my leading books in this category are meant to guide a journey of ideas, let's begin with American novels that trace personal journeys.

Mark Twain wrote the quintessential American novel, a work of art that rivals Homer or Shakespeare. And the titular hero of *Huckleberry Finn* is the quintessential American boy. "Not a freckle is missing," as H. L. Mencken put it. **Willa Cather's** sketches open up entire worlds. *Death Comes for the Archbishop* is a story about faith and struggle in the Southwest, written in language as sparse and beautiful as the land in which it's set. (For the Cornhusker Edition of this book, we'll substitute Cather's *O, Pioneers!*—which is an early novel about perseverance on the plains of Nebraska and a book that hinted that Cather would become one of the great American women writers of the last century.) **John Steinbeck** set another story of a tough journey in the West, as he followed the Joad family to California during the Dust Bowl in *Grapes of Wrath.*

James Baldwin wrote of his alienation as a black and gay man growing up in Harlem with an abusive Baptist minister as his stepfather. *Go Tell It on the Mountain* is a disturbing book in many aspects. It illustrates the ways in which religious life can turn hypocritical and repressive.

A few years ago, when a North Carolina school district tried to ban **Ralph Ellison's *Invisible Man*** from high school reading lists, one board member claimed that he "didn't find any literary value" in the story of a black man "hiding in the world," living underground, stealing electricity from Monopolated Light & Power, and trying to make sense of his life and his place in America. But trying to find your place is a theme deeply familiar to most reflective teens as they navigate the transition to adulthood.

Category 10 . . . and 13 . . . and 16:
The Great Conversation

Right about now, many readers are fuming over what's missing from this starter canon. We already mentioned the lack of poetry, and the lack of an explicit history category. And I couldn't decide what to do with the books that seemed to form up a "prison literature" category. Yet others will regard my emerging list as insufficiently attuned to the experiences of the marginalized, either historically or in America.

How could he neglect *this*, but include *that*?!

Good. That's the point. Even if you hate most of my emerging list, but you've come to know more about *why* you hate it, then congratulations. That's progress.

Our lists most certainly should be debated—and humbly revised. They are necessarily imperfect, incomplete, and full of omissions. Are we all going to agree on how to resolve this riddle? Of course not.

But those debates can only commence in a meaningful way once there is a priority set from which to work. We can only add and subtract from our lists once there are trial lists from which to add and subtract. That's what my list is, a starting attempt—it is a work in progress.

The above books are obviously not the only books Melissa and I have our children reading (see the Stepping Stones at the end of this chapter). We strongly urge them toward both "quantity and quality." Sort of like how you regain a healthy appetite after you've had the flu, we first urged our kids just to read more of whatever books they loved when they were younger. Then, after they acquired the reading bug—that is, after the appetite had been solidly awakened—we began to substitute more meat and vegetables for the cotton candy on which they previously supped. Ultimately, only a great diet of excellent reading material can sustain a long and happy life.

Whether you start out with the above list as an opening bid or choose to go another direction completely, the most important thing is to read early and often, and impart that habit to your children, too. Without someone to guide kids, they are all but guaranteed to read terrible books, or no books, and perhaps never achieve the kind of healthy, liberal freedom toward which these enduring storytellers aim to take us.

If a whole generation grows up having become habituated to reading, then even if we don't start them off with the same readings, we'll have prepared and positioned them to enter into meaningful wrestling with their neighbors about a core set of texts that we should tackle together. Both their preparedness and their empathetic debating will strengthen our shared ability to stand in the face of the forces seeking to pull us apart.

RAISE THEM AS IF THEY'LL RULE SOMEDAY

Imagine you are Aristotle, an underemployed teacher, and you've just landed a job tutoring Alexander, who will eventually be known as "The Great" and conquer lands from Greece to northern Africa to the Middle East and across much of Asia. What does Alexander need to know? Who does he need to be? What does he need to read?

Or envision yourself as nanny-tutor to a princess who will one day take the throne. Or plot your plan of attack if you were simply a parent raising a future ruler . . . because you are—this is actually you. If you are now or will one day be an American parent, then you have this high calling to raise a ruler. For in America, the people rule. And thus our people need to be fit to rule. Not just some class of elites—but all of us.

Nothing in the American ideal depends on everyone being rich. Nothing necessitates universal college graduation. But the sustenance of this free republic does require an equalitarian vision that all of us are fit to rule—maybe not making every specialized decision, but at least making informed judgments about to whom "we the people" delegate the daily business of governing and deciding. Otherwise, this historically unique experiment in self-government will have run its course.

The truly free have always required literacy. There is a reason why teaching slaves to read has historically been illegal across slave-holding cultures. And there are thus reasons why America's descent toward functional illiteracy as the digital age flowers should frighten us. For the watchfulness—and thoughtfulness—of fully formed adults is the only lasting guardian of liberty.

This list is meant to be a conversation starter, not the last word. Argue about it. Start modestly, build your categories, stack your books, reshuffle your shelf . . . and draw your kids into the conversation, the debate, and the categorizing. Soon enough they will also have a little shelf of favorite books and the makings of a fine and sharable and debatable list of their own—and therefore also the foundation necessary to join in the broader debates about a national canon.

STEPPING STONES TO A READING ADDICTION

The "Century Club" Reading Challenge

My friend Tevi Troy used to work for President George W. Bush, who was and is (contrary to public caricature) a reading machine. Tevi created this challenge game called the "Century Club." To be in the club, you needed to read one hundred books in a year. That's pretty impressive. Quite a few people can read two solid books in a week, for instance at the beach in the summer or sitting by the fire over Christmas week—but knocking out almost two per week for an entire year is daunting.

After competing against the president and his chief political advisor, Karl Rove, for one year (President Bush won), Tevi brought the concept home to his four children. At first, he and his wife Kami let their kids read relatively light books to set them on the path to one hundred. But as they developed the habit of reading, their mom and dad added more challenging titles. Quantity is important for forming the habit, but quality is the long-term goal.

Melissa and I stole their idea for our kids two years ago. They haven't succeeded yet—at finishing a full hundred in a calendar year—but it has become a healthy, behavior-shaping goal. When the girls were right around 13, we let them first pick just over half of the books in their sequence. But as weeks and months passed, we made them propose a handful of the books (usually three or four), and we selected from that list the book they'd read next—*if* we regarded any of the menu they gave us as rigorous enough. If they didn't, we just selected something not on their menu. In general, they have enough healthy appetites about their reading that they want to be in the driver's seat, so they continue to propose books that stretch them progressively more.

While drafting this chapter and thinking about how to get kids addicted to reading quantity, so that we as parents might also start substituting in more quality, I asked one of my daughters, "If an 8-year-old cousin wasn't in the habit of reading, and your job was to create an addiction, what books would you push at him or her?" Never lacking in certainty, she produced her list in twenty minutes:

1. *Tales of Magic* by Edward Eager
2. *Percy Jackson* (series) by Rick Riordan
3. *Boxcar Children* (series) by Gertrude Chandler Warner
4. *Frindle* by Andrew Clements
5. *Magic Tree House* (series) by Mary Pope Osborne
6. *Castle in the Attic* by Elizabeth Winthrop
7. *The Secret School* by Avi

I then put roughly the same thought experiment to another of my daughters, "If a 12-year-old cousin wasn't in the habit of reading, and your job was to create an addiction, what books would you push at him or her?" Her list appeared almost as quickly:

1. *100 Cupboards* by N. D. Wilson
2. *Chronicles of Narnia* (series) by C. S. Lewis
3. *Mysterious Benedict Society* by Trenton Lee Stewart
4. *Alex Rider* (series) by Anthony Horowitz
5. *Wingfeather Saga* by Andrew Peterson
6. *Harry Potter* (series) by J. K. Rowling
7. (a bit more challenging) *A Wrinkle in Time* by Madeleine L'Engle

Then my wife, not wanting to be left out, chimed in: "The key to all of this, you know, is getting them to love books even before they could conceivably read. And for that, you need the right little bookshelf of read-aloud books for your little ones." Her best recommendation for where to start is with the tremendous lists in *Honey for a Child's Heart: The Imaginative Use of Books in Family Life* by Gladys Hunt.

NINE

⇒>●⋲⋲

MAKE AMERICA
AN IDEA AGAIN

*Civic Mis-education * Don't Seek Protection from Competing Ideas*
*What Makes Us Exceptional? * The Poetry of the Founders*
*What Tocqueville Reminds Us * Many Identities, Shared Values*

America is not just a great nation; it is an idea. Ireland is a great
nation, a beautiful nation, filled with great people—but it is not an
idea. America is an idea.

—Bono

I AM AN OPTIMIST AND I BELIEVE THAT AMERICA'S
best days lie ahead. Our Constitution has given us powerful institutions
whose very power stems from the fact that they are self-limiting, allowing
us the liberty and agency to pursue our dreams. But I'd be lying if I didn't
acknowledge concerns about three trends: (1) the accelerating technologies that are, quite simply, going to make a lot of our current jobs disappear; (2) the coming-of-age crisis that has been the central subject of this
book, which I believe has resulted in a generation of kids who will have a
tough time dealing with #1, not to mention playing their roles as active,
engaged citizens; and (3) the fact that in times of economic disruption,

we invariably see the rise of people who offer quick fixes, nativist campaigns, and more centralized power as a way out.

We are going to need America's children to rise to their best in the years to come, because a nation of adult-children cannot be a nation of self-governing people.

A plea for *self*-discipline and *self*-control is the one and only dignified alternative to discipline and control from without. For in this broken world of lawless souls, there will be control; there will be government. Order-seeking and security-seeking people, as well as those in search of power for their own purposes, will invariably seek to hold back the chaos of the world. The question is whether people will control themselves or submit to the control of another.

A republic is the only form of government, the only social arrangement, that seeks to make individuals preeminent in their own self-control, their own self-possession. A republic is thus at once liberating *and scary*. For it both requires and assumes adults, not subjects. And this is a rare state of affairs in political history.

Children do not govern themselves, of course. They don't know how to. They have to be taught and they have to learn self-governance. In a healthy society, they migrate from a phase of parental control to partial self-control, and then to full independence. These developmental and transitional phases should be periods when they are thought of as "little citizens"—people on the way to becoming self-controlled. We don't think this way today.

Well-functioning citizens share a collective memory of how and why and toward what ends our polity came to be. Adult-citizenship presumes a substantial level of self-awareness and impulse control; it knows both rights and duties. Sadly, the United States today suffers from widespread collective amnesia. As a result, many Americans coming of age today don't understand the country they're inheriting. They've not heard our story. And thus many of them don't even know what they don't know.

CIVIC MIS-EDUCATION

Thomas Jefferson famously warned, "If a nation expects to be ignorant and free in a state of civilization, it expects what never was and never will be." What's happening now in this country is that we're reaping the fruits of the last fifty years of ceasing to talk in a meaningful, public way about what unites us—about what the American experiment was attempting, why it was and is extraordinary, and the challenges we must perpetually rise to if we're going to remain Americans.

Ronald Reagan famously preached that "freedom is a fragile thing and is never more than one generation away from extinction." If you don't pass along the meaning of America to the next generation, it is in danger of being lost. Everything that we cherish—freedom of assembly and dissent, the rule of law, civic engagement, small-r republican liberty—requires constant gardening, and tending, and embrace, and revivification. This is not something that can be neglected without consequence.

We need to go back to Reagan—not because you did or did not, or would or would not have voted for him, but because he was presiding at the last moment when we talked seriously about what America means for all Americans. This is not because he was a Republican rather than a Democrat, but largely because the Cold War against expansionistic Soviet communism forced us to explain who we were and why we differed. And his warnings about passing on the meaning of America resonate today, precisely because we now see the consequences of what happens when we fail to teach our kids what America means.

Yes, "failure" is the right word. We have failed. We referred in chapter 2 to the "lukewarm citizenship" of a generation that knows little to nothing about what government is supposed to do and is not supposed to do. The Intercollegiate Studies Institute in 2006 and 2007 tested more than 28,000 freshmen and seniors at eighty universities around the country. They were asked sixty multiple-choice questions about very elementary civic matters. The results from students at both the start and the end of their college careers were quite depressing. The average freshman scored 51 percent both years on fairly elementary questions. The average senior wasn't much better, averaging less than 54 percent.

Civic ignorance doesn't improve after graduation. According to one survey, only one-third of U.S. adults know the three branches of the federal government. More than 30 percent couldn't name even one branch of our government. We are likely safe to assume that people who can't identify the branches of government are probably equally hard-pressed to explain the roles of the different branches. Another survey found that only two-thirds of university respondents could pass the civics portion of the U.S. naturalization test—an embarrassing contrast to the 98 percent of immigrants seeking citizenship who pass. In a project by the Center for the Study of the American Dream at Xavier University, 85 percent of U.S. citizens surveyed couldn't define "the rule of law"; 82 percent couldn't name at least two of the three "unalienable Rights" mentioned in the Declaration of Independence; and 71 percent weren't aware that the Constitution is the supreme law of the land. This level of ignorance smells like the death of an experiment in republican self-rule.

To further confirm the dire state of our civics, the Newseum Institute reports that 39 percent of Americans have no idea at all what the First Amendment is about. Sixty-eight percent of U.S. adults are at least aware that the First Amendment protects freedom of speech, but far fewer know anything about freedom of religion or assembly or press or the redress of grievances.

I believe the First Amendment is the beating heart of the American experiment. The First Amendment is a roadmap for how a nation of 320 million people, with an inevitably wide divergence of opinion on theological, existential, and cultural matters, can nonetheless guard against the tyranny of the majority and can respect everyone's dignity, everyone's natural rights. Most fundamentally the First Amendment is a way of fostering a robust marketplace of ideas in a way that shouts: "We don't believe in violence in the public square." We stand together to defend others' right to speak even when we disagree with the content of their speech. We can argue about really big issues in this land, but we don't settle those intellectual and spiritual differences by force. That is the glorious American liberal tradition of ordered liberty.

At least, that's the way it's supposed to work.

But what happens when we become collectively ignorant of this architecture for public life? What happens when the generation coming of age begins embracing dangerously illiberal views on freedom of speech and freedom of religion?

DON'T SEEK PROTECTION
FROM COMPETING IDEAS

Widespread polling suggests our emerging generation lacks deep attachment to historic American liberties. The First Amendment Center's surveys now consistently find far weaker support for freedom of speech among Americans under age 30 than over age 30. This is a warning sign. In multiple surveys, between 40 and 50 percent of Americans between the ages of 18 and 30 suggest that the First Amendment is extreme. When asked why, millennials seem to believe that this foundational amendment is dangerous because you could use your freedom of speech to say something that might hurt someone else's feelings.

Think about that. Nearly half of young Americans would potentially curtail the First Amendment—arguably the centerpiece of the American experiment—because sometimes people use their freedom to say things that aren't very nice.

Let's unpack this with a basic yes-or-no scenario: either human nature and the world are or are not troubled. Once you grasp the obvious side of that fork (we are), then the question becomes what to do about the brokenness. The correctly American answer has always been for the state to stand down, for people to pursue their dreams and to seek ultimate meaning outside of politics, and for citizens to sort through their arguments and debates in a liberal, open public square by persuasion, not by either forced or prohibited speech.

Yes, some folks will surely use their freedom to say some hurtful things at times. That is a consequence of human brokenness; it is not something to be solved by governmental compulsion at the price of our liberty. Yet the younger generation is drifting rapidly from this quintessentially American answer—and toward a pre-American view that force, that the powerful, should "solve" contests of ideas and clashes of values by law, by prohibition, by silencing.

The antipathy to both freedom of speech and freedom of religion is even more widespread in elite institutions of higher learning. Bizarrely, the protests that have erupted over the past two years at colleges and universities that charge more than a quarter of a million dollars for an "education" have been explicit in their demands for *protection* from new and uncomfortable ideas. Two of my alma maters—Harvard and Yale— are increasingly hostile to ideas that fall outside a narrow ideological spectrum, according to a ratings system from the Heterodox Academy, a group of college professors who have pledged to "support viewpoint diversity." I was at Yale to give the Buckley Lecture in November 2015, the day that students' anti-speech protests reached a fever pitch—objecting to a free speech (!) conference.

Greg Lukianoff, president of the Foundation for Individual Rights in Education, has created the tragically apt phrase "unlearning liberty" for the troubling turn from freedom of expression and academic freedom toward political correctness and speech codes on our elite campuses.

Let's state it clearly: This is nearly the opposite of what the American Revolution was fought for. America declared independence from Great Britain in pursuit of liberty, not "safe spaces." Freedom, and particularly freedom of discourse and debate about the big ideas of life, death, and meaning, is the foundation of the American idea. Fleeting notions of psychological safety from having to consider competing ideas are quite nearly the opposite.

WHAT MAKES US EXCEPTIONAL?

At the beginning of President Obama's administration, a reporter asked him if he believed in American exceptionalism. After a pause, he strangely replied, "I believe in American exceptionalism, just as I suspect that the Brits believe in British exceptionalism and the Greeks believe in Greek exceptionalism."

With all due respect to the former president and his office, this misses the point entirely. It was a genuinely tragic moment in American history. Not only are we not teaching what America means, our president either rejected it or didn't even grasp what it has traditionally meant.

American exceptionalism is not some claim to ethnic or moral superiority; rather, it is a claim about the American Founding being unique in human history. The American Founding was radically arrogant in some ways. It was rooted in the new announcement of "universal and revolutionary principles, respecting the rights of man."

For much of human history, people have been governed under the principle of "might makes right." The king had a monopoly on violence and he could do whatever he wanted. And everyone else? They weren't citizens, but subjects—and they were dependent upon the king. Even with a generous king, the passive assumption for subjects across history remained prohibition, not permission. If the king didn't expressly permit something, it was assumed to be forbidden. That was the rule whether you wanted to start your own business or worship as you pleased.

America's Founders stunningly, arrogantly, looked at history and at kings, and retorted: We don't believe this is right. We don't believe government comes before people; we believe government is a tool that people create for themselves. We believe that people are created free, and they come together to fashion a government to secure their rights and to secure their liberties.

The Founders made their case in the Declaration of Independence, which laid out a lengthy list of grievances—a "long train of abuses and usurpations," in Jefferson's words—against King George III. But prefacing all of that was a grand statement of principles unlike anything ever seen before. For the patriots of 1776 sought to build their free and independent nation on certain self-evident *truths* that human beings are created equal in the eyes of God and are endowed by their creator with rights that government did not create and can never take away. They announced that those rights include life, liberty, and the pursuit of happiness. They declared that government cannot *grant* rights, but rather exists only to *protect* them. They shouted, with their lives on the line, that a government that acts without the consent of the governed is illegitimate and may be changed or overthrown.

The Declaration proclaims that America is much bigger than government. Governments are just about power—but the American founding moment screams that America is *not* fundamentally about power or coercion. America is first and foremost an idea. It is not an idea only for Americans. But it is an idea that Americans would proclaim on the world stage. Our forefathers and mothers spoke of self-evident truths and unalienable rights; they spoke not about blood and soil and tribe. To be an American meant sharing in this *proposition* laid out in the Declaration about where rights come from. You could be born an Englishman or a German or a Frenchman. But Americans are not just born; we are *made*.

And we believe—we "hold these truths."

As Abraham Lincoln said in an 1858 speech in Chicago, the Founding's self-evident truths represent "the father of all moral principle," and every American, new and old alike, has "a right to claim it as though they were blood of the blood, and flesh of the flesh of the men who wrote that Declaration." It is "the electric cord . . . that links the hearts of patriotic and liberty-loving men together."

When we talk about the American idea, this is what we mean.

THE POETRY OF THE FOUNDERS

The Declaration of Independence is the soaring claim about human dignity, and the Constitution is the outworking of the theory of what government exists to do, and why it must then be limited. The government exists to serve the people, not the other way around. The people are primary and the government is derivative, not the other way around.

The Declaration's claims about dignity and rights were literally revolutionary. And the consequent Constitution is unlike any political document ever written. Why? Because it is a negative document. It doesn't give us any rights; rather, it is the place where we the people define the few, limited powers that we choose to grant to the government. The new default setting remains that all nonspecified topics are merely rights retained by the people, or powers retained by levels of government closer to the people than the national level.

At its core, this is what the Constitution is doing: it itemizes the few powers that "We, the people" decided to give to the government so that together we can have this shared project of securing a framework for ordered liberty. The Constitution was written to *limit* what government can do—and thus to establish clearly what it cannot do. Limited government is a concept that flows directly from the American Founding's argument about human dignity and about where rights come from.

But wait . . . How do we then make sense of our rights as they are explained in the aptly named "Bill of Rights"? Isn't this the government claiming authorship for our rights? No. The first ten amendments of the Constitution are basically good-natured reminders, as opposed to an exhaustive delineation of what the people are free to do. The Founders very intentionally did not enumerate any rights inside the Constitution proper. They instead enumerated only the powers that the sovereign people were giving to the government. They understood and feared that governments inevitably want to grow, and to gobble up more power, especially at times of crisis.

The First Amendment became, by design, a giant laundry list of guarantees: the freedom of religion and the freedom of speech and the freedom of assembly and the freedom of the press and the right of re-dress and grievances—which basically means that even lobbyists have a right to exist and legitimate work to do. But these five rights are all listed as the "First" Amendment because you can't unbundle this cluster.

It would be meaningless to talk about freedom of religion without having freedom of speech. It would be ridiculous to talk about freedom of assembly without someone's being able to report and promulgate and persuade other people what was said and what happened via the freedom of the press. And so the beating heart of the American idea turns out not to be in the Constitution proper. It is rather in this enumeration of rights that does not end. That's why when you get to the Ninth and Tenth Amendments, the framers had the wisdom to say, in effect, "All of the rights we didn't list here, the people still retain all of those. And, by the way, all the powers we didn't specifically give to the federal government in the main document here, only states and local governments could ever exercise those powers. Got that? Do you hear us clearly? Good."

This is poetry.

WHAT TOCQUEVILLE REMINDS US

Often the best way to understand something is to try to see it from the perspective of a total outsider. One of the main reasons to travel (as we explored in chapter 7) is to meet and converse with people from other cultures, partly so that we can then understand the culture from which we have come.

Alexis de Tocqueville has been giving Americans a view into our own history and culture for nearly two hundred years. Initially, the Frenchman came to America to study our penal system and to advise his countrymen on whether our system might provide a good model for France. But much more broadly, he wanted to know why America was flourishing when other nations were not. What drove the economic dynamism here? What was the relationship between our entrepreneurial innovation and all the cultural pluralism and diversity that the American Constitution enabled?

Tocqueville was a French aristocrat and politician with a lifelong interest in the workings of governments. Later in his career, he helped draft the constitution of France's "Second Republic" in 1848 and served briefly as foreign minister. But in the 1830s, Europeans looked across the sea toward America and said, in so many words, "What in the world is going on with those weirdos?" Tocqueville certainly thought our country was peculiar—in a great way. He set out for America in 1831 with a friend to see "what a great republic is."

Tocqueville wasn't the first foreigner or even the first Frenchman to come to America to unravel its mysteries, but he was by far the most perceptive, and his perceptions were collected into a landmark work. Any American who hasn't read *Democracy in America* should. It's been called both "the best book ever written on democracy" and "the best book ever written on America." Part of why it is pleasant to read is that it is really a series of travel dispatches. Tocqueville spent nine months in the United States, and he met many of the most prominent Americans of the day, including John Quincy Adams, Andrew Jackson, Daniel Webster, and Sam Houston. Tocqueville's keen eye and brilliant turns of phrase allow us a new vantage point to look at our nation for the first time again.

Tocqueville initially thought that America's greatness stemmed from its formal institutions, from its laws. If the nation has such a wonderful and dynamic economy, surely it must have the most wonderful and dynamic bureaucrats, right? So he went to Washington, DC. But instead of bureaucratic innovation, he discovered an uninhabitable swamp populated by people who, with a few notable exceptions, he didn't regard as especially impressive. He was realizing that America's genius did not flow out and down from its political center. Rather, there was something about the texture and vitality of the local communities that produced the dynamism. At that time of his first visit in 1831, there were twenty-five states. Tocqueville felt compelled to travel widely, visiting two-thirds of the states, north and south.

In the states, he had his "Aha!" revelation. The meaning of America is not in its government or its elected officials. It is in our civic organizations, in the forerunners to what we think of today as the Rotary Club.

It's in the churches. It's even in the juries (something worth remembering the next time you get a jury summons). He found America in its
mediating institutions and in its civil society. And he understood why
Europeans were confused. For Europeans had an inherited framework
about how life is lived—by orderly planning based on the decisions of
the powerful. They believed in the more traditional view—that government is the nearly exclusive context in which people choose to build
projects together.

It turns out, Tocqueville explained, that Americans believe different,
almost unbelievable things. They believe in the heart. They believe in
the will. They believe in voluntarism. Americans believe in self-control,
rather than other-control or government-control. They believe in community. They believe in persuasion. They believe in virtue. That is the
meaning of "democracy in America." It is a set of shared assumptions—
he called it republican culture—that is well upstream from politics.

"Among the new objects that attracted my attention during my stay
in the United States," he wrote in his introduction, "none struck my eye
more vividly than the equality of conditions. I discovered without difficulty the enormous influence that this primary fact exerts on the course
of society; it gives a certain direction to public spirit, a certain turn to
the laws, new maxims to those who govern, and particular habits to the
governed." The *habits* of the citizens—this is a concept without which
the Tocquevillian understanding of America makes no sense.

What made America great in Tocqueville's eyes in the 1830s—and
what should make America great again—is not its politicians. America is not great because it has the best governing bureaucracies. Rather,
America is great when its people share a belief in the Rotary Club and
the PTA, the synagogues and churches, the small businesses and local town meetings—all the places where free people freely assemble to
serve and to build lives together. All of those things are moved by the
democratic spirit that Tocqueville brilliantly chronicled. That spirit, he
wrote, "creates opinions, gives birth to sentiments, suggests usages, and
modifies everything it does not produce."

Does democracy sometimes produce excesses? Absolutely. As much
as Tocqueville lauds democracy, some of his most insightful commentary focuses on the dangers of democracy's possible drift toward despotism, toward unbounded populism, toward the tyranny of the majority.

He saw that equality encouraged individualism, which in turn discouraged people from fully participating in public life. He sensed the drift toward materialism, which could undermine a shared sense of civic purpose. He warned of a democratic despotism that "covers the surface of society with a network of small complicated rules, minute and uniform, through which the most original minds and the most energetic characters cannot penetrate, to rise above the crowd."

No framework for public life has ever unleashed more creativity, prosperity, or dynamism than this republic born of the American idea—and yet, no human endeavor is perfect, not even the most perfect democratic republic ever seen. "I believe that in all governments, whatever they may be, baseness will attach itself to force and flattery to power," Tocqueville wrote. "And I know only one means of preventing men from being degraded: it is to grant to no one, along with omnipotence, the sovereign power to demean them." That antidote is the habit of self-discipline, self-restraint, and *adult* self-control.

MANY IDENTITIES, SHARED VALUES

What American government is fundamentally about, at the federal level, is maintaining the architecture or framework that enables us to live life in a pluralistic society. That's all. Or to borrow from Abraham Lincoln, the Constitution is the silver frame, and our free society—the free coming together of people pursuing happiness—is the apple of gold. Everybody who is advancing a vision for what a good life looks like in a pluralistic society should have a shared desire for our people to be thriving and vibrant and independent and free from force and coercion.

We are an exceptional people because we respect that Americans are not merely members of the polity. We all have plural identities. I'm an American. I'm also a Nebraskan. I'm a football addict and the son of a football coach. I'm a husband, and a dad, and a Christian. I'm a conservative, and a Republican, and a public official.

But the ordering of some of these loyalties matters. It would be absurd to put any particular job ahead of my family commitments. Similarly, I hope that all Americans regard their national commitments as more important than party allegiances—whereas many on the right might legitimately argue about the relative importance of their conservatism and their commitments to the Republican Party, and many on the left likewise wrestle with the relative importance of their progressivism and their commitments to the Democratic Party. And our country certainly comes before our football allegiance.

This kind of plural identity has been challenged—we fought a war over it from 1861 to 1865. Southerners thought their state citizenship trumped their American citizenship; and Northerners thought the reverse—that American ideals about equality and universal dignity trumped the views of Southern states about race. But when that war was over, we bound up our wounds together and moved forward, recognizing that full national flourishing requires us to pursue meaning amid multiple communities of belief and affection. Lincoln's "silver frame" of Constitutionalism enables many competing pursuits of happiness. Liberty empowers individuals and local communities to make their own choices. Liberty does not mandate how you live, but it does make a grand claim about your dignity and your unalienable rights—and therefore by implication it urges you to embrace a creed affirming the dignity and natural rights of everyone across the globe.

Jefferson called America a "light unto the nations." Lincoln said that we are "the last, best hope of earth." Martin Luther King preached that we would "rise up and live out the true meaning of [our] creed . . . that all men are created equal." Reagan resuscitated the Puritans' echoes of biblical imagery when he likened America to a "shining city on a hill." America's greatest statesmen have soaringly declared what makes our country exceptional.

But even from their rhetorical heights—rightly singing hymns to the glories of America—they are also issuing us a stark warning against squandering our birthright. This exceptional nation cannot endure by mere inertia. If we neglect to actively transmit what this nation has stood for, if the idea of America is not reborn in our children's hearts, we will all suffer a shared orphanhood. Freedom is not merely "ours by inheritance," Reagan said. "It must be fought for and defended constantly by each generation, for it comes only once to a people. Those who have known freedom and then lost it have never known it again."

America must be taught; America must be embraced.

———— ✦ ————

THE ANCIENT GREEKS AND ROMANS distinguished between those who age like grapes maturing into fine wine and those who age like grapes souring into vinegar. Naturally, we want future generations of Americans to mature, not sour. Because Americans are *made* rather than simply born, we need to help our kids become tougher, not coarser; resilient, not rigid; engaged in real life, not lost in "virtual reality"; richer in experience, not embittered by it; leaders, not lemmings knocked around by fads and circumstance. That's adulthood rightly understood.

Let your family's quest for uplift—not just material, but more importantly moral—begin. May you find new passion to strengthen timid souls. And, as Teddy Roosevelt would say, may you see those entrusted to your care become little citizens of "great and generous emotion, high pride, stern belief, and lofty enthusiasm."

In short, may they become the kind of young men and women "who quell the storm and ride the thunder."

POSTSCRIPT

⟹>●<⟸

WHY THIS WASN'T
A POLICY BOOK

VERY INTENTIONALLY, THIS BOOK HAS NOT BEEN about public policy, traditionally understood. Four explanations for why I made this decision are worth underscoring before we part.

1. Because hard problems are never solved by fighting about competing solutions before first defining precisely what problem we seek to solve.

Creative dynamism and tension can yield wonders, but only if they are unleashed *after* a problem has been defined and agreed upon. But if the fighting about means starts *before* we agree what end—what objective—we seek, the project is doomed to failure. It will devolve into irreconcilable strife about protecting current incumbent institutions (e.g., the form of the modern high school) and settling scores about larger social and economic politics.

This book, instead, has aimed to persuade you that our shared aspiration for our teens should be that all of them arrive at adulthood as fully formed, vivacious, appealing, resilient, self-reliant, problem-solving, gritty souls. We do not want more timid souls who drift through their teens and twenties in a state of numb, passive, dependent, perpetual adolescence. We want the rising generation to be the kind of Americans who understand and emulate the vigor of Teddy Roosevelt in their citizenship, in their work, in their families.

Once we agree on this goal of independent adults, we could then start moving toward the "how?" and the "by which institutions?" questions.

2. Because the heart of the problem we are tackling in this book is well upstream from politics. We are a drifting and aimless people—awash in material goods and yet spiritually aching for meaning.

Obviously Washington is a terribly broken and dysfunctional place, but the larger share of what ails us as a nation is well upstream from politics. Culturally, we are a mess.

Politics can't fix that. No matter what legislation DC passes or doesn't pass, federal policy-making cannot fix the deeper problem. And faking it, pretending that it can—even a little bit—actually makes everything worse. It excuses us from tackling the portions that are in our own lanes, and those are big portions. It distracts us from the deeper problems that touch on our own character and the hollowness of our local communities and networks of relationships. And it tempts us toward a Manichean view of the world in which Republican versus Democrat is supposedly the deep and weighty cleavage between good and evil. Of course, that's absurd.

And so this book has worked hard to guard against a reductionism that wrongly pretends our politics either caused or can solve the vacuum that is our lack of a common cultural purpose. To be sure, there are some subset portions of the solution to our multilayered problem of coming of age that have federal policy components. But let's begin by admitting that federal policy is not the lion's share of what we require right now.

3. Because we are nowhere near having a fleshed-out menu of possible policy levers—let alone competing Democrat-versus Republican-menus— so it makes little sense to begin our discussion at the place where partisan-tribal actors will work to limit our conversation.

We need to rethink secondary education, higher education, generationally segregated youth culture, and job-retraining programs at the most basic levels. This is not a case of Republicans having great ideas but being stymied by Democrats, or Democrats having great ideas but being stymied by Republicans. This is about neither party having any ideas about how fundamental the rebuilding of our coming-of-age institutions needs to be. There is a crisis of vision in creating lifelong learners. Neither party yet has much to say.

The policy levers we ultimately pull will be complicated, historically unprecedented, and plural. That is, there is surely not any one magic bullet. We should be able to include a menu and map for discussion that incorporates a good number of policies that many of us don't like individually, because that will yield a more fruitful discussion and debate than trying to preclude serious conversation before it begins.

I have long talked about a "new GI bill for the digital age"—even though many others import to that discussion specific policies that I think can be counterproductive: free higher education, universal basic income, radically increased minimum wage, etc. I would prefer to have our policy discussion center on higher-education accreditation reform, income-share financing agreements, a new universe of job-retraining programs, and radical new freedom for governors and local school districts to experiment with public-private partnerships and work programs.

We need a big, broad, real debate. To be clear, I think that, long-term, most governmental expansions yield more unintended harm than good, so I am going to be skeptical of many of the ideas offered—but we need a healthy debate that is not predetermined by us-versus-them tribalism. So let's put a broad range of ideas on the table.

There is a nearly settled assumption among political addicts—politicians, journalists, lobbyists, advocacy organizations, most think-tankers, the 2 percent of the public that regularly watches political cable news—that the great divide in American life is political polarization. That's a serious problem, to be sure. But I think there's an even deeper cleavage in American life between the politically polarized or addicted (both right and left) and the politically disengaged—which constitutes a far larger segment of our people.

Starting a discussion of the coming-of-age crisis around policy and political differences will only further drive away the large segment of Americans that we need to reengage.

4. Because the policy discussions, when they come, will come not against a static backdrop, but in the context of a highly dynamic, rapidly changing technological environment—where many of the levers individual families and communities seek to pull will be emerging from highly diverse and competitive digital markets, not homogenous planned policy.

Consider again Salman Khan, accidental founder of Khan Academy. If you already know his story and his website, you get the point. If he isn't familiar to you, stop reading here and please return to chapter 3 of this book—or go to khanacademy.org. Sal is arguably the most important math *teacher* in the history of the world, full stop. Yet he is not a teacher in any traditional, school-based sense. And math wasn't really his thing. He was just an uncle trying to help a niece, and he sat at a technological moment. Necessity is the mother of invention.

So much of where we are headed next in education and job-retraining policy-making is going to be in a technological context that won't even exist yet when we build the policy-making framework for what comes next. Entrepreneurial coding schools are springing to life in big and small towns by the day, partly to mitigate the failures of government schools in science and math but also in response to new sectors and opportunities. Policy-makers are going to need to become more nimble—not advancing static, one-size-fits-all policies, but rather policy frameworks that can adapt and change and admit plural and partial solutions.

———

IN A SENSE, my opening claim that this book is not about "public policy" is wrong—but only if we properly define the word "public." In typical American parlance, "public policy" means "governmental policy." That's an unfortunate shorthand, because it obscures a critical distinction.

In one sense, this book is very much about public policy, so long as we understand the word "public" as "relating to the whole people."

In the UK, the terms "public" and "state/governmental" are better distinguished—such that bars and restaurants are "pubs," meaning that they are not private clubs with limited membership, but rather establishments that anyone can enter to eat. Obviously, they are not *governmental,* but they are still *public.* Similarly, a "public school" is what we would call a "private school" in the United States. The Brits have state or government schools, funded by taxpayers, and they have "public" schools, which are nongovernmental but open to anyone. The contrast there is with homeschooling or with narrowly private schools.

We would benefit from a distinction like this in American public life. For the subject matter of this book was very much about our shared, common problem with coming of age—a *public* problem that individual families will rarely be able to address sufficiently on their own in isolation, and yet not the sort of problem that government power will be able to solve either.

At the end of the day, the challenge before us is to create lifelong learners and lifelong producers. Parts of that riddle will surely touch policy, but the vast majority of the challenge is about nurturing more resilient souls. And governments cannot nurture.

We need to be able to say to our young people—and to have it be true—that they are not liabilities to be managed but assets to be developed. We need to stop warehousing our teens. We need to be able to tell them that they are important, to be able to say to them: "You're needed." That requires people who know them and have a feel for their history and their future. In short, it requires love. And love is beyond the competence of governmental policy-making.

IF TEDDY ROOSEVELT SPOKE TO A HIGH SCHOOL GRADUATING CLASS

AN AMERICAN HAS TO BE TOUGH IN MIND, IN BODY, and in spirit. Few Americans have exemplified this ideal like the nation's zealous uncle, Theodore Roosevelt.

Our twenty-sixth president ended up being one of the twentieth century's most accomplished and charismatic chief executives. But in the years after his birth in 1858, no one would have predicted either of these outcomes. Teddy was a sickly, asthmatic boy who grew up to be a cowboy, writer, police commissioner, governor, war hero, mountaineer and explorer, vice president—all culminating with two terms in the White House and a tumultuous post-presidential career founding a new political party and traveling the world.

Roosevelt won immense fame leading the "Rough Riders," an all-volunteer cavalry unit of misfits and older folks that he assembled in 1898 to fight Spaniards in Cuba during the Spanish-American War. Roosevelt's Rough Riders charged San Juan Hill and rode into legend. And when the United States entered the First World War in 1917, the "Bull Moose" hauled out his old colonel's uniform and volunteered—just shy of his sixtieth birthday—to lead an infantry unit. (Woodrow Wilson declined his request.) T. R. began planning another run for president in 1920, but died before announcing his candidacy.

Roosevelt often wrote and spoke—sometimes "softly but with a big stick," sometimes with a lion's roar—of what it means to be a good citizen. He was an unapologetic American. In his letters to his children, friends, colleagues, and the everyday Americans who wrote him throughout his public life, Roosevelt stressed the importance of cultivating the virtues necessary for good character. He was convinced that America could not thrive if Americans were not attentive to character. We should listen to him.

Very few American leaders today speak like Roosevelt did. Young Americans in particular would benefit from his voice. If he had a chance to speak to a class of high school graduates, I think he might say something like this.*

> *Ladies and gentlemen, distinguished guests, faculty, parents and family members, and, of course, graduates: thank you for the opportunity to speak to you. It's been a long time since I've delivered any sort of address, let alone a commencement. I hope you will not mind an old man, who has seen a few things in his day, making a few observations about your time and giving you a few bits of advice which will probably risk sounding platitudinous.*
>
> *I have often wondered whether there ever can come in life a thrill of greater exaltation and rapture than that which comes to one between the ages of, say, 6 and 14, when the library door is thrown open and you walk in and see all the books arrayed on your table, not as a burden, but as a wonderland of gifts. Do you yet see your books as a materialized fairy land?*

---

*Roosevelt's ideas and attitudes (and occasionally words) are drawn from the following: Theodore Roosevelt, *An Autobiography* (New York: The Library of America, 2004); Letter to Bessie Von Vorst, October 18, 1902, and Letter to James Wolcott Wadsworth Jr., January 3, 1906, both quoted in Theodore Roosevelt, *Letters and Speeches* (New York: The Library of America, 2004); "Speech to Brotherhood of Locomotive Firemen," Chattanooga, Tennessee, September 8, 1902, and "Speech to Topeka, Kansas YMCA," 1903, both quoted in William Bennett, *The Book of Man* (Nashville: Thomas Nelson, 2011); and "The American Boy," and Letter to Theodore Roosevelt Jr, August 25, 1903, both quoted in Douglas W. Philips, ed., *The Letters & Lessons of Theodore Roosevelt for His Sons* (San Antonio: The Vision Forum, Inc., 2001).

Having been a sickly boy, with no natural bodily prowess, and having lived most of my life at home, indoors, I could not hold my own against bigger, stronger, tougher boys. I was nervous and timid. Yet from reading about people I admired—ranging from the soldiers of Valley Forge to the heroes of my favorite stories—and from hearing of the feats performed by my forefathers and kinsfolk, and from knowing my father, I felt a great admiration for men who were fearless and who could hold their own in the world. I had a great desire to be like them. Until I was nearly 14, though, I let this desire take no more definite shape than my daydreams.

Then an incident happened that did me real good. In the days before inhaler devices delivered medicine for the quick relief of asthma, I was sent off to Moosehead Lake for fresh air and the space to recuperate from a nasty asthma attack. On the stagecoach ride there I met a couple of boys who were about my own age, but much more competent and also much more mischievous. They took one look at me and knew I was a victim. And so they made my life miserable. The worst part was, when I finally tried to fight them, I quickly learned that any one of them could not only handle me easily, but could do it while laughing at me and preventing me from doing any damage whatsoever to them in return.

That flesh-and-blood experience taught me what probably no amount of advice could have taught me. I made up my mind that I must figure out how to never again be put in that helpless position. And having become quickly and bitterly conscious that I did not have the natural prowess to hold my own, I decided that I would substitute in the place of nature extra effort, extra training. With my father's hearty approval, I started to learn to box. I was painfully slow and awkward, and it took two or three years before I made any perceptible improvement whatever. But I kept boxing. And eventually I came to life.

As an adult, I kept at it for exercise and for craft. I would spar regularly with prizefighters when I was police commissioner of New York City. I kept it up when I was governor of New York. I tried to maintain a routine schedule when I was president—right up until one of my sparring partners hit me so hard that I was left partially blind in my left eye. To my great regret, I had to give up my beloved pastime. So I took up jiujitsu instead.

But perhaps you hear me as a relic of an older, more poorly lit era—an era before electric lights and telephones, motorcars and moving pictures, gleaming skyscrapers and speedy transcontinental travel. An era before two great wars convulsed the world and made the country you are blessed to live in a global power unlike any since the Roman Empire. An era before radio, television, and your now internetworked computers. An era when hunger and poverty remained endemic in parts of this great land. A time of great inequality not just among the races and the sexes but also between the wealthy and the poor. You have come far and fast in many respects.

But even as I am an enthusiastic believer in the doctrine of progress, I understand that not all progress runs in a straight line. If I may be blunt—and I am always blunt: you people have some big problems.

Graduates, you are on the cusp of adulthood. Your bodies are already there in terms of reproductive abilities—but what about your minds, your spirits? You are about to get "degrees," but what do they mean? What do you have to show for being on the cusp of adulthood? Do you know where your next meal is coming from? Do you know where you will sleep tonight? Do you have plans to attend a college or university in the autumn? If your answer to all three of those questions is "yes," then bully for you. You are alive.

But barely. Just barely. And I doubt very much that you are living.

I see in your generation plenty of "busyness." A lifetime of activities has been carefully planned and calculated for maximum benefit for . . . college admissions officers. I hear laments about the stresses and demands of this age, how you are too young for the rat race. I read with astonishment how your generation is depressed and anxious. So many of you take so many medicines to alleviate the symptoms. You think you are deadening the pain—but I worry you are deadening the aliveness.

You are coming of age in the wealthiest nation on earth, and yet you seem so out of sorts. Miserable, even. Lacking purpose.

You do not know what you do not know. Are you always indoors? Could you identify a flower, other than a rose or a carnation? Have you ever seen the view from a mountaintop? Do you know the difference between a wren and a sparrow? A mockingbird and a meadowlark? I'd venture to guess not one in two hundred of you could do it. I doubt your teachers could, either.

How many books have you read this month? This year? This week? I read a book before breakfast. I expect I'll read another before bedtime. This is my usual pattern. I won't presume to dictate your pace; only to suggest that you aren't reading enough. Oh, and your glowing screens do not count. Your screens are a distraction from the world around you.

Hey, you!—in the third row, with the dyed hair, on your smartyphone—are you hearing me? Put your gadgets down and look around you! Wake up! Stand up! You need what I'm saying.

The year before I was elected William McKinley's vice president, I delivered a speech in Chicago called "The Strenuous Life." You might have read about it in your American history class. (I am told you now call this "social studies." That is not progress.)

Then and now, I would say to you that the highest form of success comes not to the man or woman who desires mere easy peace, but to the one who does not shrink from danger, from hardship, or from bitter toil—and who out of these wins the splendid ultimate triumph. I have no patience for critics who do little but point out how the strong man stumbles. They blather about how the doer of deeds could have done them better. You should learn to mostly ignore such ankle-biters. Instead learn to praise the men who are actually in the arena—and no longer just men, but any citizen who strives valiantly and who comes up short again and again. Praise those who try—because there is no effort without error and shortcoming.

I can see that I've discomforted some of you parents. But I cannot apologize for this, because you people need some discomforting from your stupor. I do not believe it is wrong to encourage your children to aspire to that kind of strenuous life. It's the kind of life that recognizes and seeks out the fulfillment of production and avoids the lethargic unfulfillment of excessive consumption. If the unexamined life is not worth living, then neither is a life of passive, slothful ease.

Do you people still believe in courage? In self-sacrifice? I saw these virtues at San Juan Hill and I saw it with my four sons, each of whom served this country with distinction. My boy Quentin was killed in aerial combat over France during the First World War. My oldest, Ted Jr., was a general leading troops in France against the Germans in World War II when he finally succumbed to a heart attack in 1944. Kermit was a major in the U.S. Army—he died in Alaska in 1943. My youngest, Archie, fought and was injured—in both world wars. America was built by these boys. And America in turn built them into men.

The nation could have avoided much suffering by shrinking from strife. Millions of mothers and fathers would have been spared mourning the loss of their sons and daughters. And we would have been the poorer for it. Thank God for the iron in the blood of your grandfathers and great-grandfathers! We wouldn't be America without the grit and resolve of these families—your families.

Your generation does not have to face the task that they faced, but you have your own challenges, and woe to you if you fail to meet them.

Here is the truth: nobody owes you anything. In this life we get nothing except through effort and hard work. You very likely have no idea of the sacrifices that were necessary to make your life possible today. I do not mean the steps your parents took to raise you in relative comfort; rather, I speak of the blood, toil, and treasure of many generations of Americans to secure liberty for them and for you. Freedom from effort in the present merely means that there has been stored-up effort from the past. A mere life of ease is not in the end a very satisfactory life. Above all, it is a life that will render those who yearn for ease ultimately unfit for serious work in the world.

Meaningful work is not primarily a matter of finding a job. Serious work is more than drawing a salary. You are said to be a generation that puts a great deal of stock in choice. But not every choice is a good or laudable one.

If a man or woman, through no fault of his or hers, goes throughout life denied those highest of all joys which spring only from home life, from having and bringing up many healthy children, I feel for them deep and sincere sympathy. A similar sympathy extends to the brave soldier killed at the beginning of a fight, or the businessman who works hard and yet is bankrupted by the fault of others. But these are by no means the saddest people. Call me old-fashioned, but the man or woman who deliberately avoids marriage and has a heart so cold as to know no passion for it is a man or woman unworthy of my respect. We are talking about a shallow and selfish person.

An easy, good-natured kindliness, a desire to live your life purely according to your own desires—these are in no sense substitutes for the fundamental virtues, the practice of strong qualities without which there can be no strong people. And make no mistake: America requires strong men and women. We need people with courage and resolution; people who scorn what is mean, base, and selfish; people of eager desire to work or fight or suffer as the case may be—provided the goal is great enough. America demands men and women who contemptuously set aside mere ease, mere vapid pleasure, mere avoidance of toil and worry.

It is no secret that I think boys and girls have different responsibilities, different roles—but I was an outspoken supporter of women's suffrage. Legal equality is a given. And I believe women are perfectly adept at all but the most physically taxing professions. But let's set aside our possible differences on gender issues so that we might agree on this fundamental point: America needs both genders to be exceedingly strong and resilient.

I have thought a bit more about the particular strengths we need in our boys, and I cannot hide the fact that I am worried that you boys are soft. America has a right to expect that our boys will turn out to be good men. In my experience, the chances are strong that one won't be much of a man unless he was first a good deal of a boy. He must not be a coward or a weakling, a bully, a shirk, or a prig. He must work hard and he must play hard. He should be able to hold his own under all circumstances and against all comers. It is only on these conditions that he will grow into the kind of American man that America needs—of whom America can be really proud.

To be considered a true adult, you need both physical and moral courage. Neither can take the place of the other. As soldiers become men they often find that there are some warriors very brave in the field who prove timid and worthless as politicians and leaders. Conversely, some politicians who show an entire readiness to take chances and assume responsibilities in civil affairs lack the fighting edge when exposed to real physical danger. In each case, with soldiers and politicians alike, there is but half a virtue. The possession of the courage of the soldier does not excuse the lack of courage in the statesman, and even less does the possession of the courage of the statesman excuse shrinking on the field of battle. You must be prepared to lose your body in a great quest.

An adult must develop his or her physical prowess up to a certain point, but eventually you will reach that point where other things count more. In my regiment nine-tenths of the men were better horsemen than I was, and probably two-thirds of them were better shots than I was, while on the average they were certainly hardier and more enduring. Yet after I had had them a very short while they all knew, and I knew too, that nobody else could command them as I could command.

I believe in going hard at everything, always—whether it is Latin or mathematics, boxing or football. At the same time I want to keep the sense of proportion. I believe in rough, manly sports. But I do not believe in them if they degenerate into the sole end of anyone's existence. Character counts for a great deal more than either intellect or body in winning success in life.

You should want to be good—not goody-goody, not for appearances, but just plain good. Do you all talk about this? Cultivate the virtues! I mean "good" in the largest sense. It includes whatever is straightforward and clean, brave and manly. Have courage. Be honest. Exercise your God-given common sense. The best people I know—the very best people—are good at their studies or their business, fearless and stalwart. And note this: they are hated and feared by all that is wicked and depraved. I want you to hate things that are worthy of your hate.

The best people are incapable of submitting to wrongdoing, and they are equally incapable of being anything but kind and tender to the weak and helpless. This requires actually preparing to protect them. I recognize that this might not be a popular thing to say in your day, but the prime reason for abhorring cowards is because, if they were good, they would have it in them to thrash those who would harm the weak if and when the need arose.

Let me say something about the real world of work. Work—the capacity for work, the well of toughness in your chest even when you don't "feel" like fulfilling your duty—is absolutely necessary. No man's life is full, no one can be said to live in the true sense of the word, if he does not work. This is necessary, and yet it is not enough. If you are utterly selfish, if you utterly disregard the rights of others, if you have no ideals, if you work simply to gratify yourself, small is your good to the community. I think even then you are probably better off than if you were just an idler or a slacker. But you are of no real use unless, together with the quality that enables you to work, you have the quality that enables you to love your co-laborers, to work with them and for them for the common good of all.

Stop pitying a man or woman because they must do hard, even painful work—so long as the work is worth doing. I don't pity workers who toil; I admire them. You know who I pity? I pity the creature who doesn't work, at whichever end of the social scale he may regard himself as being. The law of worthy work well done is the law of successful American life.

I believe in play, too—you should play and play hard when you are playing. But don't ever make the mistake of making play the main thing. The work is what counts, and if you do your work well and it is worth doing, then it matters but little in which line that work is done; the man is a good American citizen. If he does his work in slipshod fashion, then no matter what kind of work it is, or how much money it pays, he is poor. And a poor American.

Aspire to be known as a worker—as one who would be ashamed not to pull his own weight, ashamed to become beholden to someone else for what he ought to be doing for himself. No man is happy if he does not work. I challenge you to find a truly happy adult who has no work. You will not find one.

Of all miserable creatures the idler, in whatever rank of society, is in the long run the most miserable. Drink this in: if a man does not work, then nothing can be done with him. He is out of place in any community—but especially in our American community. For we are workers. We have in our scheme of government no room for the man who does not wish to pay his way through life by what he does for himself and for the community. If he has leisure that makes it unnecessary for him to devote his time to earning his daily bread, then all the more is he bound to work just as hard in some way that will make the community better off for his existence. If he fails that, he fails to justify his existence. Who cares about his bank balance?

You seek success? Adults have told you that you can be anything you want to be. That is not so. Every one of you has limitations that you will not be able to overcome. This is true; now, so what? Go and build and exercise for your fellow man the talents that you do have.

There are two kinds of success. One is the very rare kind that comes to the man who has the power to do what no one else has the power to do. That is genius. But the average man who wins success is not a genius. He is a man who has the ordinary qualities that he shares with his fellows, but who has developed those ordinary qualities to a more than ordinary degree.

You are Americans. But even more, you are men and women.

You must do meaningful work.

You must understand history and the debt you owe to your forebears.

You must understand your world and your place in it.

You must wrestle with ideas.

You must not shirk or slack off. You must work. For the fate of the Republic depends on you.

Oh, and again, you must play hard as well.

Now get to it! Commence. Thank you.

ACKNOWLEDGMENTS

GETTING THIS MANUSCRIPT FINALLY ACROSS THE finish line was a bit more painful than I had predicted—and for their patience, forgiveness, lack of cynicism (most of the time), and unconditional love (all the time), I owe a huge flying-tackle hug to Melissa, Corrie-Peach, Alex-Crash, and Breck-Dogman. These are the four life partners to whom I'd give not just a kidney but every last breath of life without having to consider it for an instant. I love you, weasels. And to my parents, who have always showed me the same sort of "we'll always be here, we'll always forgive you" unconditional love, thank you. I hope none of the stories in these pages that I told without any advance permission from you result in Mom pinching my ear.

Second, thank you to a group of friends-now-turned-parents with whom Melissa and I have been comparing notes for more than two decades on this most fundamental calling of nurturing little workers, little citizens, and eternal souls. From well before any of us actually had kids, with conversations traceable all the way back to late-night Apple Jacks in the Winthrop and Quincy Dining Halls, I'm especially indebted to Derek and Kelli Lewis, Scott and Carrie Brady, Ryan and Deena Gainor, Jonathan and Tanya Ellisor, Dave and Heather Rogers, and Ryan Taliaferro. (I would like to use each of these fellows' college nicknames, but this is a family-friendly book.) Few people get to develop deep new friendships in their adulthood, so Melissa and I are well aware of how blessed we are to have half a dozen special couples in our lives. We are passionately grateful to these friends and debate partners with whom we began a lifelong journey of parental idea-swapping in our 20s: Aerin and Dan Bryant, Teri and Tom Morrison, Lisa and Mike Horton, Sara and Brian Lee, Rana and Will Inboden, and Kimby and Lawrence Berger.

This book exists partly because of my shock, as a 37-year-old new college president, at the lack of preparedness for adulthood most 18-year-olds demonstrated as they arrived on campus at Midland University. I wouldn't have been able to serve those emerging adults, or to process what was happening to youth culture, without a core team that is extraordinary and kind: Kari Ridder, Shelly Blake, Jodi Benjamin, Ray Sass, Steve Bullock, Eliza Ferzely, Merritt Nelson, Jess Knoell, Nate Neufind, Dave Gillespie, and a rolling cast of wise and selfless board members. I'd love to work with all of you on a big project again.

Fourth, the team of big-cause, low-ego workhorses who survived sixteen months on a bus running for Senate together and then turned to stewarding our governance calling has truly become another family: Chris Barkley, Jordan Gehrke, Tyler Grassmeyer, Emily Karrs, Raven Shirley, Taylor Sliva, and James Wegmann. This project was conceived in the years before that campaign began, and many bus conversations rolling across Nebraska's beautiful ninety-three counties drifted into aspects of these chapters, and I am very grateful for both your constructive input and your "that's not how it works" push-backs.

Finally, I owe an enormous debt of gratitude to five people who know how to create a book—something that I as a regular user of books wrongly thought I mostly knew how to build. To Tim Bartlett, and the team of professionals behind your Oz-like curtain: Thanks for your steady hand, ready encouragement, and undeserved patience at so many stages of this process. One of those folks behind the curtain deserves special recognition, because of how many weekends he labored to keep us on schedule, always with a smile—so thank you, Alan Bradshaw. To Matt Latimer and Keith Urbahn: Thanks for believing in a rookie, and for being willing to speak up—again and again—when I was biting off more than I could chew or trying to say more than was necessary to make the point. To Ben Boychuk, who spent far more time on this project with me than anyone else, thank you for your brain, your library, and your hunger to learn more and to get other people's ideas right. Your passion was infectious and I learned a great deal as we would argue and as we would revise. As with so many of the previously mentioned contributors, thanks for caring about the development of not only your kids and my kids, but the kids of those who will read and wrestle with this book.

NOTE ON SOURCES
AND METHODS

*(Or: Why I Left Out Endnotes and
Kept This Bibliography Short)*

I'M A HISTORIAN BY TRAINING. BUT THIS OBVIOUSLY is not an academic book. Still, some habits are hard to break. When I was preparing the manuscript, I didn't skimp on the footnotes and endnotes. Including notes is what researchers do, after all—so it seemed like the thing to do here too.

Personally, I'm the type of reader who will stick a bookmark in the endnotes section of a book in order to flip back and forth from the main text more conveniently. I also make notes on notes, deciding where to go and read more. It's not uncommon to find some real gems in the notes. George Anastaplo, who lectured for nearly sixty years at Loyola University Chicago School of Law, famously packed his books with footnotes that often read like mini-essays.

Well, my editor wouldn't go for that. And, in all likelihood, neither would most readers. (My editor is wise.) For good and for ill, footnotes and endnotes are gradually disappearing from printed books. And in the case of titles aimed at a more popular audience, that might be fine.

Nevertheless, a writer owes his or her readers at least some explanation of sources, though without overwhelming them with information. So, in addition to a bibliographic list of works consulted in this project, here please also find a partial attempt to flag with slightly greater detail a handful of the books that made this book possible.

A book like this is the product of reading from well before there was a precise book project. Part of the fun of writing was being able to draw on so much of the great stuff I read in high school and college, and then later in graduate school at St. John's and Yale. It's impossible to account for every influence, though digging into some of the enduring works explored in chapter 8 isn't a bad place to start. It's fair to say that the thought and works of Aristotle, Augustine, Rousseau, Luther, and Calvin—so vital to my own intellectual development—are present on many of the pages here. Having thoroughly devoured their writing in my academic work, it's impossible for their influence not to seep into this project. We all stand on the shoulders of giants.

Research led to some delightful new discoveries of works that I didn't know existed before this project. In the chapter on why travel is vital, my thought was shaped in large part by my own experiences. But those experiences were in turn shaped, at least during my years as an undergraduate, in no small part by John Stilgoe's teaching. I remember fondly his lecture to mostly well-to-do undergraduates at Cambridge (my modest family finances were an outlier) about how they would not likely be able to survive very long in the wild. A day or two, tops, he said, with a shrug of indifference. Stilgoe inspired me to take a canoe trip with three buddies one memorable spring through the wilderness of Maine. As I was thinking about his lectures from a quarter century ago, I wondered what Stilgoe was working on now. I was pleased to discover not only that he is still teaching as he approaches 70 years of age but also that he published an important book in 2015, *What Is Landscape?* Stilgoe taught me a different way of seeing and listening to the world around me. I tried to convey some of those lessons in chapter 7, and I quote from his eminently readable primer on exploration, *Outside Lies Magic: Regaining History and Awareness in Everyday Places* (1998).

I knew of education historian Carl Kaestle's work on education in early America (including, notably, *Pillars of the Republic: Common Schools and American Society, 1780–1860*, 1983), but it was during the course of researching and writing the section of chapter 8 on why the United States developed as both a free country and a print culture that I revisited his important work on literacy. Kaestle's *Literacy in the United States: Readers and Reading Since 1880*, edited with Helen Damon-Moore, Lawrence C. Steadman, Katherine Tinsley, and William Vance Trollinger Jr., led in turn to the University of North Carolina Press's impressive five-volume *History of the Book in America*, of which Kaestle edited the fourth volume on the expansion of publishing and reading in the United States from 1880 to 1940. I also relied on the first two volumes of the series, *The Colonial Book in the Atlantic World* (edited by Hugh Amory and David D. Hall) and *An Extensive Republic: Print, Culture, and Society in the New Nation, 1790–1840* (edited by Robert A. Gross and Mary Kelley).

Any discussion of the history of public education in the United States would be incomplete without referring to Bernard Bailyn's groundbreaking study, *Education in the Forming of American Society* (1960), and Lawrence

Cremin's three-volume history, *American Education* (*The Colonial Experience, 1607–1783*, 1970; *The National Experience, 1783–1876*, 1980; and *The Metropolitan Experience, 1876–1980*, 1990). Although Cremin was himself highly sympathetic to the progressive education movement, which he discusses at length in his John Dewey Society Lecture, *Public Education* (1976), he was a perceptive critic and recognized the challenges and drawbacks associated with a century of progressive trial and error, as he elaborated in *Public Education and Its Discontents* (1990).

So it's fair to say the history of American education has long been a personal and professional interest of mine. But only while working on chapter 3 did I become acquainted with what might be best described as the "literature of dissent"—the so-called de-schoolers and un-schoolers and advocates of the "separation of school and state" who challenged the assumptions of John Dewey and the progressive education movement. These included conservatives such as Felix Wittmer (*The Conquest of the American Mind*, 1956), who perceived a strain of Marxism in American progressive methods, as well as leftists such as Paul Goodman (*Growing Up Absurd: Problems of Youth in the Organized Society*, 1960 and 2012, and *Compulsory Mis-education*, 1964), who believed American public schools had become too corporatized and regimented for a country founded on freedom and self-discovery. *Growing Up Absurd*, incidentally, first appeared in *Commentary* under the editorship of Norman Podhoretz well before Podhoretz moved to the right. But one of the great revelations in researching and writing this book came with the discovery of John Taylor Gatto's books—particularly his first book of essays, published shortly after he was named New York State Teacher of the Year, *Dumbing Us Down: The Hidden Curriculum of Compulsory Schooling* (1992), and a later volume, *Weapons of Mass Instruction: A Schoolteacher's Journey through the Dark World of Compulsory Schooling* (2009). Gatto, unfortunately, has a reputation as a bit of a crank and a conspiracist, which comes through in his more recent writings. But his early work is bold, path-breaking, and sadly overlooked. It's a shame we don't have more teachers like him.

Writing a book also sometimes takes you down odd paths that yield little more than an anecdote, or a fragment, or bits and pieces of trivia. Most students of colonial America are aware of the British licensing laws that placed heavy burdens on printers and led to, among other things, the development of our modern idea of freedom of speech and freedom of the press. Some students will know about the seditious libel trial of John Peter Zenger. But until the summer of 2016, I was unaware of the old English offense of "figurative treason." As it turns out, there is a doorstopper of study devoted to the subject: *Imagining the King's Death: Figurative*

Treason, Fantasies of Regicide, 1793–1796 (2000) by John Barrell, professor of English and codirector of the Centre for Eighteenth Century Studies at the University of York (the book weighs in at 760 pages and will set you back $295 at Amazon).

A more affordable and approachable academic work is Harvey Mansfield and Delba Winthrop's edition of Tocqueville's *Democracy in America* (2000). That may not be the version you want to rip apart to read in chunks, as I often advise in speeches. But theirs is the version I quote. Mansfield, who is a legendary political scientist at Harvard, and his late wife Winthrop approached *Democracy in America* with the expressed goal "to convey Tocqueville's thought as he held it rather than to restate it in comparable terms of today." That doesn't necessarily make Tocqueville easily approachable to a lay reader, but it does mean the Mansfield and Winthrop edition is loaded with helpful annotations. More popular editions published by Penguin Classics, Bantam, and Harper Perennial lend themselves to the treatment I suggest. It was the latter edition, translated by George Lawrence and edited by J. P. Mayer, that I first encountered as a college student and used for years.

Finally, writing this book offered a chance to explore literature that I had encountered only on the periphery. For instance, the chapter on aging and coming to terms with death was written largely around a popular new translation of Cicero's *On Growing Old* by Philip Freeman, titled *How to Grow Old: Ancient Wisdom for the Second Half of Life* (2016). The book is formatted like the old Loeb Classical Library editions, with the English side-by-side with the original Latin—a language whose death has been greatly exaggerated. And I confess that the Peter Pan analogy at the outset of the book was not my idea originally, but was rather a suggestion from one of my editors. That suggestion led me to J. M. Barrie's story, which was a stage play before it was a novel. As with most people who know of the Peter Pan legend, my knowledge was limited almost exclusively to the Disney version and Sandy Duncan's Broadway performance. But Barrie was a marvelous storyteller in his own right, and the original packs a far greater punch in prose than the animated version ever could.

As usual, the book is better . . .

Few of the following works have been made into movies, but many of them would be excellent.

BIBLIOGRAPHY

INTRODUCTION

Roosevelt, Theodore, Philips, Douglas W. (ed.), *The Letters & Lessons of Theodore Roosevelt for His Sons*. San Antonio: The Vision Forum, Inc., 2001, pp. 47-48

CHAPTER 1

Acs, Gregory, Kenneth Braswell, et. al. "The Moynihan Report Revisited." Washington, D.C.: Urban Institute, June 2013 http://www.urban.org /sites/default/files/publication/23696/412839-The-Moynihan-Report -Revisited.PDF

Barrie, J. M., Maria Tatar (editor). *The Annotated Peter Pan*. New York: W. W. Norton & Company, 2011

Fass, Paula. *The End of American Childhood: A History of Parenting from Life on the Frontier to the Managed Child*. Princeton, N.J.: Princeton University Press, 2016.

Manyika, James, et al., "Disruptive Technologies: Advances That Will Transform Life, Business, and the Global Economy." McKinsey Global Institute, May 2013. http://www.mckinsey.com/business-functions/bu siness-technology/our-insights/disruptive-technologies.

Murray, Charles. *Coming Apart: The State of White America, 1960-2010*. New York: Crown Forum, 2012

Putnam, Robert. *Our Kids: The American Dream in Crisis*. New York: Simon & Schuster, 2015

Rousseau, Jean-Jacques (Allan Bloom, translator). *Emile or On Education*. New York: BasicBooks, 1979

Shierholz, Heidi, and Lawrence Mishel. "A Decade of Flat Wages: The Key Barrier to Shared Prosperity and a Rising Middle Class." Economic Policy Institute, August 21, 2013. http://www.epi.org/publication/a -decade-of-flat-wages-the-key-barrier-to-shared-prosperity-and-a -rising-middle-class/.

St. Augustine. *The Confessions*. New York: Everyman's Library, 2001.

Vance, J. D. *Hillbilly Elegy: A Memoir of a Family and Culture in Crisis.* New York: Harper, 2016

CHAPTER 2

"A Nation at Risk: The Imperative for Educational Reform." Washington, DC: National Commission on Excellence in Education, 1983.

"ADHD Medication Manufacturing in the US: Market Research Report." February 2015. http://www.ibisworld.com/industry/adhd-medication -manufacturing.html.

Aleccia, Jonel. "Teens More Stressed Out than Adults, Survey Shows." NBCNews.com, February 11, 2014. http://www.nbcnews.com/health /kids-health/teens-more-stressed-out-adults-survey-shows-n26921.

Alper, Becka A., "Millennials Are Less Religious than Older Americans, but just as Spiritual." Washington, DC: Pew Research Center, November 23, 2015. http://www.pewresearch.org/fact-tank/2015/11/23/mil lennials-are-less-religious-than-older-americans-but-just-as-spiritual/.

American College of Pediatricians. "The Impact of Pornography on Children." June 2016. https://www.acpeds.org/the-college-speaks/position -statements/the-impact-of-pornography-on-children.

American Psychological Association. Stress in America: The Impact of Discrimination. Stress in America Survey, 2016. http://www.apa.org /news/press/releases/stress/2015/impact-of-discrimination.pdf

Arnett, Jeffrey J. *Emerging Adulthood: The Winding Road from the Late Teens through the Twenties.* New York: Oxford University Press, 2004.

Arnett, Jeffrey J., and Elizabeth Fishel, *When Will My Grown-Up Kid Grow Up? Loving and Understanding Your Emerging Adult.* New York: Workman Publishing, 2013.

Association for University and College Counseling Center Directors, quoted in Mistler, et al.

Bailey, Beth, *From Front Porch to Back Seat: Courtship in Twentieth-Century America.* Baltimore: Johns Hopkins University Press, 1989.

Bailey, Beth, quoted in Jeffrey Arnett, J. *Emerging Adulthood: The Winding Road from the Late Teens through the Twenties.* 2nd ed. Oxford: Oxford University Press, 2015.

Barna Group. "Proven Men Porn Survey." Lynchburg, VA: Proven Men Ministries, Ltd., 2014. https://www.provenmen.org/2014PornSurvey/ (accessed February 15, 2017).

Betkowski, Bev. "Study Finds Teen Boys Most Likely to Access Pornography." *Folio,* University of Alberta, Canada, March 2, 2007. https:// sites.ualberta.ca/~publicas/folio/44/13/09.html.

Common Sense Media. "The Common Sense Census: Media Use by Tweens and Teens." November 3, 2015. https://www.commonsensemedia.org/the-common-sense-census-media-use-by-tweens-and-teens-info graphic.

Côté, James E., and Anton L. Allahar. *Generation on Hold: Coming of Age in the Late Twentieth Century.* New York: New York University Press, 1996.

Cross, Gary. *Men to Boys: The Making of Modern Immaturity.* New York: Columbia University Press, 2008.

Cunningham, Hugh. *Children and Childhood in Western Society since 1500.* Harlow, UK: Pearson-Longman, 2005.

Fass, Paula. *The End of American Childhood.* See chapter 1.

Fry, Richard. "For First Time in Modern Era, Living with Parents Edges Out Other Living Arrangements for 18- to 34-Year-Olds." Pew Research Center, Washington, DC, May 2016. http://www.pewsocial trends.org/files/2016/05/2016-05-24_living-arrangemnet-final.pdf.

Howard, Jacqueline. "Americans Devote More than 10 Hours a Day to Screen Time, and Growing," CNN, July 29, 2016. http://www.cnn.com/2016/06/30/health/americans-screen-time-nielsen/.

Hunt, Michael, quoted in David Masci. "Q&A: Why Millennials Are Less Religious than Older Americans." Pew Research Center, January 8, 2016. http://www.pewresearch.org/fact-tank/2016/01/08/qa-why-mil lennials-are-less-religious-than-older-americans/.

Hymowitz, Kay S. *Manning Up: How the Rise of Women Has Turned Men into Boys.* New York: City Journal/Basic Books, 2011.

James, Samuel D. "America's Lost Boys." *First Things,* August 2, 2016. https://www.firstthings.com/blogs/firstthoughts/2016/08/americas -lost-boys.

Kett, Joseph. *Rites of Passage: Adolescence in America, 1790 to the Present.* New York: Basic Books, 1977.

Konstam, Varda. *Parenting Your Emerging Adult: Launching Kids from 18 to 29.* Far Hills, NJ: New Horizon Press, 2013.

Lipka, Michael. "Millennials Increasingly Are Driving Growth of 'Nones.'" Pew Research Center "Facttank," May 12, 2015. http://www.pewresea rch.org/fact-tank/2015/05/12/millennials-increasingly-are-driving -growth-of-nones/.

Lukianoff, Greg, and Jonathan Haidt. "The Coddling of the American Mind." *Atlantic Monthly,* September 2015. http://www.theatlantic .com/magazine/archive/2015/09/the-coddling-of-the-american-mind /399356/.

Mintz, Steven. *Huck's Raft: A History of American Childhood.* Cambridge, MA: Belknap-Harvard, 2004.

Mistler, Brian J., et al., "The Association for University and College Counseling Center Directors Annual Survey," 2012. http://files.cmcglobal
.com/Monograph_2012_AUCCCD_Public.pdf.

"The Nation's Report Card: Results at a Glance." National Center for Education Statistics. Washington, DC: U.S. Department of Education, 2014. http://www.nationsreportcard.gov/hgc_2014/.

Neilsen Research Company. "So Many Apps, So Much More Time for Entertainment." Neilsen Newswire, June 11, 2015. http://www.nielsen
.com/us/en/insights/news/2015/so-many-apps-so-much-more-time
-for-entertainment.html.

Palladino, Grace. *Teenagers: An American History*. New York: Basic Books, 1996.

Pew Research Center. "Millennials in Adulthood: Detached from Institutions, Networked with Friends." March 2014. http://www.pew
socialtrends.org/files/2014/03/2014-03-07_generations-report-version
-for-web.pdf.

Postman, Neil. *The Disappearance of Childhood*. New York: Vintage Books, 1994.

Rabin, Roni Caryn, "Compulsive Texting Takes Toll on Teenagers," *New York Times,* October 12, 2015. http://well.blogs.nytimes.com/2015
/10/12/compulsive-texting-takes-toll-on-teenagers/?_r=0.

Reason-Rupe. "Millennials: The Politically Unclaimed Generation." The Reason-Rupe Spring 2014 Millennial Survey. Washington, DC: Reason Foundation, 2014.

Savage, Jon. *Teenage: The Prehistory of Youth Culture, 1875–1945*. New York: Penguin Books, 2008.

Shaputis, Kathleen. *The Crowded Nest Syndrome: Surviving the Return of Adult Children*. Olympia, WA: Clutter Fairy Publishing, 2003.

Smith, Christian, with Kari Christoffersen, Hilary Davidson, and Patricia Snell Hertzog. *Lost in Transition: The Dark Side of Emerging Adulthood*. Oxford: Oxford University Press, 2011.

Spock, Benjamin. Quoted in Fass, *The End of American Childhood*. See chapter 1.

Thompson, Sonya. "1 in 3 boys heavy porn users, study shows," *Eureka Alert,* February 23, 2007. https://www.eurekalert.org/pub_releases
/2007-02/uoa-oit022307.php.

"Tool: Recognizing Microaggressions and the Messages They Send," from *Diversity in the Classroom*. University of California, Los Angeles, 2014. http://academicaffairs.ucsc.edu/events/documents/Microag
gressions_Examples_Arial_2014_11_12.pdf.

Wang, Wendy, and Kim Parker. "Record Share of Americans Have Never Married." Washington, DC: Pew Research Center, September 2014. http://www.pewsocialtrends.org/2014/09/24/record-share-of-ameri cans-have-never-married/.

Waters, Mary C., et al., eds. *Coming of Age in America: The Transition to Adulthood in the Twenty-First Century.* Berkeley: University of California Press, 2011.

Woodham, Chai. "Why Kids Are Hitting Puberty Earlier than Ever." *U.S. News and World Report,* April 17, 2015. http://health.usnews.com /health-news/health-wellness/articles/2015/04/17/why-kids-are-hit ting-puberty-earlier-than-ever. Accessed July 5, 2016.

Zimbardo, Philip, and Nikita Coulombe. *Man Interrupted: Why Young Men Are Struggling and What We Can Do about It.* Newburyport, MA: Conari Press, 2016.

CHAPTER 3

Barry, Mary Nguyen, and Michael Dannenberg. "Out of Pocket: The High Cost of Inadequate High Schools and High School Student Achievement on College Affordability." *Education Reform Now.* April 2016.

Bell, Albert L. "Three-Right Circus for Morons." *American Mercury* 44, no. 174 (June 1938).

Bestor, Arthur E. *Educational Wastelands: The Retreat from Learning in Our Public Schools.* Urbana: University of Illinois Press, 1953.

Briggs, Thomas H., quoted in Richard Hofstadter, *Anti-Intellectualism in American Life.* New York: Vintage, 1966.

Ciotti, Paul. "Money and School Performance: Lessons from the Kansas City Desegregation Experiment." Cato Policy Analysis no. 298. Washington, DC: Cato Institute, March 16, 1998. http://www.cato.org /pubs/pas/pa-298.html.

DeSilver, Drew. "U.S. Students Improving—Slowly—in Math and Science, but Still Lagging Internationally." Pew Research Center, Washington, DC, February 2, 2015. http://www.pewresearch.org/fact-tank /2015/02/02/u-s-students-improving-slowly-in-math-and-science-but -still-lagging-internationally/.

Dewey, John, quoted in Edmondson, Henry, *John Dewey and the Decline of American Education.* New York: Open Road Media, 2014. https://books.google.com/books?id=liGDAwAAQBAJ&pg=PT39 &lpg=PT39&dq=dewey+schools+%22book+knowledge%22& source=bl&ots=EdPdvPJ2Di&sig=XqQwKaQCM4lRo4GPG65I Oa3-FtM&hl=en&sa=X&ved=0ahUKEwjG-vislvTPAhVH3IMKH

TM9CpAQ6AEIIDAB#v=onepage&q=dewey%20schools%20%22 book%20knowledge%22&f=false.

"Fast Facts: Enrollment Trends." National Center for Educational Statistics. Washington, DC: U.S. Department of Education, 2016. https://nces.ed.gov/fastfacts/display.asp?id=65.

Franciosi, Robert J. *The Rise and Fall of American Public Schools: The Political Economy of Public Education in the Twentieth Century.* Westport, CT: Praeger, 2004.

Gatto, John Taylor. *Dumbing Us Down: The Hidden Curriculum of Compulsory Schooling.* Gabriola Island, British Columbia: New Society Publishers, 1992.

———. *Weapons of Mass Instruction: A Schoolteacher's Journey through the Dark World of Compulsory Schooling.* Gabriola Island , British Columbia: New Society Publishers, 2009.

Gearon, Christopher J. "Colleges Adopt Programs to Help Freshmen Adapt." *U.S. News & World Report,* September 10, 2014. http://www.usnews.com/education/best-colleges/articles/2014/09/10/colleges-adopt-programs-to-help-freshmen-adapt.

Goodman, Paul. *Compulsory Mis-education and The Community of Scholars.* New York: Horizon Press, 1964.

———. *Growing Up Absurd: Problems of Youth in the Organized Society.* New York: New York Review Books, 2012.

Hayes, William. *The Fate of Liberal Arts in Today's Schools and Colleges.* Lanham, MD: Rowman & Littlefield, 2015.

Hofstadter, Richard. *Anti-Intellectualism in American Life.* New York: Vintage, 1966.

Janak, Edward. "'Caught in a Tangled Skein': The Great Depression in South Carolina's Schools." In *Education and the Great Depression,* edited by E. Thomas Ewing and David Hicks. New York: Peter Lang, 2006.

Lagemann, Ellen Condliffe. *An Elusive Science: The Troubling History of Education Research.* Chicago: University of Chicago Press, 2000.

Lynch, Matthew. "P-16 and P-20 Initiatives: Critical for Education Reform." *Huffington Post,* March 4, 2014. http://www.huffingtonpost.com/matthew-lynch-edd/p-16-and-p-20-initiatives_b_4894357.html.

Organization for Economic Cooperation and Development, quoted in DeSilver.

Ravitch, Diane. *Left Back: A Century of Failed School Reforms.* New York: Simon & Schuster, 2000.

Redford, Jeremy, Danielle Battle, and Stacey Bielick, "Homeschooling in the United States: 2012." National Center for Educational Statistics,

Institute of Education Sciences. Washington, DC: U.S. Department of Education. November 2016.

Sayers, Dorothy L. *The Lost Tools of Learning.* London: Methuen, 1948.

CHAPTER 4

Aechylus (Robert Fagles, translator). *The Oresteia: Agamemnon, The Libation Bearers, The Eumenides.* New York: Penguin Classics, 1984

Boston Public Health Commission. "Health of Boston, 2014–2015." http://www.bphc.org/healthdata/health-of-boston-report/Documents/HOB-2014-2015/5_MaternalChild_HOB%202014-2015.pdf.

Churchill, Winston, quoted in Martin Paul. *Counting Sheep: The Science and Pleasures of Sleep and Dreams.* London: HarperCollins, 2002.

Cicero, Marcus Tullius. *How to Grow Old: Ancient Wisdom for the Second Half of Life.* Translated by Philip Freeman. Princeton, NJ: Princeton University Press, 2016.

Dreher, Rod. "This Mortal Coil," (blog post). *The American Conservative,* August 26, 2015 http://www.theamericanconservative.com/dreher/mortal-coil/.

Eliot, Andrew, quoted in David E. Stannard. *The Puritan Way of Death: A Study in Religion, Culture, and Social Change.* New York: Oxford University Press, 1979.

Fuller Youth Institute, quoted in Powell, Griffin, and Crawford.

Hine, Thomas. *The Rise and Fall of the American Teenager.* New York: Perennial, 2000.

Jackson, Andrew, quoted in Robert V. Remini. *Andrew Jackson and the Course of American Freedom, 1822–1832.* Baltimore: Johns Hopkins University Press, 1998.

Mather, Cotton, quoted in Stannard.

McPherson, Miller, Lynn Smith-Lovin, and Matthew E. Brashears. "Social Isolation in America: Changes in Core Discussion Networks over Two Decades." *American Sociological Review* 71, no. 3 (June 2006). https://archive.org/details/SocialIsolationInAmericaChangesInCoreDiscussionNetworksOverTwo.

Mencken, H. L., quoted in Thomas P. Riggio, ed. *The Dreiser-Mencken Letters.* Vol. 1. Philadelphia: University of Pennsylvania Press, 1986.

Powell, Kara, Brad Griffin, and Cheryl Crawford, "The Church Sticking Together." *Immense Journal* (September–October 2011).

Regnerus, Mark, and Jeremy Uecker. *Premarital Sex in America.* New York: Oxford University Press, 2011.

Roosevelt, Theodore. *An Autobiography.* New York: Library of America, 2004.

Schlegel, Alice, quoted in Leon Neyfakh. "What 'Age Segregation' Does to America." *Boston Globe,* August 31, 2014. https://www.boston globe.com/ideas/2014/08/30/what-age-segregation-does-america /o568E8xoAQ7VG6F4grjLxH/story.html.

Schwartz, Elliott. *Music: Ways of Listening.* New York: Holt, Rinehart, and Winston, 1982, quoted in https://www.brainpickings.org/2012/04/12 /elliott-schwartz-music-ways-of-listening/.

Smith, Wesley. "Cruel to Abandon Dying to Suicide While Preventing Others." The Corner, National Review Online, August 27, 2016. http://www.nationalreview.com/corner/439440/cruel-abandon-dying -suicide-while-protecting-others.

Stannard, David E., *The Puritan Way of Death: A Study in Religion, Culture, and Social Change.* New York: Oxford University Press, 1977.

Todd, Dennis. *Imagining Monsters: Miscreations of Self in Eighteenth-Century England.* Chicago: University of Chicago Press, 1995.

Toft, Mary. Quoted in Todd.

CHAPTER 5

Aquinas, Thomas. *Summa Theologiae.* Lander, WY: The Aquinas Institute, 2012.

Baxter, Richard, quoted in William Orme, *The Practical Works of the Rev. Richard Baxter.* Vol. 22. London: James Duncan, 1730.

Brooks, David. *The Road to Character.* New York: Random House, 2015.

Carlyle, Thomas, quoted in Daniel T. Rodgers. *The Work Ethic in Industrial America: 1850–1920.* 2nd ed. Chicago: University of Chicago Press, 2014.

Crawford, Matthew B. *Shop Class as Soulcraft: An Inquiry into the Value of Work.* New York: Penguin, 2009.

Deresiewicz, William. *Excellent Sheep: The Miseducation of the American Elite and the Way to a Meaningful Life.* New York: Free Press, 2014.

Edison, Thomas, quoted in James D. Newton, *Uncommon Friends: Life with Thomas Edison, Henry Ford, Harvey Firestone, Alexis Carrel & Charles Lindbergh.* New York: Mariner Books, 1987.

Einstein, Albert. Quoted in Walter Isaacson, *Einstein: His Life and Universe.* New York: Simon & Schuster, 2007

Fitzgerald, F. Scott, quoted in Maria Popova. "'Nothing Any Good Isn't Hard': F. Scott Fitzgerald's Secret to Great Writing." *Atlantic,* January

9, 2013. http://www.theatlantic.com/entertainment/archive/2013/01/nothing-any-good-isnt-hard-f-scott-fitzgeralds-secret-to-great-writing/266935/.

Franklin, Benjamin. *Wit and Wisdom from Poor Richard's Almanack*. New York: Dover Thrift Editions, 1999.

Grund, Francis J. *The Americans in Their Moral, Social and Political Relations (Two Volumes in One)*. New York: Augustus M. Kelly, 1971. First published in 1837.

Hesiod. *Works and Days*. Edited and translated by Glenn W. Most. Cambridge, MA: Harvard University, Loeb Classical Library 57, 2006.

Hine, Thomas, *The Rise and Fall of the American Teenager*. New York: Perennial, 2000.

Jane, Talia. "An Open Letter to My CEO." Medium.com, February 20, 2016. https://medium.com/@taliajane/an-open-letter-to-my-ceo-fb73df021e7a#.4s0e8m18o.

Jefferson, Thomas. Letter to George Washington, August 14, 1787. http://tjrs.monticello.org/letter/98#X3184736.

Manton, Reverend Thomas. Quoted in Ryken, Leland, "The Original Puritan Work Ethic," *Christianity History*, Number 89, Winter 2006. http://www.christianitytoday.com/history/issues/issue-89/original-puritan-work-ethic.html.

O'Connor, Flannery (Sally Fitzgerald, editor). *The Habit of Being*. New York: Farrar, Straus, Giroux, 1979.

Riesman, David, and Warner Bloomberg Jr. "Work and Leisure: Fusion or Polarity?" In *Abundance for What? And Other Essays*, edited by David Riesman. New Brunswick, NJ: Transaction Publishers, 1993.

Roosevelt, Teddy, quoted in Albert B. Hart and Herbert R. Ferleger, eds. *Theodore Roosevelt Cyclopedia*. New York: Roosevelt Memorial Association, 1941.

Ryken, Leland. "The Original Puritan Work Ethic." *Christianity History*, no. 89 (Winter 2006): http://www.christianitytoday.com/history/issues/issue-89/original-puritan-work-ethic.html.

Weber, Max (Stephen Kalberg, translator). *Protestant Work Ethic and the Spirit of Capitalism*. New York: Oxford University Press, 2011.

Widdicombe, Ben. "What Happens when Millennials Run the Workplace?" *New York Times*, March 19, 2016. http://www.nytimes.com/2016/03/20/fashion/millennials-mic-workplace.html?_r=0.

Williams, Stefanie. "An Open Letter to Millennials Like Talia . . ." Medium.com, February 20, 2016. https://medium.com/@StefWilliams25/an-open-letter-to-millenials-like-talia-52e9597943aa#.aj0716ava.

CHAPTER 6

Bernstein, William J. *The Birth of Plenty: How the Prosperity of the Modern World Was Created.* New York: McGraw-Hill, 2004.

Brooks, Arthur. *The Conservative Heart: How to Build a Fairer, Happier, and More Prosperous America.* New York: Broadside Books, 2015.

Epictetus. *Discourses, Books 3-4, Fragments, The Enchiridion.* Translated by W. A. Oldfather. Cambridge, MA: Harvard University Press/Loeb Classical Library, 1928.

Ford, Thomas. Quoted in Sellers, *The Market Revolution.*

Fukuyama, Francis. *The Great Disruption: Human Nature and the Reconstitution of Social Order.* New York: Free Press, 1999.

Galbraith, John Kenneth. *The Affluent Society.* Boston: Mariner Books/Houghton Mifflin, 1998.

Goodman, Paul. *Growing Up Absurd: Problems of Youth in the Organized Society.* New York: New York Review of Books Classics, 2012.

Holiday, Ryan and Stephen Hanselman. *The Daily Stoic: 366 Meditations on Wisdom, Perseverance, and the Art of Living.* New York: Portfolio (Penguin Publishing), 2016.

Kochhar, Rakesh. "How Americans Compare with the Global Middle Class." Pew Research Center, July 9, 2015. http://www.pewresearch.org/fact-tank/2015/07/09/how-americans-compare-with-the-global-middle-class/. Accessed May 3, 2016.

Kotkin, Joel, *The City: A Global History.* New York: The Modern Library, 2005.

Montesquieu, Charles-Louis de (Thomas Nugent, translator). *The Spirit of the Laws.* New York: Cosimo Classics edition, 2011.

Murray, *Coming Apart.* See chapter 1.

Packard, Vance Oakley. *The Waste Makers.* Brooklyn, NY: Ig Publishing, 2011.

Riesman, David (with Nathan Glazer and Reuel Denny). *The Lonely Crowd.* New Haven, CT: Yale University Press, 1961.

Rousseau, Jean-Jacques. *Emile.* Translated by Allan Bloom. New York: Basic Books, 1979.

Rubin, Gretchen. *Better Than Before: What I Learned About Making and Breaking Habits—to Sleep More, Quit Sugar, Procrastinate Less, and Generally Build a Happier Life.* New York: Broadway Books, 2015

———. *The Happiness Project: Or, Why I Spent a Year Trying to Sing in the Morning, Clean My Closets, Fight Right, Read Aristotle, and Generally Have More Fun.* New York: Harper Paperbacks (revised edition), 2015.

Sedley, David. In *The Cambridge Companion to the Stoics,* edited by Brad Inwood. Cambridge: Cambridge University Press, 2003.

Sellars, John. *Stoicism.* Berkeley: University of California Press, 2006.

Sellers, Charles. *The Market Revolution: Jacksonian America, 1815-1846.* New York: Oxford University Press, 1991.

Smith, Christian, et al. *Lost in Transition: The Dark Side of Emerging Adulthood.* New York: Oxford University Press, 2011.

Veblen, Thorstein. *The Theory of the Leisure Class.* New York: Dover Publications (Dover Reprint Editions), 1994.

CHAPTER 7

Boorstin, Daniel J. *The Image: A Guide to Pseudo-Events in America.* New York: Vintage, 1992.

Gibbon, Edward. *Memoirs of My Life.* London: Folio Society, 1984.

Goethe, Johann Wolfgang von. *Italian Journey.* Translated by W. H. Auden and Elizabeth Mayer. London: Folio Society, 2010.

Kotkin, Joel. *The City: A Global History.* New York: The Modern Library, 2005.

Lewis, C. S. *Essay Collection and Other Short Pieces.* Edited by Lesley Walmsley. London: HarperCollins, 2000.

Steinbeck, John. *Travels with Charley in Search of America.* New York: Library of America, 2007.

Stilgoe, John. *Outside Lies Magic.* New York: Walker and Company, 1998.

Thoreau, Henry David. *Walden; or, Life in the Woods.* New York: Library of America, 1985.

Twain, Mark. *Innocents Abroad.* New York: Library of America, 1984.

———. *The Adventures of Huckleberry Finn.* Berkeley, CA: University of California Press, 1985.

CHAPTER 8

Aronowitz, Stanley and Henry Giroux. *Postmodern Education: Politics, Culture, and Social Criticism.* Minneapolis, MN: University of Minnesota Press, 1991.

Bijan, Stephen. "You Won't Believe How Little Americans Read." *Time,* June 22, 2014.

Bloom, Allan, *The Closing of the American Mind: How Higher Education Has Failed Democracy and Impoverished the Souls of Today's Students.* New York: Simon & Schuster, 1987.

292 THE VANISHING AMERICAN ADULT

Bloom, Allan and Harry V. Jaffa. *Shakespeare's Politics.* Chicago: University of Chicago Press, 1997.

Bureau of Labor Statistics. "American Time Use Survey—Summary." Washington, D.C.: U.S. Department of Labor, June 24, 2016. https://www.bls.gov/news.release/atus.nr0.htm

Burlingame. *Abraham Lincoln: A Life* (2 vol.). Baltimore: Johns Hopkins University Press, 2008.

Dusbiber, Dana. "Teacher: Why I don't want to assign Shakespeare anymore (even though he's in the Common Core)." *Washington Post,* June 13, 2015. https://www.washingtonpost.com/news/answer-sheet/wp/2015/06/13/teacher-why-i-dont-want-to-assign-shakespeare-anymore-even-though-hes-in-the-common-core/

Eliot, Charles W. (editor). *Harvard Classics* (51 volumes). New York: P. F. Collier and Son, 1909.

Febvre, Lucien and Henri-Jean Martin. *The Coming of the Book: The Impact of Printing, 1450-1800* (3rd Ed.) New York: Verso, 2010.

Franklin, Benjamin. "Apology for Printers" (1731). Quoted in Pasley, Jeffrey L., *"The Tyranny of Printers": Newspaper Politics in the Early American Republic.* Charlottesville, VA: University Press of Virginia, 2001.

Fried, Johannes (Peter Lewis, translator). *The Middle Ages.* Cambridge, MA: Harvard-Belknap, 2015.

Füssel, Stephan. *Gutenberg and the Impact of Printing.* London: Routledge, 2005.

Garcia, Emily. "'The Cause of America Is in Great Measure the Cause of All Mankind': American Universalism and Exceptionalism in the Early Nation." In *American Exceptionalisms,* edited by Sylvia Söderlind and Jamey Carson. Albany: SUNY Press, 2011.

Gottlieb, Agnes H. and Henry Gottlieb. *1,000 Years, 1,000 People: Ranking the Men and Women Who Shaped the Millennium.* New York: Kodansha America, 1998

Hart, James D. *The Popular Book: A History of America's Literary Taste.* London: Oxford University Press, 1950.

Hirsch, E. D. *Cultural Literacy: What Every American Needs to Know.* Boston: Houghton Mifflin Co., 1987.

Hirsch, E. D., Joseph F. Kett, and James Trefil. *The Dictionary of Cultural Literacy: What Every American Needs to Know* (1st edition). Boston: Houghton Mifflin Co., 1988.

Jefferson, Thomas. *Writings.* New York: Library of America, 1984.

Kamarck, Elaine C., and Ashley Gabriele. "The News Today: 7 Trends in Old and New Media." Center for Effective Public Management, Brookings Institution, November 2015.

Kirsch, Adam. "The 'Five-foot Shelf' Reconsidered." *Harvard Magazine*, November–December 2001. http://harvardmagazine.com/2001/11/the -five-foot-shelf-reco.html.

Kovarik, Bill. *Revolutions in Communication: Media History from Gutenberg to the Digital Age*. New York: Bloomsbury Academic, 2015.

Lewis, C. S. *Mere Christianity*. San Francisco: HarperSanFrancisco, 2001.

MacCulloch, Diarmaid. *The Reformation: A History*. New York: Viking, 2004.

Mumford, Lewis. *Technics and Civilization*. Chicago: University of Chicago Press (reprint edition), 2010.

Postman, Neil. *Amusing Ourselves to Death: Public Discourse in the Age of Show Business* (20th Anniversary Edition). New York: Penguin Books, 2005.

Rutherfurd, Livingston. *John Peter Zenger: His Press, His Trial and a Bibliography of Zenger Imprints*. New York: Dodd, Mead & Company, 1904.

The Trial of John Peter Zenger. Federal Hall National Monument, National Park Service. https://www.nps.gov/feha/learn/historyculture/the-trial -of-john-peter-zenger.htm.

CHAPTER 9

"Americans Know Surprisingly Little about Their Government, Survey Finds." The Annenberg Public Policy Center of the University of Pennsylvania, September 17, 2014. http://cdn.annenbergpublicpolicycenter .org/wp-content/uploads/Civics-survey-press-release-09-17-2014-for -PR-Newswire.pdf.

Basler, Roy P. (editor) *The Collected Works of Abraham Lincoln*. New Brunswick, NJ: Rutgers University Press, 1955.

Berns, Walter. *Making Patriots*. Chicago: University of Chicago Press, 2001.

Dickey, Jack. "The Revolution on America's Campuses." *Time*, May 31, 2016. http://time.com/4347099/college-campus-protests/.

Intercollegiate Studies Institute American Civic Literacy Program. "Our Fading Heritage." Wilmington, DE: Intercollegiate Studies Institute, 2008. https://www.americancivicliteracy.org/2008/summary_summa ry.html.

Jefferson, Thomas. *The Works of Thomas Jefferson*. Edited by Paul Leicester Ford. Vol. 11: *Correspondence and Papers, 1808–1816*. .New York: G. P. Putnam and Sons, 1905). http://oll.libertyfund.org/titles/807#Jeff erson_0054-11_455.

Lincoln, Abraham. "Speech at Chicago, Illinois." July 10, 1858. http://
    quod.lib.umich.edu/l/lincoln/lincoln2/1:526?rgn=div1;singlegenre
    =All;sort=occur;subview=detail;type=simple;view=fulltext;q1=Let
    +us+discard+all+this+quibbling.
Lukianoff, Greg. *Unlearning Liberty: Campus Censorship and the End of
    American Debate.* New York: Encounter Books, 2012.
Mullin, Benjamin. "A Third of Americans Can't Name any First Amend-
    ment Rights." The Poynter Institute, June 24, 2014. http://www
    .poynter.org/2014/a-third-of-americans-cant-name-any-first-amend
    ment-rights/256743/.
Newseum Institute/*USA Today.* "The 2016 State of the First Amendment."
    Washington, DC: Newseum Institute, June 2016. http://www.new
    seuminstitute.org/wp-content/uploads/2016/06/FAC_SOFA16
    _report.pdf.
"One in Three Americans Fail Immigrant Naturalization Civics Test."
    Xavier University News Release, April 27, 2012. http://www.xavier.edu
    /campusuite25/modules/news.cfm?seo_file=One-in-Three-Americans
    -Fail-Immigrant-Naturalization-Civics-Test&grp_id=319#.V4-292V
    gHdk.
Reagan, Ronald. "First Inaugural Address, Governor of California." Janu-
    ary 5, 1967. https://www.reaganlibrary.archives.gov/archives/speeches
    /govspeech/01051967a.htm.
Tocqueville, Alexis de. *Democracy in America.* Edited and translated by
    Harvey Mansfield and Delba Winthrop. Chicago: University of Chi-
    cago Press, 2000,

AFTERWORD

Bennett, William. *The Book of Man.* Nashville: Thomas Nelson, 2011.
Philips, Douglas W., ed. *The Letters and Lessons of Theodore Roosevelt for His
    Sons.* San Antonio: The Vision Forum, Inc., 2001.
Roosevelt, Theodore. "The American Boy," May 1900. Quoted in Philips,
    Letters and Lessons.
———. Speech to Brotherhood of Locomotive Firemen, Chattanooga,
    Tennessee, September 8, 1902. Quoted in Bennett, *Book of Man.*
———. Letter to Bessie Van Vorst, October 18, 1902. Quoted in Roos-
    evelt, *Letters and Speeches.*
———. Letter to Theodore Roosevelt Jr., August 25, 1903. Quoted in
    Philips, *Letters and Lessons.*
———. Speech to Topeka, Kansas YMCA, 1903. Quoted in Bennett,
    Book of Man.

―――. Letter to James Wolcott Wadsworth Jr., January 3, 1906. Quoted in Roosevelt, *Letters and Speeches*.

―――. *An Autobiography*. New York: The Library of America, 2004.

―――. *Letters and Speeches*. New York: The Library of America, 2004.

INDEX

Adams, John, 217–18
Adams, John Quincy, 254
ADHD, 37
Adler, Mortimer, 221–2
adolescence
  definitions of, 14–15
  perpetual, 2, 6, 8, 14–18, 110, 259
  See also coming of age
adult-children, 2, 51, 54, 100, 246
adulthood
  emerging adulthood, 43, 52–3, 81, 86, 145,   ˜58, 168, 210, 211
  legal definir
  markers o{
  quarter-l'
adulting,
Aeschyl'   ˙3
affluer   ˙so
    ˙   ˙. and consumption
age   ˙n, 18, 93, 98, 205.
    ˙ee also* generation segregation
American Civil War, 29, 34, 36, 48, 64, 65, 72–3, 235–6
Amish, 17, 161
anxiety
  age of, 164–8
  and college students, 38
  and parents, 95
  status, 24
Aquinas, Thomas: *Summa Theologica,* 134, 234

Arendt, Hannah: *Origins of Totalitarianism,* 237
Aristotle, 9, 114, 133, 134, 154, 228, 233, 234, 241
  Ethics, 233
  Politics, 236
Arnett, Jeffrey Jenson, 52–3. *See also* adulthood: emerging adulthood
Augustine of Hippo, 9, 23–4, 27–8, 228
  Confessions, 23, 233
Aurelius, Marcus: *Meditations,* 169
Avi: *The Secret School,* 243

Baby Boom generation, 18–21, 37, 42, 92
Bailey, Beth, 33
Baldwin, James: *Go Tell It on the Mountain,* 239
Barrie, J. M.: *Peter Pan,* 13–14
Baxter, Richard, 129–30, 168
Bell, Albert L., 62–3
Benedict, Ruth, 95
Bestor, Arthur, 69
Bible, 134, 187, 213–15, 225
  Genesis, 133, 229, 232
  Psalms, 103
  Proverbs, 131
  Ecclesiastes, 110
  Matthew, 232
  Romans, 229, 232
  Corinthians, 43

Bloom, Allan: *The Closing of the American Mind,* 222
Bonhoeffer, Dietrich: *Letters and Papers from Prison,* 230
Boorstin, Daniel, 181, 183
boredom, 46, 84, 111–12
Briggs, Thomas H., 68–9
Brooks, Arthur, 152–5
Brooks, David, 144
Bush, George W., 242

Call of Duty: Black Ops (video game), 39
Carlyle, Thomas, 134
Carter, Jimmy, 29, 63
Cather, Willa
  Death Comes for the Archbishop, 239
  O, Pioneers!, 239
Catholicism, 21, 42, 43, 73, 188, 214
character-building
  and adolescence, 15
  and democracy, 255
  and education, 21, 26–8
  and generation/age segregation, 86, 103–4, 116
  and grit, 6, 7, 46, 55, 78, 85, 122, 145, 259, 270
  habits of, 83–4, 85–7
  and intellectual fragility, 44–6
  and limited consumption, 86, 151–75
  and politics, 260
  and reading, 87, 207–28
  and republicanism, 7, 133, 164, 255
  and resilience, 6, 7, 8, 30, 36, 46, 103, 111, 115, 168, 178, 190, 211, 223, 258, 259, 263, 271

self-reliance, 2, 5, 7, 8, 22, 40, 259
  and self-restraint, 80, 125, 166, 256
  and travel, 86–7, 177–206
  and work ethic, 86, 122, 124, 129–39, 143–4, 147
  and work suffering, 9, 103–4, 120, 133, 138–40, 143–5
  See also virtue
Chase, Chevy, 177
Chaucer, Geoffrey, 228, 231
  Canterbury Tales, 234
Chesterton, G. K.: *Orthodoxy,* 230
Christianity, 27, 43, 103–5, 129, 134, 146, 228, 230, 232, 233–4, 256
  Catholicism, 21, 42, 43, 73, 188, 214
  Protestantism, 21, 42, 214
Churchill, Winston, 113
Cicero, Marcus Tullius, 89, 102–3, 213, 219
  On Old Age, 95
Ciotti, Paul, 62
civic education, 218–21, 245–58
civil rights, 20
Clements, Andrew: *Frindle,* 243
Clinton, Bill, 63
Cold War, 21, 193, 200, 247
Columbia University's Teachers College, 25, 68
coming of age, 1–2
  rites of passage, 16–17, 32, 43, 55, 96, 99, 137, 192
  See also adolescence
coming-of-age crisis, 1–8, 10, 22, 46, 125, 245, 261, 262
consumerism and consumption
  and age of anxiety, 164–8
  and comfort, 171–3

consumerist captivity, 155–7
and fashion, 163–4
and happiness, 152–5
and Industrial Revolution, 160–2
limited consumption, 86, 151–75
luxury, 5, 86, 127, 163–4, 168,
171, 182
meaningful production versus, 9,
18–19, 86, 122, 124, 173, 269
and millennials, 155–8
and necessity, 157–60
stepping stones, 174–5
and stoicism, 168–71
and technology, 6
using-and-discarding, 156, 167
Core Curriculum, 222, 224. *See
also* reading
Coulombe, Nikita, 39
Counts, George, 68
Crawford, Matthew, 133
Shop Class as Soulcraft, 132
curiosity, 81, 111–12, 139, 144,
178, 181, 182, 193, 200, 205,
210

death, 22, 86, 106–7, 110, 153,
158
death as central fact of life, 95–9
dying well, 100–104
infant mortality, 97, 196
Declaration of Independence, 20,
216, 218, 235, 248, 251, 252
deferred gratification, 26, 125, 152,
156, 166, 173
Democratic Party, 19, 203, 223,
257, 260
Democratic-Republican Party, 162
depression, 4, 37, 38, 106, 268
Deresiewicz, William, 144
de-schooling, 279. *See also*
homeschooling

Dewey, John, 22, 25–8, 66–8, 70,
79
Democracy and Education, 67
Humanist Manifesto, The, 67
"My Pedagogic Creed," 67
Diamond, Jared: *Guns, Germs, and
Steel,* 237
Dirty Rotten Scoundrels (film), 200
disruption, 7, 10, 19, 28, 30, 53,
73, 128, 163–7, 203, 215–16,
246
Donnelly, Joe, 203
Douglas, Stephen A., 211, 236
Douglass, Frederick, 135
*Narrative of the Life of Frederick
Douglass,* 236
Dreher, Rod, 103–4
Druhe, Clara, 94
Dust Bowl, 157, 239
Dylan, Bob, 96

Eager, Edward: *Tales of Magic,* 243
Edison, Thomas, 133, 212
education
achievement gaps, 62
compulsory attendance, 19, 34,
60, 65, 70, 71
Department of Education, 62, 63
Dewey on, 22, 25–8, 66–8, 70,
79
and digital revolution, 73–4
and funding, 61–4
"grade 13," 74–7
homeschooling, 73–4, 111, 262
homogenized schooling, 60–1,
69, 70, 76–7
hybrid learning, 73–4
and immigration, 64–6
learning how to learn, 77–82
Nation at Risk, A, 72
P-16 framework, 73–7

progressive, 25–7, 68–9
public education, 26, 36, 57–60,
    63, 66, 68–9, 71–2, 262
school prayer, 20
schooling as distinct from,
    59–61
secondary schooling, 19–20, 34,
    37, 62, 64, 68–9, 76–7, 260
social promotion, 63, 76
STEM programs, 238
traditionalist versus pragmatist
    view on, 21–2
trivium, 79
Einstein, Albert, 132, 212
Eisenhower, Dwight D., 44
elders, 17, 19, 80, 54, 93–5, 134
Eliot, Andrew, 98
Eliot, Charles W., 220–1, 227
Ellison, Ralph: *Invisible Man*, 240
employment. *See* work
Encyclopædia Britannica, 221
Engels, Friedrich: *Communist
    Manifesto* (with Marx), 237
entitlement, attitude of, 6, 44, 46,
    123, 125, 139, 158, 168
Epictetus, 219
  Enchiridion, 169–70
Erikson, Erik, 15, 49
escape, 110–17
Euclid: *Elements of Geometry*, 213,
    239
European Vacation (film), 177

fake news, 208, 220
Fass, Paula, 20, 35–6, 48, 55
Federalist Papers, 236
Fertile Crescent, 159
Fitzgerald, F. Scott, 132–3
Forbes, Esther Hoskins: *Johnny
    Tremain*, 36
Ford, Thomas, 163

Foundation for Individual Rights
    in Education, 250
Founding Fathers, 10, 128, 162,
    164, 211, 218, 233, 235, 237,
    251, 252–3
Franklin, Benjamin, 128–30,
    216–17
  Poor Richard's Almanac, 128–9,
    217
freedom to versus freedom from,
    122, 124, 230, 270
Friedman, Milton and Rose: *Free to
    Choose*, 237
Fukuyama, Francis, 165–7

Galbraith, John Kenneth: *The
    Affluent Society*, 166
Garcia, Emily, 217
Gatto, John Taylor, 71–3
  Dumbing Us Down, 71
generation segregation
  adult escapes, 110–15
  awareness of mortality, 99–100
  birth, 106–10
  death as central fact of life, 95–9
  dying well, 100–104
  elders, 17, 19, 80, 54, 93–5, 134
  peers and peer culture, 8–9, 18,
    20, 91–3, 95, 139
  purposes of sex, 104–6
  stepping stones, 115–17
Generation X, 42
Generation Z, 155
Gibbon, Edward: *The History of the
    Decline and Fall of the Roman
    Empire*, 181–2
Goethe, Johann Wolfgang von, 194
Goodman, Paul, 60–1, 70–1, 166
  Growing Up Absurd, 60, 70, 166
Great Depression, 35, 40, 65,
    120–1, 157, 167, 178–9

Greatest Generation, 42, 121
grit, 6, 7, 46, 55, 78, 85, 122, 145, 259, 270
Gruden, Jon, 138
Grund, Francis, 128
Gutenberg, Johannes, 212–16

Haidt, Jonathan, 45
Hamilton, Alexander, 162, 236
Hanselman, Stephen, 169
happiness, 9, 152–5
Harden, Blaine: *Escape from Camp Fourteen*, 102
Hayek, F. A.: *The Road to Serfdom*, 237
Hegel, Georg Wilhelm Friedrich, 67
helicopter parents, 2, 46, 116
Henley, William Ernest, 112
Hine, Thomas, 95
Hirsch, E. D.: *Cultural Literacy*, 222–3
Holiday, Ryan, 169
Homer, 177, 219, 228, 239
    Odyssey, 233
homeschooling, 73–4, 111, 262
Horowitz, Anthony: *Alex Rider* (series), 243
Hunt, Gladys: *Honey for a Child's Heart: The Imaginative Use of Books in Family Life*, 243
Hunt, Michael, 42
hunting, 96–7, 100–101
Hurst, Erik, 39
Hutchins, Robert Maynard, 221–2
Huxley, Aldous: *Brave New World*, 238

idleness, 6, 130–1
immigration, 120, 135, 202
    and assimilation, 48, 50

and education, 21, 50, 65
    and parenting, 55
    and U.S. naturalization test, 248
    waves of, 64–5, 219
Industrial Revolution, 28, 131, 160–2, 213, 236
intellectual fragility, 44–6
International Justice Mission, 102
Islam, 231, 232

Jackson, Andrew, 103, 254
Jackson, Jesse, 223
Jacksonians, 163, 168
Jane, Talia, 126–8
Jay, John, 236
Jefferson, Thomas, 133, 162, 164, 168, 206, 212, 237, 246, 251, 257
    syllabus for citizenship, 218–21
Jeffersonians, 163
jobs. *See* work
Judaism, 16, 21, 43, 64, 231, 232

Khan, Salman, 74, 261
Khan Academy, 74, 261
Kim Jong-un, 102
King, Martin Luther, Jr., 228, 257
    "Letter from a Birmingham Jail," 230
Kuhn, Thomas: *Structure of Scientific Revolutions*, 239

L'Engle, Madeleine, 108
    Wrinkle in Time, A, 143
Lewis, C. S., 184
    Chronicles of Narnia, The, 243
    Mere Christianity, 230
Lewis, Michael: *Moneyball*, 231
Lincoln, Abraham, 211, 236, 251, 256, 257

Lincoln-Douglas Debates, 211, 236
Lipka, Michael, 42
literacy, 10, 26, 36, 51, 63, 95,
    209–13, 217–18, 221–3, 242.
    See also reading
Lucretius: *On the Nature of Things,*
    239
Lukianoff, Greg, 45, 250
Luther, Martin, 146, 215–16
    Bondage of the Will, 234
    Commentary on Galatians, 232
luxury, 5, 86, 127, 163–4, 168,
    171, 182
Lynch, Matthew, 76

Machen, J. Gresham: *Christianity
    and Liberalism,* 231
Madison, James, 162, 212, 236
Mandela, Nelson, 112, 115
    Long Walk to Freedom, 230
Mann, Horace, 65
Mann, Kate, 44
Manton, Thomas, 129
marriage, 11, 32, 39, 41–2, 52, 53,
    84–5, 108, 154, 270–1
Marx, Karl, 131
    Communist Manifesto (with
    Engels), 237
Maslow, Abraham, 49
Mather, Cotton, 97
McCain, John, 112–13, 115
media, 50–1. *See also* social media;
    television
Mencken, H. L., 105, 135, 239
microaggressions, 1, 45–6
middle class, 20, 28, 35, 37, 131,
    164, 196
Midland University, 2–3, 47, 92,
    122–3, 125–6, 145, 224
military, U.S.
    Marine Corps, 17

Navy SEALs, 17
    reasons for enlistment, 101
millennials
    and civics, 43–4, 249
    and consumerism, 155–7, 167
    and grit, 55
    and perpetual adolescence, 52–3
    and religious participation, 42
    and socialism, 44, 237
    in the workplace, 46, 125
Mills, C. Wright: *White Collar,*
    166
Mintz, Steven, 36
Montesquieu, 164
Monty Python, 97
Morissette, Alanis, 170–1
Moynihan, Daniel Patrick, 19
    "Moynihan Report Revisited"
    (Urban Institute), 19
Mumford, Lewis, 212
Murray, Charles, 19, 153–4
music, 111, 114

narcissism, 19, 23, 24, 93
National Assessment of Education
    Progress (NAEP), 10, 43–4
Negroponte, Nicholas: *Being
    Digital,* 231
New Deal, 65
Nordlinger, Jay: *Children of
    Dictators,* 102
nuclear family, 19, 80

Obama, Barack, 250
O'Connor, Flannery, 139
Orwell, George, 31
    1984, 234
    Animal Farm, 121, 238
Osborne, Mary Pope: *Magic Tree
    House* (series), 243
out-of-wedlock birthrate, 19

Packard, Vance: *The Waste Makers*, 166–7

Paine, Thomas: *Common Sense*, 217

Palladino, Grace, 49

parenting, 4, 23–8, 209
    adult-children, 2, 51, 54, 100, 246
    European approaches to, 35–6
    helicopter parents, 2, 46, 116
    intentional parenting, 146
    soft parenting, 37–50
    training wheels, 115–17

Parr, Ellen, 111

passivity, 3–4, 6, 8, 14, 24, 70–81

Paul the Apostle, 43, 228

peer culture, 8–9, 18, 20, 95, 139

Peterson, Andrew: *Wingfeather Saga*, 243

Piaget, Jean, 49

Plato, 23–4, 219, 234
    Crito, 233
    Republic, 24

polarization, 6, 21, 46, 224, 261

policy, 259–63

Pope, Alexander, 219, 225

popular culture, 21, 50, 106, 139, 152, 170

pornography, 40

Postman, Neil, 31, 50–1, 54, 168
    Amusing Ourselves to Death, 50
    Disappearance of Childhood, The, 50–1

poverty, 156, 225
    and coming of age, 17
    global statistics, 158
    Teddy Roosevelt on, 268
    travel as means to witness, 195–6

prescription medications, 37–8

production
    economic, 132, 154, 156, 161, 166, 212–13
    meaningful, 9, 18–19, 86, 122, 124, 173, 269

progressive education, 25–7, 68–9

progressive movement, 48, 65

protest era (1960s), 20–1

Protestantism, 21, 42, 214

Puritans and Puritanism, 89, 97–8, 129–31, 135, 207, 257

Putnam, Robert, 19

Ravitch, Diane, 69

reading, 207–8
    on the American Idea, 235–6
    Century Club reading challenge, 242–3
    conversion narratives, 230–1
    and digital distraction, 208–11
    and early America, 216–18
    Greek, 232–3
    habit of, 208–11
    humanistic science, 238–9
    importance of, 87, 207–8
    and invention of the printing press, 211–14
    Jefferson's syllabus for citizenship, 218–21
    literary canons, 221–8
    marketplace of ideas, 214–16
    on markets and economics, 236–7
    prison literature, 230, 240
    Sasse family canon, 228–41
    stepping stones, 242–3
    theology, 232–4
    on tyrants and totalitarianism, 237–8

reading comprehension, 10

Reagan, Ronald, 247, 257

realism, 16, 23, 25, 36–7, 78, 103
recession, economic (2008), 18
Regnerus, Mark, 106
religious participation, 42–3
republican government
    and education of youth, 224
    liberty, 247
    localist, 162
    nationhood, 8
    self-rule, 248
Republican Party, 203, 206, 247, 256–7, 260
republicanism
    and consumerism, 163
    and luxury, 163, 168
    virtues and character, 7, 133, 164, 255
resilience, 6, 7, 8, 30, 36, 46, 103, 111, 115, 168, 178, 190, 211, 223, 258, 259, 263, 271
Riesman, David, 131
    The Lonely Crowd, 166
Riordan, Rick: Percy Jackson, 243
rites of passage, 16–17, 32, 43, 55, 96, 99, 137, 192
romanticism, 23–5, 36, 80, 171, 230, 234
Roosevelt, Theodore, 10, 100–101, 133, 140, 168, 258–9, 265–74
    Autobiography, 100, 266
    letter to son, 9
Rousseau, Jean-Jacques, 9, 23, 27–8, 114
    Emile, 24, 139, 171–2, 234
Rove, Karl, 242
Rowe, Mike, 134
Rowling, J. K.: Harry Potter (series), 243
Rubin, Gretchen, 154
Ryken, Leland, 129–30

Sasse, Elda and Elmer, 119–23, 135
Sateré-Mawé people, 16
Sayers, Dorothy, 78–81
Schlegel, Alice, 93
Schwartz, Elliott, 111
Science, Technology, Engineering, and Mathematics (STEM), 238
screen time, 4, 38–9
Scripture. See Bible
self-reliance, 2, 5, 7, 8, 22, 40, 259
self-restraint, 80, 125, 166, 256
Sellers, Charles: The Market Revolution, 163, 237
Senate, U.S., 6, 19, 112, 197, 202–3, 206, 225, 276
sex, purposes of, 104–6
Shakespeare, William, 210, 219, 231, 233, 234–5
    Hamlet. 225, 235
    Julius Caesar, 235
    King Lear, 235
    Macbeth, 225, 235
    Sonnets, 235
Shaputis, Kathleen, 52–3
Shawshank Redemption, The (film), 146–7
Silent Generation, 42
Smith, Adam: The Wealth of Nations, 237
Smith, Christian, 43, 53, 155–6, 158
Smith, Wesley, 103
Snyder, Zack, 16
social media
    #adulting, 1
    #firstsevenjobs, 135–6
    #FromTheRanch, 141–3
    and algorithms, 6
    Facebook, 220
    and "fake news," 208, 220, 226

Instagram, 1, 127, 191
Medium, 126
and oversharing, 125
and screen time concerns, 4, 226
Twitter, 1, 135, 141
Socrates, 78, 151, 169
Solon, 53–4
Spock, Benjamin, 48, 49–50
Steinbeck, John, 186–7, 191–2, 195
Grapes of Wrath, 239
Travels with Charley in Search of America, 186
Stewart, Trenton Lee: *Mysterious Benedict Society,* 243
Stilgoe, John, 189–90
Stoics, 104, 169–70, 219
stoicism, 103, 121, 142, 166, 168–71, 173
Stoppelman, Jeremy, 126
storytelling, 114, 117, 135, 187
suffering, 23, 86, 153, 156, 159, 165–6, 270, 271
and character, 103–4
and work, 9, 138, 140, 143–5

300 (film), 16
teen pregnancy, 19
"teenager," use of the term, 34
television, 9, 49, 51, 154, 178, 210, 219, 238, 268
Thatcher, Margaret, 173, 207
Thoreau, Henry David, 194
Thucydides, 218
History of the Peloponnesian War, 204, 233
Tocqueville, Alexis de, 36, 245, 253–6
Democracy in America, 236, 254–5, 280
Toft, Mary, 107–8
Tolkien, J. R. R., 230

totalitarianism, 53, 102, 233, 237–8
toys, childhood, 37, 72, 157
travel, 177–80, 192–205
learning how to see, 188–92
light travel, 86–7, 174
and seeing contrasts, 185–8
stepping stones, 205–6
tourism as distinct from, 181–4
trigger warnings, 44–5
Troy, Tevi, 242
Twain, Mark, 57, 196
Adventures of Huckleberry Finn, 193–4, 239
Innocents Abroad, 177

Uecker, Jeremy, 106
United States, 245–6
American exceptionalism, 250–2
Bill of Rights, 252–3
civic education, 218–21, 245–58
and competing ideas, 248–50
Constitution, 162, 235–6, 245, 248, 252–4, 256
as creedal nation, 7, 10
Declaration of Independence, 20, 216, 218, 235, 248, 251, 252
shared values, 256–7
un-schooling, 61, 279
using-and-discarding, 156, 167

Vance, J. D., 19
Veblen, Thorstein: *The Theory of the Leisure Class,* 164
video games, 27, 39, 151, 172, 175
virtue, 21, 166, 173, 181, 266, 271–2
deferred gratification, 26, 125, 152, 156, 166, 173
etymology of, 51
eulogy versus resume, 144

republican, 7, 133, 164, 238, 255
work suffering, 9, 138, 140,
    143–5
See also character-building
Voice of the Martyrs (periodical),
    102

Warner, Gertrude Chandler:
    Boxcar Children (series), 243
Washington, George, 162, 212
Weber, Max, 130
well-being, 9, 145, 155
    emotional, 45
    financial, 41
Williams, Robin, 156
Williams, Stefanie, 127–8
Wilson, N. D.: *100 Cupboards,* 243
Wilson, Woodrow, 265
Winthrop, Elizabeth: *Castle in the
    Attic,* 243
work
    cattle ranch lessons, 139–44

detasseling corn, 136–8
employment, 18, 29, 41, 90, 129,
    133, 154
first jobs, 135–9
knowledge work, 29–30, 161
stepping stones, 147–9
and suffering, 9, 138, 140, 143–5
Teddy Roosevelt on, 9
vocation, 8, 29, 129–30, 136,
    154
walking beans, 137
work ethic, 16, 18, 86, 90, 113,
    122, 124, 129–39, 143–4, 147,
    209
World War I, 265, 269
World War II, 113, 120–1, 201,
    204, 270

Yelp, 126–7, 200

Zeno of Citium, 169
Zimbardo, Philip, 39